Mama

Marijke Lockwood

Mama

Printed by Digital Print Australia
135 Gilles Street
Adelaide
SA 5000

For information address mickiedaltonbooks@lycos.com

First Printing 2012

ISBN: 978-0-9873069-7-5

Print book and ebook distributed by
DoctorZed Publishing
www.doctorzed.com

PRINTED IN AUSTRALIA

Published by The Mickie Dalton Foundation
Kempsey, NSW
Australia

Dedications

Margaretha Wegman-Dobber 1921–1958 - Mama #1
Josina Wegman-Dobber 1920–current - Mama #2

*Some people are lucky to have been given a
wonderful mother.
How lucky am I to have had two amazing women I
had the privilege to call 'Mama'*

Acknowledgments:
Lidy van Soest
Ineke and Harry van der Hoogte
Michael Davies
*Thank you - without your support, encouragement
and input, this book would not have been completed
or published.*

Foreword

This book is based on my recall of events from 1958 to 1962 (and some flash-backs prior to this period). Some of the details may be disputed by others, but they are as I recall them.

Some of the names of the characters in this book have been changed due to my young age when these events took place, I am unable to recall all the names of the people involved. Although the events/conversations are vivid, some names escape me or are confused in my memory (especially those of the nuns at the orphanage and schools).

Throughout the book I use my siblings' 'Australian' names. Some, like me, kept their Dutch names, for others it was easier to have their call-names translated into Australian equivalents:

Dutch Name	Australian Name
Willie	Wil
Ans	Ann
Joop	John
Marijke	Marijke (Ma/ray/ke)
Arnold	Arnie
Truusje	Trudy
Greetje	Margaret
Lidy	Lidy – (Lee/dy)
Ineke	Ineke – (Een/eh/ke)
Tiny	Tiny – (Tee/ny)

(Two sisters who are not mentioned in my memoirs were born after the period of this book: Bernadette - 1963 and Cisca – 1964: a total of 12 children.)

Chapter 1

7 September 1958 – Amsterdam, The Netherlands

"Marijke."

The deep authoritative voice of Sister Geertruida broke into the hopscotch game I was playing with my two best friends at the orphanage; Hennie, a chubby girl with a cute freckled face, and Ursula, a Polish girl. We'd taken the opportunity to play in the playground after we finished our lunch of sandwiches and soup in the dining room. We had to be back in class in fifteen minutes. After two days of rain, we relished the sunshine.

"Mother Superior wants to see you in the visitors' room," continued Sister Geertruida.

"But, Sister, I haven't done anything wrong today, honest."

My ten-year-old mind was spinning. *What did I do this time?* I was in trouble often, but I struggled to think of what I could have done that would cause me to have to see Mother Superior. I'd never been sent to Mother Superior before. *This must be really bad.*

I looked up, expecting Sister to be scowling at me. But instead, her eyes were gentle.

"No, you're not in trouble, Marijke. Mother Superior and your Papa want to speak with you and your brothers and sisters."

* * * *

The Catholic orphanage (De Voorzienigheid) was situated in the heart of Amsterdam. This city, with its famous canals and narrow cobbled streets originally meant for horses and foot traffic, had many attractive old buildings. The orphanage didn't fall into this category. The long dark brick wall with its evenly spaced windows faced a narrow street. It was four stories high and its only other feature was six long cement steps which lead to a heavy carved wooden front door.

The name, 'De Voorzienigheid' was chiselled into a cement block above the door. The Sint Maria School adjoined the orphanage.

The internal playground was asphalted. It had a monkey bar, a sandpit to one side and a large tree near the far wall. The whole area was surrounded by sombre dark buildings and a high brick wall. Although dismal, we made our own fun. In 1958, a lot of areas in Amsterdam still bore the scars of war.

Most other children in De Voorzienigheid were orphans. Our family situation was different in that both our parents were alive. Mama had been ill on and off over the previous five years. Whenever she had been admitted to hospital for surgery or treatment, we went to the orphanage. As there were nine children under fourteen, Papa was unable to look after us as well as work.

Originally the orphanage was for girls only, but from early 1958 boys were accepted. This time my two brothers and five of my six sisters were also there. My eldest sister, Willie, was placed with an aunt and uncle who lived near the high school she attended.

Papa, a tailor, wasn't able to look after nine children on his own. He was a proud man who worked extraordinary long hours in an effort to earn sufficient to support us.

As well as working for a boss during the day, he took in private work, often sewing late into the night. I can still see him sitting on his sewing table neatly stitching, his legs crossed beneath him, thimble on his middle finger. Click, click, click. He worked methodically and meticulously. A treadle sewing machine sat next to the large table and a small light hung from the ceiling. He'd sit there for hours, the only break when he ran out of cotton and had to rethread the needle, or when he'd hop off the table to use the sewing machine.

We were used to going into the orphanage. It became our second home during Mama's illness. We weren't told what was wrong with her, but we knew she always came home when she was well enough.

When we returned to the orphanage early July 1958, the nuns had kept our name tags on the drab clothes we were provided with from our previous stay. I remember thinking, *'They must have known we were coming back.'*

Each Sunday afternoon Papa collected us to visit Mama in the hospital. We made drawings and little books for her, which she loved. She'd give each one of us a hug and a kiss and invite us to sit on her hospital bed. Mama was an avid story teller, and loved talking to us about her childhood and her family and their experiences through the war. She had a vivid imagination and was able to bring any story to life. I loved to watch her animated face as I listened to her equally animated voice.

* * * *

Sister Geertruida led me inside to join my brothers and sisters; thirteen-year-old Ansje (Ann) and twelve-year-old Joop (John), nine-year-old Arnold, seven-year-old Truusje (Trudy), six-year-old Greetje (Margaret), five-year-old Lidy, and Ineke who had turned three the previous week.

Together, we followed the nuns to the front room of the orphanage, which was situated down a long dark corridor.

I wonder what this is about? I thought, as I held hands with Trudy and Lidy. Ann took Margaret and Ineke's hands. The boys followed close behind. Sister Geertruida opened the dark wooden door and said almost reverently, "In you go children," then stood aside for us to enter.

The room contained a heavy wooden table surrounded by twelve chairs. The floral upholstery on the chairs was frayed and faded. A pot plant with a large red flower stood in the centre of the table.

A single light globe dangled from the high ceiling above the table. The walls were painted dark green. Besides the table and chairs the only other piece of furniture was a matching sideboard. On the left side it held a statue of the Virgin Mary holding the baby Jesus. A statue of Jesus, his arms outstretched, his red heart embedded with a crown of thorns, stood on the right. A single candle in a bronze holder stood between the two statues, its flame casting a gentle glow around the otherwise drab room.

Willie sat on a chair to the right of Mother Superior, and Papa next to Willie. We walked around and kissed them hello, then Mother Superior motioned for us to sit down. Never having been asked by the nuns to sit at a table with them, I tentatively took a chair.

Willie started playing with a strand of her hair, a sign she was nervous. She twirled the strand around her index and middle fingers. Ann looked straight ahead and had her hands tightly clasped on her lap.

John sat nonchalantly looking around, as though to say, I don't know what all the fuss is about. Tall and gangly, he always came across as being cocky. He'd been in trouble a few weeks earlier, when he took a dare from some of the other boys to sneak into the girls' dormitory and say hello to one of the girls whilst she was in bed.

He had succeeded, but was caught on his way out. To say he was in deep trouble with the nuns was an understatement. John told me later he decided that whatever the nuns wanted to talk about that day could not be anywhere near as bad as his last meeting with Mother Superior.

I looked around the room. The whole family was here, except for Mama. Papa looked like he'd been crying, which upset me. Papa was a strict man. He didn't often show his emotional side. I'd never seen him cry before.

Papa wasn't an affectionate man, but he loved playing with us whenever he had the opportunity. Tickling us was his favourite pastime. He got great delight out of our squeals and giggles. I don't recall him ever telling me he loved me or was proud of me, but somehow, I always knew. Later in life I would resent this for a period of time, but whilst I was a child growing up it didn't occur to me that he might not love me. I just knew he and Mama loved us unconditionally.

"Ouch," I yelped, as I realised I'd bitten my fingernail to the quick. The taste of blood in my mouth made me withdraw my finger quickly. *I hate that I bite my nails. I always get into trouble, and I don't even realise I'm doing it until it hurts, or someone growls at me.* Mama and Papa had tried so many ways to get me to stop, from putting mustard on my nails to wrapping my hands up in bandages, all to no avail.

Papa looked up then lifted his glasses to wipe his eyes. I couldn't stop looking at him, wondering what could be wrong. He nervously started polishing his glasses with his hankie.

Mother Superior gave a little cough, and looked around at us with concerned eyes. "You're probably wondering why you're here," she said softly. After a pause, she continued. "As you know, your Mama's been in hospital for quite a long time this time."

"Is she coming home? Can we go home, Papa?" an excited John asked in an expectant voice.

He hated living at the orphanage, and the severe restrictions placed on him. The nuns hadn't yet learned to cope with boys. It was a whole new experience for them, and the boys' shenanigans were not appreciated.

Papa answered, "No John, Mama is very sick and can't come home. That's the reason you've been called here, so I can explain what is happening."

I felt my chest tighten as I saw Papa swallow hard. His voice sounded hoarse.

Mother Superior took over.

"The doctors have tried everything to make your mama better, but the good Lord has decided that He would like to take your Mama to heaven very soon. Your Papa's going to take you all to the hospital now to see her. She'll receive her Last Rites this afternoon, which is a very special Sacrament, preparing her to go to heaven. Your Papa wants you all there to see her receive this sacrament, and to pray with her and for her."

I tried to absorb what was being said. *Mama receiving her last rites? My Mama going to heaven? But that can't be true. God cannot take our Mama, we need her, I need her.*

I struggled with these thoughts and with the idea of Mama dying. I wanted to scream, but no sound came out. My ten-year-old mind tried to take in the enormity of this news. *Mama should come home. Mama always gets better and comes home...*

A lump settled deep in my throat and I felt tears flow freely down my face. I looked up to see Papa and Willie crying quietly. Then Ann started to sob. Trudy let out a wail and then started to sob loudly. (It was many years later Trudy told me she didn't understand what was happening. She cried because I was crying.)

"Go and get ready to go to the hospital," Mother Superior's voice quivered as she too struggled with tears.

"Should we get dressed in our Sunday clothes? This is a Sacrament, like Baptism and First Holy Communion. So it's a special occasion, and we should get dressed up," I said between quiet sobs. Although I was a tomboy, I knew Mama liked us to look nice, and so did Papa. We may not have had much, but our Sunday clothes were special. They were often hand me downs, or lovingly made for us by Mama.

"Oh my child, yes, I think it is a very important occasion. Run along quickly, all of you. Get changed into your Sunday clothes. Hurry. Then come back to this room. Papa will wait for you."

As I changed in the dormitory, my mind was in turmoil. *How can this be?* The only thing I knew about death was when I found a dead bird when I was about six years old. Mama had gently wrapped the bird in some soft paper and had helped me bury it. She'd explained about death in a simplistic way. And now my Mama was dying? *Are they going to put her in the ground too?*

Chapter 2

When we arrived at the hospital we were greeted by grandparents, aunts, uncles and cousins. Both Mama and Papa were from large families. Papa was one of seventeen children; Mama one of ten.

Father Hartog, our parish priest from Amsterdam North, greeted us and led us into Mama's room. Candles were lit and Father Hartog commenced the service. His monotone voice droned on, but I wasn't listening. I stared at Mama in the bed. She was so thin; her cheekbones stood out in her yellow coloured face, her closed eyes sunk deep into their sockets. I could see the bones in her hands through her paper-like skin, as if she were translucent.

Mama had been slim in her younger years, but during her illness and pregnancies she had put on quite a lot of weight. But now she was skinnier than anything I had ever seen.

She drifted in and out of consciousness during the service. Every now and then her lips moved along with the prayers being said.

After the service was finished, we were taken into a large corridor outside Mama's room. Relatives wandered around as if in a daze. Most were quiet or holding whispered conversations.

Each of us was invited back into Mama's room individually to say goodbye to Mama. How can a ten year old say goodbye to her Mama?

I walked in and began to cry as I looked at her. I wanted to climb on the bed and cuddle up to her. Mama's eyes were closed. It was all too much to bear. I tried to pray, but prayer failed me.

Both Mama and Papa were devout Catholics, and their faith had carried them through so many tribulations; the war; her illness. Now here she was, aged thirty seven, Mama to nine children, and she was dying. How could God want to take her? *God is supposed to be good and kind, and this is not good, it is mean!*

I stood there with tears rolling down my face. Mama opened her eyes and gently took hold of my hand. Her fingers felt cold and clammy. She looked at me, and then gently pulled me forward. "Don't cry for me, Marijke, I'm going to heaven to be with my Lord." I felt a slight pressure on my hand, and then she closed her eyes again.

I was ushered out for the next person to go in for their farewell. I don't know if she spoke to anyone else when they said their goodbyes. But it is one of the most profound memories I have of my Mama. She was dying, but she gathered enough strength to speak to me; to try to make me feel more at peace with her passing.

Outside the room Ann was sobbing loudly and some aunties were trying to console her. I heard one say, "Poor Ann, she's so close to her Mama, she'll miss her more than any of the other children."

I wanted to scream out, "I love Mama just as much as Ann, and I will miss her too." But I didn't. I withdrew into myself and kept quiet, crying silently.

8 September 1958

The next morning I was taken out of class and once again taken to the front office. All my brothers and sisters were already there. Papa arrived and told us in a broken voice, "Mama died this morning."

I have been told by my siblings that I sobbed, but for some reason, I cannot remember much of the rest of that day, except that the nuns decided we should all go back to class. They said that it was better if we kept busy.

During our lunch-break some of my friends asked why I had been called out. When I told them my Mama had died, they hugged me, and asked me to join in their game.

In bed that night I couldn't stop crying. I tried to imagine never seeing Mama again. I hid my head under the blankets so as not to wake the other girls in the dormitory. I don't know what time it was when a hand gently touched my hair. I looked up to see one of the nuns looking at me. She bent over and whispered, "I'm pleased you're crying and grieving, that's a good thing - God bless you child." She again stroked my hair and left.

This was very confusing to me. *Why is she pleased that I am crying? Crying isn't good; it means I am sad. How can that be a good thing? Can't she understand that my Mama has died? Shouldn't she be sad that I am hurting so much that I need to cry? Shouldn't she have tried to console me?*

I so desperately needed someone to give me a cuddle or a hug. I didn't know how my sisters and brothers were coping, but I felt terribly alone in my pain. Even though I didn't understand the full implications of Mama's death, I knew my life would never be the same again.

10 September 1958

As was tradition, Mama's body was laid out in a coffin in Mama and Papa's bedroom in our apartment in Amsterdam North. The day before Mama's funeral, one of the nuns escorted us to have a viewing of Mama.

The sight of Mama in the white satin lined coffin embedded itself in my mind. It was an emotional experience, yet it gave me some comfort. Mama looked at peace. Her eyes were closed, and I thought she had a gentle smile on her face. There were flowers and candles around the coffin. She wore a long white gown. I thought she looked like an angel. I couldn't stop looking at her.

Papa took a couple of photos of Mama laid out so peacefully. Yet to this day I am unable to look at these, which seems strange considering that my recall is that of her looking so at peace.

The nuns took us back to Amsterdam North for Mama's funeral the next day. To this day I don't have any memory of the funeral. It was obviously too painful.

Chapter 3

We were taken back to the orphanage after Mama's funeral. That night in bed I tried to pray, but my emotions were in too much turmoil. "God, why did you take my Mama? Why can't you let her come back to us? Mama always said you can perform miracles. You can let her come back. Why couldn't you have made her better?"

Life went on. I ate. I slept. I went to school and played with my friends. But inside I was confused and grieving. Each morning when I woke up I had a gnawing feeling inside of me, like something was going to happen, but I didn't know what.

At the orphanage all the other children had lost parents; most of them both parents. But we didn't discuss our personal backgrounds, and were never encouraged to do so.

One Saturday, a couple of weeks after Mama's funeral, my best friend, Fietje, from Amsterdam North, came to visit me at the orphanage. Fietje had been my best friend at school since kindergarten. She was as short as I was tall.

"Hello, it is so nice to see you!" I said excitedly.

"I've missed you so much, Marijke. I miss your family and your Mama too. When will you come back to Amsterdam North?" she asked.

"I don't know," I said, as I had no idea. I hadn't thought about going home since Mama died. Other children at the orphanage never went home, so I assumed we would just stay there. Now that Mama was gone, who would look after us?

I cried when Fietje left. She was the first person who had said she missed Mama. The nuns had prayed for Mama and the Sunday after she died Mass in the chapel had been dedicated to her. But nobody talked about her.

"You're not as much fun like you used to be," Ursula said one day. "Don't you want to be our friend anymore?"

I shrugged my shoulders and looked from her to Hennie.

"I'm just sad. My Mama died."

"Well, I don't know what you're so sad about. You should be happy that you still have your Papa and all your sisters and brothers. Hennie and I don't have any family." With that, the two of them walked away from me.

I thought about that and felt a bit guilty, but I still didn't feel any better. *Nobody understands how I feel, not even my friends.*

On the twenty-first of October, Trudy celebrated her eighth birthday. Papa picked us up and took us for an outing to the zoo for a special treat. But it just wasn't a birthday celebration as I knew it. Mama had always made our birthdays special. Even in the toughest times, she ensured we received a present, and she'd bake a birthday cake. The whole family lined up at breakfast time, oldest to youngest. The first person in line would hold the candle-lit cake. As the birthday person entered the room, we all sang Happy Birthday together.

Each family member had a little gift behind their back. We took turns to kiss the birthday person and wish them a Happy Birthday. Then we'd proudly produce the gift from behind our back. It might only be a small lolly, or a yo-yo, but it was given with love and pride.

My birthday was coming up and I wasn't looking forward to it for the first time in my life. I didn't want to turn eleven without Mama.

Even though my brothers and sisters were in the same orphanage, I didn't see much of them. We were split into age groups, and the boys were separated as much as possible from the girls.

I was the only girl from our family in the ten to twelve age group, with Ann and Trudy the closest to my age, but three years my senior and junior. Ann was in the big girls area; from thirteen to sixteen years old. Trudy and Margaret were in the group from six to nine. The two youngest sisters, Lidy and Ineke, were in the littlies group, aged from two to six.

Although I was surrounded by people, I felt isolated; unable to talk to anyone. It never occurred to me the nuns may be approachable. That had not been my experience with any of the nuns I had dealt with throughout my life. I'd always had a fear of nuns and other religious people, like brothers and priests. I believed they could see into my very soul; they were holy people, and God gave them special powers to see all the wrong deeds and thoughts I had.

On Sunday the second of November, Papa collected us and took us for a walk in a nearby park.

When we returned to the orphanage we were once again ushered into the front room, where we were met by Mother Superior. I didn't like that room. As far as I was concerned it was a bad news room.

So it was a pleasant surprise when Papa said, "How would you all like to come home in about two weeks?"

"Yes!" The answer came in unison.

"Do you remember Tante (Aunty) Jos, one of Mama's cousins?"

I vaguely remembered a tall lady, always elegantly dressed, who attended various family functions.

"Aunty Jos has agreed to become our housekeeper. She will come each morning, and go home each night after dinner."

"When will we go home, Papa?" I asked excitedly. *Maybe I can be home for my birthday.*

"I've organised with Mother Superior for you to come home on Sunday, the sixteenth of November."

"But Papa, why can't we go home on Saturday?"

"Why? What difference does one day make, Marijke?" Papa sounded a bit annoyed.

"Papa, it's my birthday!" *I can't believe you would forget my birthday.* Of course I didn't understand he had far more pressing matters to deal with since Mama's death. But I wanted to be home for my birthday. I knew it still wouldn't be the same, but it would be better than here at the orphanage.

"Oh Marijke, I forgot, I'm sorry. Of course, you can all come home on your birthday. I'm sure Aunty Jos will bake a special birthday cake for you."

"Thank you Papa," I replied, pleased to have my way.

"Oh, and one other thing, we're moving house before you come home. We're moving to Amsterdam South, so Aunty Jos can travel to and from her home easier."

"No, Papa, we can't move. Papa, please, I want to go back to my old school, with my old friends." *I don't believe it! What else is going to change in my life?*

"That's just not possible, Marijke. We've already signed the lease on the new apartment and we're moving this week. By the time you come home, everything will be settled."

"No, Papa, please don't make me change schools again, please!" I began to cry. I looked around at my brothers and sisters. They were all quiet and seemed quite happy to move to another school.

Papa looked up at Mother Superior. "Would it be all right if Marijke continues her schooling here?"

She nodded in agreement.

"How would that suit you, Marijke? It's not so far to travel from Amsterdam South to here."

I looked at Papa, and then at Mother Superior. Although I really wanted to go back to Amsterdam North, and to the school I had attended since kindergarten, I knew this was not possible.

"Yes, I'd like that. I like this school and I have some friends here."

"That's fine by me, Marijke," Mother Superior said, "but you will have to ensure you get to school on time. OK?"

"Yes Mother, I will. Thank you."

"Well, that's settled then. I'll come and collect you all after you finish your morning school on Marijke's birthday." Papa looked relieved.

I felt a little guilty that I had kicked up a fuss, but the thought of moving house, and changing schools was overwhelming me. I would have to make new friends all over again. It was all getting too much; everything seemed to be getting out of control. My life was changing at will and I couldn't do anything about it.

After Papa left, Mother Superior asked me to stay for a chat, telling the others to return to their rooms.

"I hope you realise that we don't usually let children from outside the orphanage attend our school. But you are a good student, and I understand that it would be really difficult for you to change schools again. So I've made this concession. Please don't let me down. Keep your grades up, and make sure you help your Papa as much as you can. Promise?"

"Yes Mother, I will."

As I left the room I felt Mother Superior had understood what was going through my mind, and my wish not to change schools. I suddenly felt a bit more optimistic about my future. I'd still be able to remain friends with Ursula and Hennie and some of the other girls here.

Chapter 4

I woke up early on my birthday, and stripped my bed in the dormitory. "I'm going home today, I'm going home today," I sang to myself. *But where is home?* My excitement was mixed with trepidation. *Will there be a birthday cake and a present for me? Will Papa have remembered?*

Saturdays were half school days. I had trouble concentrating in class, but finally the bell rang. I ran from the class to the dormitory to collect my few personal belongings, and change into my own clothes. I skipped down the steps, and almost knocked Sister Geertruida down the stairs.

"Marijke, please slow down. You know you're not allowed to run down the stairs or in the corridors." But she didn't sound too annoyed, she had a half smile on her face.

"Sorry Sister." I tried to hide the excitement in my voice, but not very successfully.

"I believe you're leaving us today. Oh, by the way, Happy Birthday."

"Thank you Sister."

"Maybe we'll see you again some time." *Oh, I hope not, I never want to come back here again.* I knew the nuns were good to us, but I never ever wanted to come back here, ever!

"Go have your lunch and your Papa should be here soon to take you home."

I walked to the dining room, and gulped down my sandwiches and a glass of milk.

After prayers I said goodbye to the other girls and headed for the front door. I was the first one there, but was soon joined by my brothers and sisters. I hadn't seen them yet that morning, and they all wished me a happy birthday. Papa walked in a couple of minutes later. Mother Superior wished us all the best and we walked outside. *Yes! I'm going home AND it is my birthday.*

We caught the tram to Amsterdam South, and then we walked about five minutes down a wide street before we arrived at our new home.

I looked around to familiarise myself with this new area. Opposite was a kindergarten and playground, with high steel fences and gates. Before opening the front door, Papa told us that when he and Mama were first married in 1942 they had lived in this street. Willie and Ann were both born there before the family moved to Amsterdam North at the end of the war.

This was the first time I'd heard Papa talk about Mama since the day she died, and I choked up.

Papa opened the front door and we all climbed the two flights of stairs up to our new apartment. Of course new apartments were really renovated old apartments. These were some of the ones that didn't get damaged in the war. It all felt strange, and a chill ran through me. I didn't want to go inside. Mama wouldn't be there waiting, like she had always done in the past.

Papa opened the door and let all the others in, but told me to stay outside. "Just a couple of minutes, we'll call you inside when we're ready." The door closed behind him.

As I stood there I felt confused, scared, excited and angry. Angry that Mama would not be there when the door opened. I was confused about my feelings and emotions.

"Today is my eleventh birthday." I said out loud, trying to cheer myself up. I stood there and waited for the door to open to let me into my new home and new life.

"OK Marijke, you can come in now."

I tentatively walked through the door into a hallway and then another door which was being held open by Papa, into what was obviously our new lounge-room.

As I walked in the familiar strains of Happy Birthday started up. Everyone sang in full voice and Willie was holding a birthday cake with eleven burning candles.

Aunty Jos was standing at the back of the room holding a parcel, also singing along.

After three cheery "hip, hip hoorays," Ineke gave me a kiss on each cheek, as was the Dutch tradition; wished me Happy Birthday in her sweet three year old voice and handed me a little bar of chocolate. Next was Lidy with a small packet of colouring pencils, and so on. When it was Willie's turn, she lowered the cake so that I could blow out the candles. Papa came over with Aunty Jos; they wished me Happy Birthday; gave me the traditional kisses and handed over the wrapped parcel.

I opened it carefully, and saw a polished wooden box. I ran my fingers across the beautiful wood, then opened the lid and found a lift out compartment. Underneath were a couple of reels of cotton, and in the compartments some needles, pins, a thimble and a pair of scissors. My own sewing box, I felt very grown up with such a present and thanked Papa and Aunty Jos. She had a gentle smile on her face "Do you like the sewing box Marijke?"

I didn't have to lie, something I was well known for when it suited me. I really liked the box, as I loved sewing, knitting and crocheting.

Aunty Jos went to the kitchen, which was at the back of the apartment, and brought back orange cordial for everyone. The cake was a delicious chocolate cake, and Papa carefully cut it into eleven wedges, with one piece bigger than the rest, which was served to me first as the birthday girl.

I relished the cake and the attention I was receiving. Since the day Mama received her last rites I had not felt special, but right then I certainly did.

Sitting around the table Papa said that when we finished our cake he'd show us around the apartment.

I looked up and saw Aunty Jos looking at me.

"Are you enjoying the cake Marijke?" she asked quietly.

"Yes thank you, it's really nice," I said as I looked at her a little more closely. She looked older then the last time I'd seen her, which had been at Mama and Papa's twelve-and-a-half year wedding anniversary. Although she was not beautiful, I thought she was quite pretty, but not as pretty as Mama.

Her short hair was dark and permed; she wore a floral dress, which was quite fashionable. She also wore a full length apron, just like Mama used to wear. I was soon to discover this was her standard dress mode whenever she was doing any housework.

Enjoying the cake, my sisters and brothers were happily chatting about being home, and wanting to explore our new neighbourhood. I joined in, and for a little while I felt happy.

"Now everybody," Papa interrupted, "as I told you, Aunty Jos will come here at eight o'clock each morning, and go home after we've finished dinner. I need you to help her as much as you can. I know you can all do things around the house, because you did it for Mama when she was sick."

Bang! I felt a sharp pain go through my chest. *How can I be sitting here enjoying my birthday?* I had forgotten about Mama for at least half an hour. Guilt overwhelmed me. Papa mentioning Mama had brought me back to my reality, and I wanted to cry.

Papa continued, "Aunty Jos and I have made up a roster of your chores, so there'll be no misunderstanding of what's expected from each of you. We can talk about that tonight."

"Come on, let's go upstairs and look at the bedrooms."

The thumping of so many feet going up the wooden stairs to the third floor echoed loudly. Lidy took my hand going upstairs. She looked up at me with her deep blue eyes.

"Marijke, this is not our house, but did you see? It was our table and our chairs and all our other things."

I looked at her, "Yes, but this is our house, Lidy, this is where we live now."

"Are we going to stay here forever? And will Mama come back then?"

"No, Mama's dead, Mama will never come back, she's in heaven."

There, I had said it out loud for the first time; I almost choked on the words. Would it become easier if I said it more often?

Chapter 5

The apartment had three upstairs bedrooms. Willie's room was no more than a little alcove off the main bedroom. There was just enough space to hold a single bed and a small wardrobe.

The two boys shared the second bedroom. With two single beds and a small wardrobe. It was also very compact, as were all the rooms in the apartment. But we didn't have much in clothes or personal belongings anyway, and we didn't know any better. All our friends and families lived in similar apartments. For Amsterdam it was quite normal.

The largest bedroom fronted the street, with a window overlooking the kindergarten. In the room were two double beds, one with a wooden frame; the other folded up against the wall, a curtain pulled across it when not in use. When that bed was down, there wasn't much room to move. But when the bed was folded up, there was floor space for us to get dressed and play.

"Now girls, Aunty Jos and I think it will be best if Lidy and Ineke, being the two youngest, sleep with Ann. She can take care of them if they wake during the night. Marijke, Trudy and Margaret, you three will share the other bed."

"And Marijke, you have to remember that it is very important you do not wet the bed, as it will make too much washing for Aunty Jos."

Oh Papa, I will try so hard not to wet the bed, I silently vowed to myself. Mama and Papa had taken me to a special doctor a couple of years before, because I still wet the bed. The doctor told them I'd grow out of it. As I had always shared beds with my sisters, it was embarrassing. Even at the orphanage I regularly wet the bed, much to the disgust of the nuns. I was publicly embarrassed by them by having to strip my bed in front of the other girls. Then I'd be lectured about being too lazy to get up to go to the toilet. It became so embarrassing that sometimes I tried to hide it from the nuns by making my bed quickly.

But they seemed to know, and shamed me more for not being honest. I couldn't win and the humiliation overwhelmed me at times. At least at the orphanage I had a single bed, and didn't wet anyone else.

As I got older and it didn't stop, I became paranoid about it. Each night I told myself I'd wake up for sure, and tonight I'd stay dry. Yet, night after night, I dreamt that I did wake up and was sitting on the toilet. Then I'd feel the warmth go up my back and down my legs; I'd wake up and realise that I'd done it again. I'd be so upset, especially as my younger sisters didn't wet the bed, not even Ineke.

"Marijke, you will be responsible for making your bed every morning and Ann you will be responsible to make your bed." Papa's voice brought me back from my thoughts.

"Papa, can Lidy, Ineke and I have that bed please?" Ann asked, pointing to the wooden bed. Ann had always been the motherly type from a very young age. She had Papa's dark wavy hair, and dark eyes.

"Yes, if you want, it doesn't really matter to me. Are you okay with that, girls?"

We all nodded. I liked the idea of having the fold up bed, because I figured that once the bed was folded up, the extra space was for those who slept in that bed. If they got the comfortable bed, we should have the extra space for playing. It didn't take long to realise it didn't really work out that way!

"Look everybody, we have a shower. I particularly requested it from the landlord before we moved in. I told them with so many of us we really need it."

The pride in Papa's voice was obvious as we followed him through the door into the little alcove next to the stairs. He loved wheeling and dealing and took great pleasure in having a win. He'd brag about any wins for days. I learned as I got older that he didn't talk about any deals he hadn't won.

A shower in an apartment was not common, as public bath-houses were used on a weekly basis by most people. In Amsterdam North we didn't have a shower. Now we not only had a shower, but also a small hand basin for washing ourselves and cleaning our teeth; such luxury.

How Mama would have loved to have had a shower, I thought.

Mama and Papa had instilled cleanliness in us from a very early age, and our weekly bath had always been a Saturday night ritual.

I had a suspicion Aunty Jos had something to do with getting the shower installed. We soon found out that she was extraordinarily concerned and fussy about cleanliness, hygiene and appearances. Having worked as a housekeeper and cleaner for such a long time, she was fastidious to a fault.

"You can all go unpack your things you brought home with you today, and then come downstairs to spend some time with Aunty Jos. She wants to talk with you and get to know you all better. She has cooked dinner for us tonight, your favourite rice pot Marijke. Then after dinner she'll go home."

With this Papa went downstairs. We started unpacking the paper bags the nuns had given us with our few belongings.

The left side of the wardrobe had six drawers, one for each girl. The right side had hanging space, but not much was needed as we only ever had a couple of dresses each.

I opened my drawer, and saw my underwear neatly folded, next to them were my few personal belongings. We never had many toys. My most prized possession was a doll Mama and Papa had given me for my sixth birthday.

It wasn't a big doll, but I loved it dearly; it was a black doll with tight curly hair. I didn't know anyone else who had such a doll. Mama had knitted a pretty pink dress for it and had helped me to knit little booties, of which I was very proud.

And there was my doll, in the drawer, looking at me with her beautiful dark eyes. I picked her up and held her to my chest and started to cry.

"What's the matter?" Margaret asked. I knew she wouldn't understand why this doll had suddenly brought back the tears, I couldn't explain it myself. I was just so pleased to see something familiar. Dolly had always been my confidant, I could tell her anything, and I loved her so.

I quickly wiped my eyes with the back of my sleeve, and gave Margaret a hug.

"Nothing, I just missed my doll so much, I'm happy to see her."

When I'd finished unpacking I placed my doll on the one chair in the room; gave her a kiss, and promised her she'd never be put in a drawer again.

I was back downstairs when the doorbell rang. Papa told John to go downstairs to see who it was. A minute or so later my god-mother, Mama's sister, Aunty Rie walked in. She came over and hugged me, planted two kisses on my cheeks and wished me a Happy Birthday. She handed me a parcel wrapped in pretty pink crepe paper, with a big white bow on it.

I was pleased to see her. She looked a lot like Mama, and she always spoiled me because I was her god-daughter. She loved giving me nice things that Mama and Papa couldn't afford. I quickly undid the bow, being careful not to tear the paper. Inside was a big ball of soft pale blue wool, a crochet hook, knitting needles and a pattern book. I thanked her and showed her my sewing box.

We sat down and Papa played his favourite record on the gramophone. We started to sing along to the song, "If I was a little white duck, swimming in the water." Funny how that was Papa's favourite song, as he hated being in water, except for his shower. He never went swimming, he never even put his feet in the water.

We sang some other songs. Then Willie said they'd rehearsed a special performance for my birthday. The four little ones sang a little Dutch song, dancing around the lounge-room. They were so cute, when they finished they bowed, and we all clapped. Their eyes beamed as they accepted the applause.

The afternoon flew by, and it wasn't long before Aunty Rie had to leave to catch her tram and train home. She lived in Rotterdam, which was quite a distance to travel. With the weather getting quite cold and windy at this time of the year, she wanted to get home before dark.

As it was my birthday I didn't have to help with any of the chores, so I went back upstairs; picked up my doll and sat on the chair.

I hugged her again, and closed my eyes, imagining Mama downstairs preparing my dinner. Although I had enjoyed the afternoon and was pleased with the cake and the presents, it felt strange. Not only because Mama wasn't there, but because this new apartment did not feel like home.

I sat there for a while and remembered the day Mama and Papa had given me Dolly for my birthday. "This doll is special," Mama had said.

"She is black like Black Piet, who brought you to me."

Mama told me many times I had been a present from Black Piet when I was born. For as long as I remembered my birthday was the first day of the Saint Nicholas season, which ends with a celebration on the fifth of December each year, with festive family parties when gifts and surprises are exchanged.

Between mid November and December five each child placed one shoe under the hearth or mantelpiece each night. If you'd been a good boy or girl, Saint Nicholas's helper, Black Piet, came down the chimney and put a little gift in your shoe; usually a St. Nicholas biscuit called Taai Taai, or a lolly or chocolate of some sort.

However, if you'd been naughty you received nothing. We were told that if we'd been really bad Black Piet would take us away in his sack.

There were times I didn't get caught being naughty by Papa or Mama, but Black Piet still put something in my shoe, so I thought he wasn't very smart. As we were told that Saint Nicholas could see everything we did, Black Piet should have known I'd been naughty.

Mama used to tell me, "In 1947 I placed my shoe under the mantelpiece, and I must have been extra good that year because when I woke in the morning, there you were, peacefully asleep in my shoe."

I could never get enough of this story and asked her to repeat it to me time and time again.

"Mama, if Black Piet brought me, how come I am not black?" I asked her. For some reason I always wanted to have dark skin.

"Well, because you are our girl. Although you are special because Black Piet brought you to us, you are not Black Piet's baby."

Mama had a different story for each of my brothers and sisters as to why they were special, but I loved my story best of all.

As I sat there cuddling my doll, I started crying again. I would never again be told by Mama that I was her special gift. I felt confused and ungrateful to everybody who had gone to so much trouble to make my birthday special. Life was just too complex at that moment, having to deal with all the changes.

Chapter 6

"Marijke, are you coming down for dinner?" Willie called from downstairs. "We're all waiting for you."

I wiped my eyes, put my doll back on the chair and went downstairs.

I joined my siblings around the table and Papa said grace, another family ritual. We always said our morning prayers together, grace before each meal and a prayer of thanks after each meal. We also said evening prayers on our knees, which usually consisted of the Rosary.

Aunty Jos put the big pot of rijstebrij (milk rice) on the table. We had big bowls, and Papa dished up the rice with a large ladle, a thick and rich milky mass. We were given a little dab of butter to spread over the top. This melted, creating a thin layer of yellow puddles, which was then covered with dark brown sugar, and the finishing touch was a sprinkling of cinnamon.

I loved this dish, not only for its sweet taste, but it actually satisfied me. I had a veracious appetite, and most days I didn't feel full when we left the table.

I savoured every mouthful, and when Aunty Jos offered a second helping I gladly took it. On top of the cake we'd already had I was really full that night.

After dinner Willie and Ann helped Aunty Jos clear the table, do the dishes and clean the kitchen.

"I enjoyed sharing your birthday with you today Marijke. I'll see you all tomorrow at eight o'clock."

With that Aunty Jos kissed each of us goodbye, went downstairs where she kept her bike, and left.

"Okay everybody, we need to have a family discussion as to how these new arrangements are going to work," Papa said.

"Aunty Jos and I made up a roster. I'll put it on the wall in the kitchen so you can check if you're not sure. But it hasn't changed much since before, except now that you're all a little older, you may have to do more than you used to do." Papa spoke with authority. When Papa used this voice we knew better than to argue with him. He was the head of the household, and he was to be obeyed.

Before we went to the orphanage, whenever Mama was sick and at home, Papa used to wake me up early.

"Marijke, can you get up and help me cut the lunches? Mama is sick this morning, and you are the quickest and best at making sandwiches."

This compliment worked every time, and as I was a born early riser, I proudly helped Papa cut the lunches. They'd be neatly lined up in their brown paper bags on the kitchen bench by the time everybody else got up.

Papa advised that from now on this would be one of my regular duties. Willie and Ann were to help the younger children get washed and dressed. All this had to be done before we sat down for breakfast. We had all our meals together, including breakfast.

Ann offered to undertake the ironing after school, as she enjoyed this chore, and used to do it when Mama was sick.

John and Arnold were upset that they also had some chores to do, as they considered there were enough girls around to undertake these jobs. But it was their job to get the table set and cleared for breakfast each morning. And of course, they had to make their own beds. Aunty Jos washed up the breakfast dishes once we'd gone to school and Papa had left for work.

"When you come home from school, if you have any homework, you always do that first," Papa said. "Aunty Jos will ask for help if she needs any to prepare dinner. If she asks you to do something, you will do it. Do not complain to her, as she is doing her best to do as much as she can. It isn't easy for her to come and help look after this big family, and we must show our appreciation. If I hear that anyone has been disobedient or I hear any complaints, I'll make sure you get punished."

We all knew Papa's punishments, which usually consisted of having to go to bed without dinner, or a good spanking on the back side. Papa never used any implements (although he often threatened to,) but believe me, Papa's right hand was a weapon in itself. When he was angry the marks on your bum reflected the level of his anger.

"If you go visit your friends or go outside to play, tell Aunty Jos where you are, and always be home by half past five."

There was another roster drawn up for evening chores, taking turns at setting the table; clearing the table; washing the dishes; wiping them, and another to put them away.

Willie and Ann were to take turns from not having to do these chores to help the little ones get ready for bed, making sure they cleaned their teeth and washed themselves properly.

After Papa finished talking, Ann offered to get Lidy and Ineke ready for bed. As Mama used to do in the cold weather, pyjamas and nighties were laid over the heater in the lounge-room to warm up. Ann, who had already put their nighties over the heater, picked them up and took Lidy and Ineke upstairs.

After they were settled in bed Papa told us, "We've also worked out bedtimes for everybody. It's basically the same as before, except Trudy and Marijke who've had a birthday since then. You can both go to bed half an hour later."

"You mean I can stay up until half past eight now, Papa?"

"Yes, Ineke and Lidy at seven o'clock, Margaret at half past seven, Trudy and Arnold at eight o'clock, and you at half past eight. John at nine o'clock, Ann at half past nine and Willie at ten o'clock."

"What would you like to do now, seeing it's still your birthday?"

"Papa, I think you forgot about Black Piet. Shouldn't Ineke and Lidy have put their shoes under the mantelpiece?" I asked.

"Goodness me, I forgot. Ann, go and see if they are asleep yet."

Within seconds Lidy and Ineke came rushing down stairs, excited looks on their faces. They had no idea about dates yet, so this was an unexpected surprise for them. They put their shoes near the heater, turned around with big smiles on their faces, and sang a spontaneous Saint Nicholas song. We all joined in and laughed at their delight.

"Now to bed quickly, or Black Piet may not come," Papa said.

"But Papa," Margaret said, "I don't think Black Piet knows where we live. How will he find us?"

"Don't you worry, Saint Nicholas knows where all children live, and he will have told Black Piet we are here."

"Can we play a game of cards please?" I asked after they were settled back in bed. "I would like to play Casino." Our family was big on board and card games.

It was soon half past eight, and time for bed. Tomorrow would be Sunday, which meant a routine of getting up at eight o'clock, going to Sunday Mass at nine, and then coming back for a Sunday breakfast.

I changed and washed, got dolly off the chair and looked at Margaret and Trudy already asleep. I remembered I'd promised Papa I would try not to wet the bed, so I ran downstairs and made sure I went to the toilet again. "I'm eleven now, and I am NOT going to wet the bed anymore!" I promised myself.

The double bed wasn't very big, but we were used to sharing, and besides on cold nights we kept each other warm. There was no heating upstairs, so body heat was appreciated.

I tried to get between my two sisters, but there really wasn't enough room. Each one of them was facing their side of the bed, with their backs touching. I tried to push my legs between them and push them apart, but with no luck. Then a brainwave hit me; I gently pinched each of them on their bums. Although they didn't wake up they moved simultaneously, giving me time to quickly squeeze between them. The heat of their bodies had already warmed the middle of the bed. What a great benefit to be the oldest in the bed. I snuggled down with dolly and lay with my eyes wide open reliving the day. Did I only leave the orphanage that afternoon? So much had happened.

I still felt lonely, but it was lovely to feel surrounded by my two sisters. It was somewhat comforting to not be in a bed on my own.

But I didn't feel like I was home. The orphanage had felt more like a home to me than this apartment. *If Mama was here I'm sure it would feel different.*

I turned onto my right side, clutching my dolly between me and Trudy. I said my own personal little prayer, or rather, I talked to Mama. When we'd said prayers with Papa after dinner he'd prayed especially for Jesus to give peace and rest to

Mama in heaven. I now closed my eyes, trying very hard to imagine Mama resting in heaven; one of God's angels.

"Mama, please help me not to wet the bed. Mama I miss you so much."

The next thing I knew Papa was gently shaking me. "Marijke, I know it's early, but do you need to go to the toilet?"

I sat up, confused as to where I was. Looking around, memories about yesterday's homecoming came back to me. Then I looked at Papa and gave him a great big smile.

"Papa, I'm not wet! Papa, I didn't wet the bed!" I was so excited, I quickly climbed over the still sleeping Trudy and gave Papa a big hug. He hugged me back before I raced down to the toilet.

I knew that Mama had helped me stay dry. I never wet the bed again from that day on.

Chapter 7

The Monday after my birthday I started travelling to the school at the orphanage. Sometimes Aunty Jos allowed me to use her bike. When I had to walk I often waited near the tram stop, which was less than five minutes from home. When passengers alighted, some threw used tickets on the ground. I collected them up and checked if any of them were still valid. Nine times out of ten I was successful and I'd catch the next tram to school. The walk was about half an hour, and in the cold winter months could be quite miserable, especially when the snow was ankle deep.

I never told anyone about looking for tram tickets, as I thought Papa and Aunty Jos would consider it dishonest. Looking back I realise Papa would've been proud of me, as he was quite a scrooge himself. He was not averse to taking advantage of systems to gain an advantage, especially relating to money.

Life settled down; we got used to having Aunty Jos around. She spoke quietly, and like Mama, I don't recall her ever losing her temper. I didn't make her life easy, nor did some of my brothers and sisters. We resented her fussiness, and the way she'd tell Papa if anything had not been done to her liking. Papa dealt with us after she went home, dishing out punishments like having to do extra chores, being grounded, or the dreaded spanking.

Aunty Jos was also part of a large family; her father had passed away when she was quite young. Her mother, who was still alive, had been unable to cope with raising six children on her own. They'd been placed into a Catholic home, similar to the orphanage we'd been in. She was brought up very strict by the nuns, and when she left the home, she became housekeeper to various families. Because she was fussy and quick, she was hired by wealthy families. I never understood why she'd never married, as she was quite attractive.

Although softly spoken and gentle, she did let you know when she was displeased. She'd shake her head and let out a big sigh. She certainly told us when things were not to her liking or standard. Her standards were high, very high, especially in the areas of cleanliness and hygiene.

If it was my turn to do the dusting, for example, she'd run her index finger over the most inconspicuous place, like the top of a door. If a little dust showed on her finger, I'd have to dust the whole room again, from top to bottom. Similarly with cleaning and clearing the sink, making beds and any other chores. They had to be done perfectly. Of course, these rules applied to all of us, not just me.

If one of us really upset her or made a cruel remark, she'd turn around and walk away. Sometimes I saw tears well up in her eyes. But she never punished us; she left that up to Papa. Mama used to do the same, although she certainly used to tell us what she thought of our behaviour, and sometimes sent us to our rooms.

After Papa arrived home for dinner, one or more of us would be told to join him in the lounge-room. There he passed out whatever punishment he felt was suited to the crime. I dreaded his hands, he smacked hard, very hard, always on the backside, leaving red finger marks.

I found it difficult to bond with Aunty Jos, and her fussiness frustrated me. Sometimes I told her that she couldn't tell me what to do, or tell her that she was too fussy.

Willie told me years later that she was very angry and hurt after Aunty Jos came. She'd been made responsible for so many things during Mama's illness and after she died. When Aunty Jos came, she felt she was relegated to being a child again. It was good enough for her to be considered an adult when it had suited Papa.

Ann told me she'd resented Aunty Jos' role. Ann believed she owed it to Mama to look after Papa and the others in the family. She said she couldn't understand that, at the age of almost fourteen, she wasn't considered responsible enough to be in charge. She used to enjoy helping with things, and felt she was denied what she felt should have been her role.

The younger ones took to Aunty Jos quite well and she was extremely patient with them.

Mama used to have a lovely singing voice, and encouraged us all to sing and dance. Mama and Papa met each other whilst both performing in a local amateur musical. Papa also enjoyed singing and could hold a note. Now that Aunty Jos was our housekeeper, we often heard her sing and hum.

Singing was one of the many happy memories I have of my childhood, both before and after Mama died. We sang when doing our chores together, danced around with the tea towel, or grabbed a sibling and just do a jig of some sort. Papa loved having the radio on, and he had a gramophone, but only owned a couple of records. These would be played again and again; we all knew the words of each song backwards.

As a family we made up plays and songs, with Mama's input and encouragement. Every time an aunt or uncle, Oma or Opa, or of course Mama or Papa celebrated a birthday, you'd think we were the Von Trapp family! All the adults moved their chairs around the room for our performance. We made costumes from newspaper and bits of material. Mama sometimes let us use bed sheets and towels to wrap around each other. She also used to buy crepe paper, and we helped her make our costumes. We'd sing and dance for the family; the adults cheered and clapped, making us feel proud.

For my tenth birthday I'd received a brand new recorder from Mama and Papa. We had a recorder class at school, which I loved. I was able to play a tune from listening to it, and didn't need sheet music, although we had to learn how to read music as part of this class.

After Aunty Jos came into our family she continued all these family traditions, and actually encouraged them. There was a sense of normality when we practiced together to entertain the family.

That I don't recall either Mama or Aunty Jos losing their temper with me is amazing, as I was definitely no angel, and probably got into more trouble than all my brothers and sisters put together. I told lies when it suited me, and used to steal some lollies or biscuits. As these were luxuries in our family, Mama and Aunty Jos always knew how many they had. I also occasionally took money from Mama's purse, maybe five or ten cents.

This was quite a lot of money then, as you could buy two salted liquorice lollies for one cent. I'd go to the corner store and buy my lollies, eating them on the way to school, really savouring them. Once I stole a whole guilder, a small fortune, from brother John. He had raised this through his bob-a-job work for scouts.

Looking back on this I have to laugh at my stupidity. I found the guilder on the floor in the upstairs hall; it must have fallen out of John's pocket. I went outside for a while then ran back inside.

"Mama, Mama, look what I found outside."

Mama looked at the guilder in my hand, and started to say something, when, at the same time, John came running downstairs from his bedroom.

"I've lost the guilder for scouts," he cried, tears pouring down his cheeks. He'd worked so hard, doing each job for five cents.

Of course, Mama put two and two together, and came up with four. Mama got the truth out of me, and said she was very disappointed in me, and worried about my dishonest streak. Of course Mama told Papa. He told me years later that they'd been so concerned about me, an appointment had been made to take me to a psychiatrist. However, due to Mama's illness, this was cancelled, and I never made it to the couch.

"You are our naughtiest child," Papa said on more than one occasion.

I realise now that I was looking for attention, and I continued these bad habits well into my teens. Subconsciously I didn't receive the attention I craved. I never stole anything outside the home, although I wasn't averse to tell a lie to anyone if it got me out of trouble. Negative attention was better than no attention at all.

Margaret told me, "I used to see you get into trouble, and I'd be good, because I was too scared to get into trouble with Papa."

Papa and Aunty Jos continued our family traditions, and we received our little nightly Saint Nicholas gifts, culminating into the feast of Saint Nicholas on the fifth of December. This was always a big celebration day in our family. A Saint Nicholas procession wound itself through Amsterdam. We'd excitedly stand in the cold outside, enjoying the big floats, bands, clowns and all the Black Piets. And then, last of all, there was Saint Nicholas, on his big white stallion, with his beautiful red mitre, and his golden staff.

religious feast day in our household, having received gifts on the day of Saint Nicholas.

Each night, after evening prayers, we gathered around the tree and the nativity set, which also had candles placed in front of it. Papa lit all the candles, and we sang Christmas carols. Oh, how I loved Christmas time in our family.

This year, although Mama was not there, Papa said a special prayer for her before our singing, which gave me the comfort that she was there with us.

On Christmas Eve we stayed up late and attended midnight Mass. We walked to church arm in arm, all sat together in church, enjoyed the formal Mass and sang along with the choir. The scent of incense and Mir again gave me a sense that Mama was there with me. She had not forsaken me, she was there with me.

After Mass, parishioners wished each other a Holy Christmas. We walked home together again in the cold. It had snowed whilst we were at Mass, and the joy of a white Christmas had become a reality.

Once home, the first thing Papa did was lay the baby Jesus in the little crib of our nativity set. After that we enjoyed a cup of hot chocolate, and Dutch rusks sprinkled with little sugar balls, coloured white and pink. This was our Midnight Christmas Mass breakfast.

We slept in the next morning, and when we got up, Papa and Aunty Jos, who'd arrived before we woke, had prepared a formal breakfast table. A bowl full of highly polished red apples, built into a pyramid, had been placed on the table. Each apple had a lit candle on it, creating a beautiful centre piece. As Mama had always done, strips of red and green crepe paper were laid from side to side across the white table cloth, which was actually a sheet.

When we were dressed, we had a full Christmas breakfast. This consisted of fresh bread rolls, boiled eggs, thinly cut ham, cheese, and tea. I loved Christmas, the smells, the sounds, everything about Christmas. Thank God, Christmas this year still had that same feeling, emotion, and most of all faith and love in our family. Mama was with me in spirit, because her Christmas traditions had not changed.

Winter that year was very cold, with the canals frozen over, giving us the opportunity to take shortcuts across the ice when going to school or church.

New Year's Eve was also a celebration; the decorations were still up. We sang Christmas carols, and enjoyed the special Dutch treats which Papa cooked in oil, then sprinkled with icing sugar, called Olie Bollen (Oily Balls). These were similar to doughnuts, but with fruit in them, and sprinkled with icing sugar. We only ever had these on New Year's eve. Aunty Jos had made the traditional salmon, potato and red beet salad, with lots of mayonnaise. I always looked forward to these once a year treats. Aunty Jos' version of the salad was the same as Mama's, delicately decorated with sliced egg, gherkins and thin strips of red beet.

The Christmas season for us ended with the feast of the Three Kings, which was celebrated on the sixth of January each year.

Mama used to make a special fruit cake for the feast of the Three Kings. She placed a bean into the cake, and whoever got the bean in their piece of cake was King or Queen for the day.

No chores, giving commands within reason, to the rest of the clan, and choosing the evening's menu. I'm sure Mama knew exactly where the bean was, because as I got older I realised we all seemed to be King or Queen in turn.

On the seventh of January, we pulled down our Christmas tree and decorations. We helped Papa drag the tree and branches to a square in the local area. All others in the neighbourhood did the same. After dark, everybody gathered around this huge pile of pine trees. It was ceremoniously lit, and created a huge bonfire, with branches exploding and sending pine needles, glowing from the fire, high into the air. We'd stand around ooohing and aaahing, and the warmth from this huge bonfire was lovely on a cold winter's night.

When we arrived back home, Mama used to have a large pot of hot chocolate already on top of the stove, and we wrapped our gloved hands around the steaming mugs, warming us inside and out.

Aunty Jos and Papa continued with these family and neighbourhood traditions, creating as few changes to our lives as possible.

The cold winter of 1958 continued into 1959, and things settled down. Aunty Jos took sick in early March and then she contracted pneumonia. She ended up in hospital for about a week. One of Papa's sisters and her husband came to help out until Aunty Jos was better again.

It was while she was in hospital that Papa called us in for a family meeting after dinner.

"I have some good news to share with you," Papa said. "Aunty Jos and I have decided to get married. When she gets home from hospital, you can start calling her Mama."

No, no, no. Papa, this cannot happen. No. I have a Mama; I don't want a new Mama. No, this can't be true!

I looked at Papa with tears welling up in my eyes. He had a big grin on his face, beaming from one ear to the other. A couple of the little ones were laughing and clapping, but I saw the pain and confusion in some of my brothers and sisters' eyes. If Papa noticed, he did not let on.

"We'll be married on the thirtieth of April, the Queen's birthday holiday. You can all attend the wedding, and Aunty Jos will then come to live with us as your new Mama"

I got up from the table before Papa could see my hurt and my anger. I ran upstairs and threw myself on the bed. How could he think of marrying another woman? He loved Mama; she had only been dead six months. How could he now want to marry Aunty Jos? *Papa, I can't call Aunty Jos Mama. Aunty Jos is NOT my Mama. I can't do it, I WON'T!*

Tears streamed down my face, my sobs stifled by the pillow. I thumped the now wet pillow with my fists. *Mama, how could Papa have forgotten about you so soon? I don't want a new Mama. Why did you die and leave me?*

Chapter 8

After some time, my sobbing subsided. The pillow was drenched, and my eyes swollen. I lay there for a while longer, not knowing what to do. *Should I go down and tell Papa he can't get married to Aunty Jos, and more importantly, that I won't be able to call Aunty Jos Mama?*

I knew I'd like to do that, but also that I wouldn't. Papa didn't take kindly to having his decisions questioned, and it had sounded like a fait-accompli. I was sure that this was not a debatable topic, and nothing I said or did would change Papa's mind.

I don't care Papa, I am NOT calling that woman Mama. My Mama is in heaven, she's only been dead six months.

I sat up on the bed and hugged my dolly, surprised no-one had come looking for me yet.

They don't even care that I'm up here. Papa's down there, smiling and grinning, happy he's getting married again. He can't love Aunty Jos, he loves Mama. We still pray for Mama every day. What would she think about all this?

Mama, please help me to understand. I don't want Papa to marry Aunty Jos. Why can't we just go on like we are? That's working. It's not like when you were alive, but we are a family again. Why do things have to keep changing all the time?

"Marijke." Papa spoke quietly. I hadn't heard him come upstairs. "Are you coming downstairs to join us for dinner?"

He must have noticed my swollen eyes, but didn't say anything.

"I'm not feeling well, can I stay up here and go to bed?" I didn't look him in the eyes, I couldn't look him in the eyes. Right then I hated him.

"Okay, can I get you anything?" His voice did sound concerned. *Go away, that's what you can do. Don't marry that woman, that's what you can do.*

"No, thank you," I said, rather rudely and abruptly. If he noticed, he didn't comment.

He left the room, and I threw my head down on the pillow again, but this time my tears wouldn't come. I felt an anger, no, a rage, well up and take over my whole body. I began to shake, and I clutched dolly so hard, I almost broke her.

I hate you Papa, and I hate Aunty Jos. How can you forget about Mama so quickly?

I finally got up, undressed, washed and cleaned my teeth. I had to go downstairs to go to the toilet, so I tip-toed down, hoping no-one would hear me.

"Are you okay?" Ann asked as I came down the stairs. She walked over to me and hugged me. "Are you all right?" she asked again.

I nodded, knowing if I spoke, I'd cry again. Ann didn't look like she had cried. *Why aren't you upset? Do you want Papa to marry Aunty Jos?* I thought.

"I need to go to the toilet, and I'm feeling sick, so I'm going to bed," I said, opening the toilet door to escape.

After washing my hands, I crawled into bed, and hugged my dolly to my chest as if my life depended on her. My mind was spinning; confused, angry, hurt. Every emotion washed over me. I wanted to scream, yell, and throw things. Anything to get rid of this anger and the fear of more changes in my life.

I must have drifted off from emotional exhaustion. I woke up when Margaret climbed into bed next to me. I rolled over to hug her. I was in desperate need to feel another human being.

"Isn't it exciting, Marijke? Papa and Aunty Jos are getting married. Papa said we can all go to the wedding, and we will all have new dresses and new shoes, and everything." Her young voice was full of awe and excitement.

I pretended to be asleep, and didn't answer her. *Am I the mean one? Am I being selfish? Why doesn't anyone care Papa has forgotten about Mama?*

I rolled over again to the other side, so as not to let Margaret see the tears well up again.

I woke up early the next morning, feeling sad. I'd dreamt about Mama, and the time she had gotten really angry when I was about four or five years old. Not angry with me, but with a man walking down the street. I had been so proud of my Mama that day. When it came to her children, she had always been protective and loving. Nobody dared say anything against us, and her motherly instinct, as well as her temper, could flare quite quickly.

It had been a cold winter's day, snow on the ground. Mama was wrapped up in her grey and well worn woollen coat, the only one I ever remember her in. She also had a scarf tied around her head, to keep out the wind. I always thought Mama looked so pretty with the colourful scarf around her head.

The older children had gone to school, and we were on our way to get some groceries. Trudy was a baby in the pram, and Arnold sat on a little seat on the front of the pram. I walked with Mama, tightly holding her hand, whilst she pushed the pram with the other hand.

Suddenly, a man came running down the street towards us, obviously in a hurry. The footpath was quite narrow, and with the pram, there was not a lot of room for him to get past. As he approached he tried to sidestep us, and slipped in the snow, almost landing on top of me.

"Get out of my way, you little piece of human being!" he yelled at me, as he tried to balance himself.

This statement made Mama really angry. I didn't recall ever having seen her angry like that before. "Don't you DARE call my daughter a piece of human being! She is a complete human being. She may be small, she's only a child. But she is a complete human being!" Mama's voice could be heard all the way down the street.

The man had gathered himself by then, and just stared at the angry looking woman with her little brood. He looked terrified, as if he thought Mama might attack him. He took one look at her angry face and blazing eyes, and decided to retreat.

Oh, how proud I was of my Mama; that she'd stood up to the man, but more, because it had made me feel important. I was a whole human being, not a piece of one.

I lay in bed, remembering that event, and the dream which had brought it back to me; feeling Mama's presence.

I climbed over Trudy's still sleeping body, and crept downstairs, trying not to wake anyone else. As I arrived downstairs, Papa met me in the hallway.

"Good morning, Marijke," he said, as he gave me his usual morning kiss and hug.

"Good morning, Papa." I pecked him on the cheek, and got into the toilet to escape. I didn't feel like talking to him. I was afraid I might get into an argument about last night.

But as per usual, the decisions had been made, and there were no further discussions. When Aunty Jos arrived, Papa wished her a good morning, and gave her a kiss on the cheek. This was the first time I'd seen any show of affection between the two of them. I turned around and stormed off into the dining room. By now the other children were up, and arrived downstairs for breakfast.

When saying Grace, Papa asked God to give peace to Mama, and then said, "Dear Lord, bless our new Mama, and thank you for making her part of our family, Amen."

"Amen." Everybody else responded, before crossing themselves. My mouth closed tightly. I did not say Amen, because I did not want Jesus to bless a new Mama. I crossed myself and left the table, getting ready for school.

As the days and weeks progressed, everyone started calling Aunty Jos 'Mama', and she smiled sweetly at the name, obviously pleased that she seemed to have been accepted. I had no choice but to do the same. The first few times were very difficult, but eventually it became the norm. But when I called her Mama, it didn't have the same meaning it had for my real Mama. This title had now become a name to me, not an endearment.

Although I sensed something was missing, I enjoyed going to school at the orphanage, and was doing well. I was in grade five and was equal dux of the class. I did well in all subjects, picked things up quickly, and got on with the other girls in class and the teachers. I enjoyed the rivalry between myself and another girl, also called Marijke, for gaining the highest marks in almost all subjects. We usually ended up getting equal top marks, or coming in first and second.

Except for history. I loathed history with a passion. Actually, not the lessons, as I enjoyed learning about the past. It was the emphasis on specific dates and times when major world or local events had occurred. I couldn't see any sense in knowing these dates, they were not important to me. Who cared if it was the 7th of May of a certain year, or the 17th? Well, the teacher did. Come test time, my details of events were always spot on. But when it came to the questions on dates, I did not do well, bringing my marks down dramatically.

I recall receiving one test paper back, where the teacher had written in big red letters: "When are you going to learn your dates, Marijke?" I never did, but I still got reasonable marks for this subject. The other Marijke loved history and always beat me in this subject. I excelled at maths and Dutch, and usually pipped her on these subjects. So all in all, we had a healthy rivalry, which kept us both working hard.

It was also at this time I noticed my body starting to change, although I was extremely naïve in this area. As Mama had been sick for so long we had never had a mother to daughter chat about these things. I knew nothing about sex, or the bodily functions relating to this.

My breasts were developing, and little tufts of hair appeared in places they hadn't grown before. I did accept these changes without question, as my older sisters had developed in front of my eyes, so obviously it was part of growing up.

We used to have religious instructions every day at school. Right from when we started kindergarten, this was an important part of the curriculum in all Catholic schools.

All my teachers had always been nuns. Up to that stage of life, I believed that teachers were all nuns, or brothers in the boys' schools.

One day, our teacher introduced the topic for the day as 'personal hygiene'. I thought it a funny topic for religious instructions.

"Now, girls, most of you, or at least some of you, will have noticed that your bodies are changing. This is a special gift from God. Your bodies will change over the next few years, until you become fully grown young women. God has been good to us, and has made sure that when you grow up, your bodies will be able to have children. To do that, your bodies need to develop the way God has planned."

Her voice was very serious, and she looked around the classroom as she spoke, from one to the other. You could have heard a pin drop. As all the other students were orphans, I assumed they were in the same situation as me. They'd never been told about these things.

"There's one thing I really MUST impress upon you. You will be young ladies soon, no longer children. And with that comes the need for hygiene and self respect. You must ensure you always keep those parts of your bodies clean and covered. But you must also make sure that, as God's children, and as future mothers of his children, your body stays pure. You must not sin, girls. You must not let good feelings override your chastity." She paused after this statement, again looking around the class slowly and seriously.

"One of the first things you have to remember as you develop into women, you do NOT touch those sacred parts. You keep them clean, make sure they are washed, but NEVER touch them."

What is she talking about? What parts of my body are sacred? And how can I wash these parts, and not touch them?

"Okay, girls, let us get on with our regular lesson now," she said.

I guess that was the end of my lesson on the facts of life and the birds and bees. I didn't have a clue, I wasn't going to ask a nun to explain and show my confusion. I hated not understanding, and didn't want to show the rest of the class how dumb I was, as that might damage my reputation as a top student.

But, this worried me for years to come. I certainly did not have a close enough relationship with my new Mama to ask her. Besides, she was very prim and proper, and I didn't think she knew anything about such things. It must be something God had told the nuns, as His special messengers, to pass on to us. I didn't even discuss this with my older sisters.

Whenever I had my shower, I would wash myself, and look at my developing body with confusion. Now which part is sacred? *I think it must be my breasts, they are the only things I can see are really changing, apart from the hairy bits. But how can I wash them, but at the same time not touch them? And why not?*

Chapter 9

Before Mama went into hospital the last time, she'd bought some really nice material and patterns. She was a good seamstress, and had started to make all the girls a brand new dress. This was very exciting to me, because mostly I received hand-me-downs. Clothes went from Willie to Ann, and then from Ann to me. By then they would be well and truly worn, but still in perfect condition. Papa and Mama always made sure we learned from a very young age, that no matter how poor we were, or how little we had, we always looked after everything. Never a hem to hang out, or a button missing. Any seams which looked like bursting, were reinforced, and socks darned on a weekly basis.

For each of us to get new dresses had been an exciting prospect. But of course, once Mama had gone into hospital, this project had been put on hold.

One day, Aunty Jos, now our new Mama, asked me to come into Papa's little sewing room, off the lounge-room. There, spread out on the big sewing table, lay the material and the pattern for my new dress.

"Marijke, I know Mama was going to make you this lovely dress. I'm going to do it for you now, and you can wear it to our wedding. I'll make all the girls' dresses that your Mama couldn't do because she was sick. Then we'll all go shopping for new shoes. I need to take your measurements, because I have noticed that you have shot up quite a lot, and you have started to fill out."

I looked at the beautiful pale blue material, and the white binding which would offset the seams. The pattern was one Mama and I had chosen together, and I thought it was the most beautiful dress pattern I had ever seen.

"Thank you, Mama, that will be really nice. Can I help you with the sewing, because I'm pretty good at it. And then you won't have so much to do."

"Why, thank you, that'll be very nice. I'll let you know when I get to those parts you can do, like sewing the buttons on, and hemming. Is that okay?"

"Yes, I'd like that. Then I can use my sewing box, and my reels of cotton."

This was the first time I had called her Mama without thinking about it. It wasn't until later that day I realised that Aunty Jos had become the Mama of our home. Not *my* Mama, but *a* Mama. It was sort of acceptable to me now, and although my memories of Mama were with me daily, they became less painful as time passed. I still had some very sad moments, but they were not as painful as they had been in the past.

The preparations for the wedding were in full swing. Apparently there was some consternation about this union within various family circles, as it was so soon after Mama's death. But I did not hear any of this, and got caught up in the excitement of the new clothes and shoes. The wedding itself did not excite me too much, but by now I had accepted that this was going to happen.

One evening, when we were playing a game of cards, Mama and Papa were giggling about something, and then Papa started tickling Mama. This had always been one of Papa's favourite past-times, tickling us. I looked at them, and suddenly felt angry. How could he do this? He used to tickle my Mama, and she used to laugh so loud. She had been very ticklish, as were all of us kids. And obviously this Mama was also ticklish.

I jumped up, threw my cards on the table, and stormed off, furious. *I can't watch Papa do this to her. He's forgotten about Mama, he can't do this to another woman!*

"Marijke, get back here. What's the matter with you?" Papa demanded.

I put my head around the door. "If you don't know, then I won't tell you!" I yelled. I grabbed my coat and ran downstairs. I slammed the front door, and ran down the street.

It was already dark, and it was cold, but I didn't feel the cold. I was mad. *I can't go back, I will run away. I can't watch Papa tickle this Mama. He probably never loved Mama at all, or he would not have forgotten her so quickly.*

I stopped running, and walked around a couple of blocks, trying to get rid of my anger. I started to feel the cold wind, and realised I was out in the dark by myself. *Where can I go? Maybe one of my friends' homes?* But my friends were either living in Amsterdam North, or at the orphanage. I certainly didn't plan to go to the orphanage, and Amsterdam North was too far. Besides, I was getting spooked out there, in the dark by myself.

I walked back home, and had to ring the bell for someone to let me in. I waited a minute or so, before John opened the door for me.

"You're in big trouble now!" he said meaningfully. "Papa is really mad at you for going out like that." He had a smug look on his face, like he enjoyed me getting into trouble.

When I got back upstairs Mama had left, and Papa asked me to come into his sewing room. He looked really angry, but I was angry too.

"What do you have to say for yourself, young lady? That was very bad behaviour, and if you don't tell me what led to your outburst, I'll punish you."

"I don't want to tell you, because you'll get mad at me," I said defiantly.

"I'm already mad at you, so tell me, what was that all about?"

"I don't want to tell you. I just want to forget about it!" I was getting angry again.

"Mama thought she had upset you, but didn't know why. She was very hurt when she left. I think you owe her an apology."

"I owe HER an apology?! I don't owe HER anything! She is NOT my mother!"

He leaned down, and gave me a hefty slap across my backside. "Ouch! I hate you! I hate being here. She is NOT my Mama, she's NOT!"

Another smack. "You are drawing the blood from under my nails!" Papa shouted. "Mama has done so much for you, and you treat her like that."

"I wasn't angry with her, Papa, I'm angry with you!" Tears were now pouring down my face. "You haven't been the same since Mama died!" Another smack.

Papa was shaking now, and he also had tears in his eyes. "Go to your room, go to bed. I will deal with you tomorrow. Don't dare say another word!" He stomped out of the room, and I followed him out, not looking at the enquiring eyes of my siblings as I walked through the lounge-room.

Sobbing, I ran up the stairs, and once again, threw myself on the bed. I cradled my dolly, still shaking, and still feeling the sting of Papa's smacks.

Mama, please help me. I hate Papa, I hate this Mama. Life's not fair. Why did God take you away, and change our lives like this? God, how can you do this to our family? How can you do this to me? A good God wouldn't make me hurt this much!

I continued to sob, and eventually fell asleep with my clothes still on. When Margaret came to bed, she woke me up. I got changed into my nightdress, washed, and walked downstairs to go to the toilet.

As I came out of the toilet, Papa walked past me in the hall. He didn't say anything, he just glared at me, and I glared back at him. I think that was the first time, when I had been home, that I didn't say good-night to Papa, or anyone for that matter. No good-night kisses and hugs. I went back upstairs, and got into bed. Margaret was asleep on the far side of the bed, with her back to me. I crawled in beside her and lay awake for a long time. When

Trudy came to bed I pretended to be asleep. But sleep did not come for a long time.

When are these changes in my life going to stop? I want my old life back. Back in Amsterdam North, back with my friends and especially back with Mama.

But I knew this could never happen. In the end I felt sad, my anger had dissipated. I just felt very sad and alone once again. *Nobody understands how I feel. Why is life so difficult?*

On the morning of twenty-four April, Papa and Mama were married for the State. In Holland, ministers and priests don't have legal powers to marry for the state, only for the church. The church wedding is not seen as a legal marriage. Couples wishing to have a church wedding, first have a State Wedding which, in those days, generally took place in a registry office. Some couples undertook both on the same day, others chose to separate the two events, first having a simple state wedding, with only a few witnesses and family members in attendance, and a more elaborate wedding at a later date.

Papa and Mama decided on having two separate days. They were both extremely religious and the state wedding did not have any sentimentality attached to it.

The twenty-fourth was also Willie's sixteenth birthday. It was this that was celebrated on the day, not the wedding. I don't believe any of us attended the ceremony, I know I didn't. We went to school as normal, and after arriving home, had cake and our usual birthday party of song and dance.

On the morning of the church wedding I awoke early. It was the Queen's birthday, a public holiday, which meant all family members could attend the big wedding. The Queen's birthday in Holland has always been a big celebration, with parades, floats, and people hanging out flags of red, white and blue, with an orange sash; representing the Royal House of Orange.

But this year the day was about Papa and Mama's wedding. We all got dressed into our new outfits. I loved my new dress, especially as I had helped Mama with some of the work. I had hemmed it twice, as my first effort wasn't good enough for Mama. But this time, I didn't mind, as she was a beautiful seamstress, and was teaching me how to do it properly.

"Marijke, with big steps you get home quickly. But by taking your time and doing it properly, you can take great pride in your workmanship," Mama said when I had finished the hem.

I must admit, it was obvious that you could see the hem clearly on the outside of the dress, with the long stitches I had used. I was always an impatient person, in that I liked to see things finished within a reasonably quick time frame.

Mama unpicked the hem carefully, so as not to damage the material. She then showed me how to make small stitches, and only pick up one thread of material at a time, not pulling the thread too tight. As the skirt part of the dress was quite full, it took me longer than I liked. But when I finished it, with Mama's support and encouragement, I was very proud of myself. I thought it looked professional, just like Papa and Mama's stitching.

Wearing this dress for the first time made me feel really pretty. With brand new white socks and my blue shoes, I felt like a princess. Papa had cut all our hair, to save money, and although I wasn't overly pleased with the result, I combed it so it looked soft and shiny.

The day was bright and sunny, and quite warm for that time of year. I'd love to say how wonderful the wedding was, but I can't. I have no memory of that day except getting ready and feeling pretty. I have studied the photos, and know I was there. But even after all these years I still can't recall it; it is locked away with Mama's funeral. My sisters and brothers have told me it was a lovely wedding, and the food was delicious, and that we were all allowed to stay up until the end of the long festivities.

After the wedding, Mama moved into the apartment, and into Papa's bedroom. Although I didn't like this idea, at least it wasn't into my Mama's bedroom, as we had moved.

Things continued as before, with the odd conflict between brothers and sisters. I occasionally overheard my older siblings discuss their frustrations with Mama. Sometimes one of us would say something cruel when we didn't agree with her, and as always, Papa dealt with the punishment.

But things settled down, and that summer was lovely, as it was the first time in quite a few years we had spent our summer vacation at home. I continued with my gymnastics, which I had started when I was in Grade 3, in Amsterdam North. I was quite good at it, except for the beam. I was extremely agile, even being able to wrap both my long skinny legs around my neck at the same time. But I never had a stable balance and I was terrified of the beam, always falling off.

I enjoyed the ring and floor exercises. I won a gold medal for my floor exercises when I was in Grade 3. Mama hadn't been able to come, as she had been sick in bed. But she was so proud of me, her eyes shone when I brought the medal home. She let me hang it above our bed on the wall.

That first summer after the wedding, when Papa had some free time of a weekend, he sometimes decided we'd all go for an outing.

"Why don't we all go to the Amsterdamse Bos (Amsterdam's Bush)?" We helped cut sandwiches for a picnic lunch, packed some blankets and walked to the park. We sang songs as we walked there, holding hands and swinging the bags of sandwiches and cordial bottles.

In the park was a swimming pool, which was free to the public. This was such a treat. I was a strong swimmer, but didn't realise that at the time. I just knew I loved being in the water. Papa and Mama never went in, neither of them were fond of water. Papa couldn't swim, and Mama was more worried about the germs which might be floating around in the water.

They sat on the blankets and watched us with smiles on their faces, while we played with the younger children in the water.

We squealed and laughed and had so much fun together. When we were called out for lunch, we were ravenous from all the activity. Eating lunch we had to fight off the wasps, which terrified me.

Then we had to wait at least half an hour before being allowed back in the water.

During that half hour the little ones played in the playground, while some of us sat around telling stories or singing a song together. I have such fond memories of these special family moments.

One morning Mama said, "How would you all like to come to the zoo today?"

The response was one of pure joy. *The zoo! Wow!*

"I want to take everyone as a special treat. It is my thank you for helping me be part of your family," she said, with a warm smile.

We were excited, getting ready in the quickest time. While I was helping Mama cut lunches, I asked her, "Can I cut some of the crusts off so I can feed the animals?"

"Yes, of course, but I don't know if you're allowed to feed any of the animals. Which animals do you think would eat bread?"

"The birds, I know the birds eat bread and crumbs, because Mama used to put the breadcrumbs out on the window sill all the time," I informed her.

"Marijke, that's a lovely thought. You should've told me. We'll also put all the breadcrumbs out on the window sill from now on. If I forget, will you promise to remind me?"

"Yes, I will." I felt so happy that another one of Mama's traditions would now be continued, and that I was given the responsibility to make sure it happened.

The day at the zoo was wonderful, and I could see that Papa and Mama enjoyed seeing us have such a good experience. I threw some of the bread crumbs into the birds' cages, and shared this joy with my brothers and sisters. We also threw some of the crusts to the monkeys, and laughed at them grabbing at the crusts and then chasing each other for them.

When we came to the duck pond, we also gave them some crusts. Then we all sang Papa's favourite duck song. We danced around and laughed, and Mama and Papa joined in. A few people stopped and watched us, and clapped when we finished.

I didn't want to go home at the end of the day. I loved seeing all the animals, and learning about them. Especially the giraffes, they looked so elegant with their long necks.

Throughout my childhood I had often been called a giraffe, due to my long slim neck. At first I used to get upset when called a giraffe. Then Mama told me that a long neck is one of the seven signs of beauty. She told me a long neck is elegant. After that I savoured the name, and here they were, my namesakes.

When we arrived home, Mama asked me to help her prepare the evening meal. As I was peeling the potatoes, she said, "Thank you for thinking of the birds. It shows you have a kind heart, and I'm pleased that you told me about putting the crumbs on the window sill."

I wasn't too sure how to respond to this compliment, so I looked at her and smiled. She smiled back at me. "I loved today at the zoo, you looked like you were really enjoying yourself," she said.

"I did, Mama. I love watching animals, and I think the monkeys were really funny," I said, my face showing my pleasure.

Mama gave me a spontaneous kiss on the cheek, which was not something she did as a rule. I kissed her back. We looked at each other and smiled. Just then, I felt close to her; this was a special moment.

A few weeks later an aunty and uncle I'd never heard of before came to visit us. We were introduced to them as Aunty Rie and Uncle Theo, from Australia. I didn't even know where Australia was, but it sounded so exotic.

Aunty Rie was a cousin of both Mamas, and had grown up with them. Aunty and Uncle had moved to Australia just after the war, one of many migrants looking to improve their lives from the dismal conditions in Europe.

We gathered around them, listening to the wonderful stories they told us about their life in Tasmania, a small island state of Australia. They told us of the many opportunities there, the beauty of its flora and fauna and the wild animals. They showed photos of wonderful houses you could build and own in Australia.

We listened in amazement. In our small world, we had no idea there were countries so different to ours. The photos of the scenery they showed us were so vastly removed from our flat country. There were mountains, long white beaches, and huge houses. The houses looked like palaces to us in comparison to the small cramped units in Amsterdam.

"Why don't you come to Australia?" they asked Mama and Papa. "We're sure you will love living there. If you come to Tasmania, there is a large Dutch community already established. We're sure you will feel quite at home there."

We all started speaking at once, "Yes, Mama, Papa, that will be nice," and, "doesn't that sound wonderful," and, "our own house, Papa, we could have our own beautiful house."

"Whoa, whoa, everybody, don't all speak at once. It all sounds wonderful, but it's not that simple. Mama and I will talk about it. If we like the idea, we'll look into it. It would be a huge undertaking, leaving behind our families and friends. And of course, it is on the other side of the world," Papa said in his authoritative voice, calming us all down.

When Aunty Rie and Uncle Theo left, we were still abuzz with the possibilities. That night I lay in bed, conjuring up beaches and big houses, it sounded wonderful and exciting. *I wonder if Papa and Mama think we should go to Australia. Do I want to go there? It sounds exciting, a new country and a new language. But it also sounds scary.* I fell asleep, dreaming of sitting in a lovely big house, on a mountain, overlooking a long sweeping beach.

When I got up the next morning, Papa was already in the kitchen. Whilst we set the table for breakfast, I asked him, "Do you think we might go to Australia, Papa?"

"I don't know, there are a lot of things to think about. But, Mama and I are going to look into it. If we think it's suitable, it could mean a new beginning for the family. What do you think, Marijke?"

Papa is asking my opinion? Wow, he thinks I am old enough to give him my opinion!

"I don't know either yet. It sounds exciting and I think it would be a really good place to live. But it also sounds scary, because they don't speak Dutch, and it's so far away. What would happen if we don't like it there, Papa? Can we come back again?"

"I don't think that would be so easy, that's why we have to make sure we really want to do this. It's a big step for the whole family, and we need to be one hundred percent sure that it is the right thing to do," Papa said.

I floated around on air the rest of that day. I felt that Papa had given me a chance to give my opinion on a really important matter, and had taken my opinion seriously.

Chapter 10

A week after the visit by Aunty Rie and Uncle
Theo, they came back for dinner. They were a fun
couple. I guessed them to be in their late forties.

Mama and Papa had made some initial
enquiries about migrating to Australia.

"If we go there, what would be the housing
situation?" Papa asked them.

"It's very different from here in Holland. Nearly
all houses are privately owned. Some people invest
in houses to rent out. When a house becomes
vacant, the owners advertise in the local newspaper,
or through a real estate agent. You then apply,
negotiate the rent, and if you are lucky, the rental
house is yours. There are some government homes
for the under-privileged, but there is a long waiting
list for those. These are quite small, although still
larger than these apartments in Amsterdam. Most
people obtain bank loans, and build their own
house, or have it built for them. You pay off a
mortgage over twenty-five years, and the house is
yours."

I listened intently to the conversation between the adults, fascinated and excited by the thought of having a brand new house, with gardens and a back-yard to play in. They also described that a lot of people had their own chickens, and had fresh eggs daily. Wow, what a luxury that would be.

A few weeks later Papa told us at the dinner table that he and Mama had put in an application to migrate to Australia. "Now don't get over excited, because this is just an inquiry, and there are lots of hurdles to overcome before we could be accepted."

"Papa, if we go to Australia, how do we get there?" I asked. Only ever having travelled on trams and trains, and the ferries across the river between Amsterdam North and Centrum, I wondered how we would get there, to the other side of the world.

"I believe that most migrants travel by boat. It takes about five weeks. We'd probably leave from Amsterdam or Rotterdam, through the Suez Canal, the Red Sea, then on to Australia."

I got my atlas out at school the next day, and traced the trip with my finger. *Wow, that looks such a long way. Holland is but a tiny speck in the world.*

I told Hennie and Ursula we might move to Australia, but they laughed.

"Marijke, is this one of your wishful stories? How much would that cost? Your Papa could never afford to pay for such a trip," Ursula said.

I was hurt that they didn't believe me, but at the same time, what they said sounded reasonable. How could we afford it? We didn't consider ourselves poor, because we didn't know any better. But I did know that Papa worked very long hours to make ends meet, and there was never much money over for luxuries.

When Papa came home from work that evening, I rushed over to give him his welcome home kiss. Before he could settle down in his armchair, I asked, "Papa, how can we go to Australia? It would cost lots of money, and how would we get everything over there, all our furniture and other things?"

"Whoa, girlie, slow down, not so many questions at once. And don't forget, I told you last night, we are only looking into it at this stage, just preliminary enquiries."

"Yes, I know, but I have been doing a lot of thinking, and I looked on the map. Australia's on the other side of the world, and they speak English, and we don't."

"Okay, one thing at the time. If we decide to go, AND get approved by the Australian government, they will pay for us to move there. They will also move all our belongings there. It will only cost us a few guilders. Secondly, we can start some English classes. Willie speaks some English and Mama does too. And when you go back to school after the summer holidays, you'll be in Grade six, and you will be learning English and French."

I took this all in, and decided to stop asking questions. I would research about Australia in the school library books. Should Papa tell us that we would be going to go to Australia, I'd have a lot of knowledge about where we were going.

About two weeks later, just before school started again, Papa told us we had to go on the train to Rotterdam, to an information session on Australia. *Yes! A trip by train! I love travelling by train.*

We set out together, enjoying the ride, the sun was shining and I felt good. Once again we started singing as a family in the train, much to the delight of the other passengers.

In Rotterdam, we walked to the government buildings. I loved Rotterdam, it seemed to have a personality very different to Amsterdam, and was a large seaport. Many barges and ships entered Rotterdam to ply their ware throughout Europe. Rotterdam was the main marine entry point to Europe, so was very busy, and in those days,

Holland was the primary ship building nation in the world.

Inside the impressive building we were met by an Australian representative, and shown into a theatre like room. Nice velvet red chairs, nothing like I'd ever seen before, so plush, were lined up in rows. A big screen stood at the front of the room, and after an introduction by the Australian representative in reasonably good Dutch, the room was darkened and an 8mm film starting showing the lifestyles of Australians.

We were all agog, and Papa wasn't able to contain our excitement after we came out, although he tried.

That evening Mama and Papa filled in all sorts of forms they'd been given in Rotterdam, to apply to migrate to Australia. They received a reply within a week, requiring each family member to undergo a medical check.

Another trip to Rotterdam, this was such a treat! Twice in one month, and this time we had a day off school, as the first semester had started a week earlier.

The medical examination was comprehensive, each of us going in separately, starting from the youngest. We sat in the waiting room for a long time, having a half hour lunch break. Mama had brought sandwiches and cordial, which we had outside in a little park near the surgery.

By the time we arrived home it was close to dinner time. Mama was an organised person, and had prepared the vegetables and potatoes before we left home.

Dinner that night was very noisy, to the extent that Papa started to get angry. It had always been a rule that, at the dinner table, we were seen but not heard, unless we were spoken to by the adults. But the excitement of having been to Rotterdam again, and the feeling that we would probably go to Australia got the better of us. In the end Papa joined in, with Mama listening and smiling.

A couple of weeks later a letter arrived from the Australian Consulate. Mama hadn't opened it when it arrived. She always kept the mail for Papa to open. As soon as he came upstairs, we clustered around him while he slowly sliced open the envelope with a knife.

We watched Papa's face with baited breath, but it didn't give anything away. When he'd finished reading the letter, he handed it to Mama. "Here, you read it," he said. I thought his voice sounded disappointed, or worried.

Mama read the letter, this time we all watched her expression. Her face fell, which gave us an indication that maybe we would not be going to Australia.

I had to ask, I was too impatient to wait, "Papa, Mama? Are we allowed to go to Australia?"

Papa looked at Mama, and then back to us. He slowly shook his head. We turned our attention back to Mama, who was also shaking her head.

"But, Papa, why not? We're good people, why don't they want us in Australia?" I was annoyed, it did not seem reasonable.

"They say here that I did not pass the medical test," Papa said sadly. "Apparently the stomach ulcers I had surgery for a few years ago are considered a risk they are not prepared to take."

I felt my shoulders slump, and as I looked around the room, a rather sombre mood had taken over from the optimism of only a few minutes ago.

"Oh, well," said Papa, "We haven't lost anything, now have we? If we hadn't applied we would still be in the same place as we are now."

"But you haven't been sick for a long time, so why is it a worry now? You are healthy." Willie said. "I don't understand, that was a long time ago."

"Well, they've made a decision, and we can't do anything about it," Papa said. "Let's set the table and have dinner. I don't know about anyone else, but I'm starving."

The dinner table was very quiet that night, and we didn't sing as we cleared the table and did the dishes. It had been such an exciting and scary concept, we'd all been drawn into the possibility of going to the other side of the world.

We celebrated different birthdays over the next couple of months, including my twelfth birthday.

Although I didn't understand why, I was quite off some days, feeling moody and depressed, yet other days I was on top of the world. Of course, they were my hormones starting to come into play. Although I was still very skinny, I was quite tall and my breasts were developing at a steady rate.

It was towards the end of November that another letter arrived from the Australian Consulate. Once again, we waited with baited breath for Papa to come home from work. We all kept looking out the windows to see if we could see him riding his bike down the street. When we saw him, a couple of us ran down the stairs to meet him, and tell him about the letter.

"Don't get too excited," Papa said, "It's probably just a confirmation that we were not successful."

Again, we watched Papa slowly open the envelope, but this time there was no doubt about the letter, as Papa's mouth turned up into a big wide grin.

"We've been accepted to go to Australia," he said, trying to keep his voice in check. Mama came up to him quickly and rubbed his back while she read the letter over his shoulder.

"Why did they change their mind, Papa?" I asked.

"Apparently Australia is short of females, and they need more girls or women to help populate the country. They have reviewed all the declined applications, and as we have seven girls, they've decided that my health problems are not serious enough to not accept us."

"I would like everyone to go to bed early tonight, as Mama and I will have a lot of things to talk about. We have not yet decided if we will actually go to Australia. We need to weigh up our options."

We all agreed, but we didn't get to sleep early. We talked late into the night, excitedly planning our new life in Australia. I participated in these discussions, but in the back of my mind I was getting concerned. Now that the possibility was real, I realised that, if we did go, my life would once again be turned upside down. Leaving all my friends behind, especially Fietje, and our large extended family: all the aunts and uncles, and my beloved Oma, Papa's mother, my cousins and my God-mother.

I lay awake for hours, excitement intermingled with fear and trepidation. I must have fallen asleep eventually.

The next morning, I felt tired and had a headache. I told Mama and Papa that I wasn't feeling well, and they let me stay home from school.

After the other children had gone to school and kindergarten, Mama came upstairs to check on me. I pretended to be asleep, I was too worried where all this might be heading. I was confused, mixed emotions combined with hormones swinging my moods from euphoria to depression.

Chapter 11

The next morning I got up early, and started to cut lunches. I actually beat Papa out of bed, and though I hadn't had much sleep, I felt remarkably awake. As I was spreading the bread with margarine, my mind wouldn't stop thinking about yesterday's events.

What can be the worst thing that can happen if we go to Australia? I can learn a new language, and I've always made friends easily. Can we come home if it doesn't work out? I guess if I don't like it, and Mama and Papa want to stay, I can wait a few years and then come back when I'm an adult.

"Marijke, you're up early this morning." Papa's voice made me jump. "You're almost finished with the lunches, thank you."

"I was awake anyway, Papa. I can't stop thinking about Australia, and what it will be like."

"Well, Mama and I talked about it a lot last night. Now, you mustn't tell anyone else yet, but I think we will go. We feel it'll be a new start for all of us. After everything that's happened over the past eighteen months, with Mama dying, and now with your new Mama, it might be good to get away from all the memories, and start again."

"When we will go?" I hoped not too soon, as I wanted time to finish Grade six. It was important to me to finish dux of the school before going to high school.

"Not for a few months I would imagine," Papa said in response to my question. "Mama and I think about May or June next year. We do have to wait until all government arrangements are in place. And we need inoculations against various diseases. It will take some time. But don't forget now, not a word to any of the others. Mama and I are still discussing the final details, we'll tell everybody when we've made our decision."

Soon, everybody was up and getting ready for school. Papa set off for work on his bike and we all went off to the various schools we attended. I decided not to look for a tram ticket that morning. I wanted to walk and think about everything. I enjoyed walking, especially if I wanted to think or work out a problem.

The half hour plus it took me to walk to school was time well spent. My head had cleared, and I was once again feeling positive about all these happenings. I was thrilled when I got to class that we were going to have our first English lesson. I don't think anyone else was as excited to learn English as I was.

When I got home I couldn't wait to show off the few English words I had learned that day. I found Mama in the kitchen preparing the evening meal. "Mama, I learned some English today, do you want to hear some words?"

Mama turned away from the sink and looked at me. "Yes, of course, what did you learn?"

"I learned boy and girl and table," I said proudly.

"That's very good. It's always nice to learn a different language," Mama said in her quiet voice.

Over dinner that night Papa informed everyone that we would definitely be moving to Australia, to start afresh. There were squeals of delight and joy from around the table.

"There's still a lot to be done, and I'm not sure how our families will take this news," Papa said. "I will tell Oma Wegman tomorrow. I don't think she'll be happy about it."

Our dear Oma, Papa's mother, was one of my favourite people in the whole wide world. She was a shortish and rotund woman, with huge thighs. Her wavy hair, dark when she was younger, had turned a delightful white. A pretty shiny white; not a grey hair to be seen. It also had a lovely natural wave in it. Oma had been large ever since I could remember, but her size wasn't an issue with me. I wasn't aware of skinny or fat. To me at that time of my life, people were people, and we were all different. It was her spontaneous laugh and her love for all her grand-children that made her special.

We also enjoyed the lolly jar next to her chair. When we visited she'd sneak some lollies to us when Papa wasn't watching. That lolly jar probably had a lot to do with her size.

At dinner the next evening, Papa told us that he'd told Oma and Opa about our planned move. Papa said, "Oma looked at me with her mouth wide open, and her dentures almost fell out. Then, when she'd gotten over the shock, she stood up, and yelled at me, "Over my dead body you will, son, over my dead body!!." Then she sat back down, and kept glaring at me."

Oma was well over sixty, and the thought of leaving her was gnawing at my stomach. Poor Oma, she'd had such a busy and difficult life, and we were a really close family. I understood she'd miss us, and we would certainly miss her. I was sure Opa would miss us too, but he was a quiet man, not given to emotional outbursts.

All the planning for our big journey was undertaken by Papa, and I'm sure Mama had a good deal of input. I didn't particularly enjoy the inoculations, but they weren't too bad.

We went through another Saint Nicholas feast, Christmas and New Year celebrations. That winter wasn't as cold as the previous one, but there was a lot of wind coming in from the North Sea. It was bitingly cold, making my nose and ears feel like they were frozen. I continued to take the trams to school whenever possible, and I had a warm duffel coat with a big warm hood. We never wore slacks or trousers, always dresses or skirts. Long woollen socks and heavy shoes, made for the cold weather, were the order of the day. Glamour had nothing to do with how we looked, except for Sundays, when we wore our Sunday best.

By about February of 1960 things started to move along. We found out we would be travelling on a ship called the *"Zuiderkruis"* (Southern Cross). It was a warship, converted to a migrant ship. The Dutch Government had three such ships transferring migrants from Holland to Australia, New Zealand and America. We would set sail on 25 May 1960, the trip to take about five weeks.

All our belongings would also be shipped to Australia, but they'd be held in storage once we arrived until we had a house to move into.

"I know it will be an inconvenience for most of you, but you will all be billeted out to family members for a few weeks before we leave," Papa said one night. "You will continue to go to school if at all possible, except for the day before we leave."

Later that evening I asked Papa who I would be staying with. "You and Ineke will be staying with Aunty Jo and Uncle Arie in Amsterdam North," he responded. "I thought you might like to go back to your old school for those few weeks and see your old friends again,"

I threw my arms around his neck. "Thank you, thank you, Papa." I was overjoyed with this news. "Can I stay with any of my friends overnight if their parents let me? Please?"

"First it will need to be okay with Aunty Jo, and of course with your friends' parents. But I don't see why not. You'll be expected to help with chores while you are there. And Aunty Jo is pregnant again, so you'll need to help her too."

I loved Aunty Jo. She was one of my Mama's sisters, and when we lived in North I used to visit her often. She lived quite close to our old church and all the Catholic schools. She was one of those disorganised, open house people, who loved being surrounded by children. She already had two of her own and was expecting her third. She made us feel welcome whenever we used to drop in on the way home from school.

"Papa, I think everything's going to be fun in Australia, and I'm excited about going on a big ship. But the best part is that I have time to say goodbye to my friends at school at the orphanage, and then I get to see my best friends in Amsterdam North again, especially Fietje. Now I can say goodbye to her too. But I think it'll be really sad leaving them all and maybe never seeing them again."

"Well, yes, that goes for all of us, Marijke. It's a big adventure, but it's also a big risk we are taking. I hope it all works out. If I tell you a secret, can you promise you can keep it a secret?

"Yes, Papa," I promised excitedly.

"You're going to have another brother or sister. Mama is expecting a baby, and she's due to have the baby on your birthday." Papa looked at me with a big grin on his face.

I wasn't quite sure how to respond to this statement. How could Papa know when a baby was going to be born? Of course, I still hadn't been told anything about the facts of life as far as the birds and the bees were concerned. But the thought of another baby born on my birthday was an exciting prospect.

"The baby will be born in Australia?"

"Yes, the baby will be born in Australia. But don't forget, don't tell anyone, okay?"

"I promise, Papa." I was still feeling privileged to have been given such a big secret.

Towards the end of April I had to say goodbye to my friends at the orphanage, as I would be living in Amsterdam North for the last month before departure. The boat was scheduled to sail from Amsterdam on the 25th May. It was difficult, yet I hadn't grasped the concept of moving to the other side of the world. I was upset that I now wouldn't finish the school year, which ended in June. But the thought of going to school in North was worth this sacrifice.

My friends asked me to send them letters when we had settled in Australia. Hennie, Ursula and I put our hands one on top of the other, and made a pledge to always be friends, forever and ever.

On the Queen's birthday, which of course was also Papa and Mama's first wedding anniversary, Ineke and I were taken to Tante Jo. She looked much fatter than she was last time I saw her. She made us feel very welcome, and took us to the attic, where she'd prepared two fold up beds for us.

The next day, I went back to my old school. It was so good to see Fietje and Hettie again, and my other friends. I stayed over at Fietje's place a couple of times. She was the youngest in a family of four, and the only girl. She'd had cancer when little, and had some nasty scarring on her bottom lip. But we had been good friends since kindergarten and I didn't notice the scarring anymore. There was a ten year age difference between Fietje and her older brothers, the youngest was twenty-two. She was very spoiled, at least in my eyes.

Fietje had so much such as her own bike, a record player and lots of records. Her bedroom was plastered with photos and posters of Elvis Presley. I had never heard of him before, but by the time we left for Australia, I was in love with Elvis. Fietje played his songs over and over, as the two of us danced around in her bedroom.

She had a warm and kind heart, and offered me several of her things to take to Australia. But I had to decline, as Papa had said we could only take one thing on the boat each. And that was going to be my doll. I was getting a bit old for a doll, but she was so special to me, she was still my security blanket.

One night when I got home after having played at Fietje's after school, Aunty Jo was sitting on a kitchen chair peeling potatoes. She had a bucket of potatoes on the floor, and a metal bowl for the peels on her belly. On the other side of her was a pot with water.

"Marijke, come over here, quick," she said. "Look the baby is kicking the bowl." Aunty Jo's face glowed. As I looked over at her, the bowl moved slightly. As I got closer, the bowl, peels and all, went flying off her lap. Aunty started laughing. She sounded so much like my Mama I caught my breath.

"I think this is going to be a very active baby," Aunty Jo laughed. "It's not even born yet, and look at the mess it's already made!" She waved her arm over the floor, where potato peels lay everywhere. When we both stopped laughing I picked up the potato peels for her. Her belly was too big for her to bend over.

"Marijke, come and put your hand on my tummy," she said quietly.

I wasn't sure what to make of that. It was only just recently I had become aware that babies grew inside a mother's stomach. To be asked to put my hand on her stomach was not something I had expected.

I tentatively put my hand on her stomach. She took hold of it, and moved it up. I felt something move.

"That is one of the baby's feet," she said, as she slowly moved my hand to another spot. "This is the other foot." As she said this, the baby kicked quite hard. Aunty said "Ouch...that hurt." But she laughed as she said this.

She slowly took my hand across her stomach, gently explaining about the baby, as I felt it move at times. At one stage I felt a little fist scrape against my hand. For once I was lost for words. I kept my hand there for a while longer.

"Aunty Jo, how did your baby get into your stomach?" I asked, totally perplexed.

Aunty looked at me for some seconds, deep in thought. "Didn't your Mama talk to you about how babies are made before she died?"

"No, she only told me that Black Piet brought me one year." This statement brought another laugh from Aunty.

"I think you need to ask your new Mama," she said gently. "I don't think it's up to me to talk to you about such things. All I can tell you is that God gives us a true blessing when we conceive a baby."

When I lay in bed that evening, I glowed with the warmth of having felt this little baby move inside Auntie's stomach. I wondered how God blessed people to get conceived. Maybe when you pray in church and ask God to conceive a baby.

The time was flying by and the last day at school came around all too quickly. Fietje's family invited me to join them after school for a farewell party.

A party, a real party, for me! How exciting. When we got there, they had so many delicious goodies. Little cakes, biscuits, lollies, cordial and ice-creams. Then they gave me a packet of lollies to take with me on the boat.

"You'll share that with your brothers and sisters, won't you?" Mrs Wessels said.

"Yes, of course, thank you very much." I was really sad to say goodbye to my friends, but I had to leave. Aunty Jo was cooking a special dinner for us tonight. Fietje and I promised to write. As with Hennie and Ursula, we also put our hands together and vowed to stay friends forever. Fietje then handed me a little parcel. "It is only small, but I want you to wear it forever," she said. Inside was a small gold locket with a photo of her inside. I put it around my neck and hugged her. "I'm going to miss you," I cried.

When I got back to Aunty Jo's house, she had cooked dinner. Just as well I had a veracious appetite, after all the things I had eaten at Fietje's house.

I packed my clothes in a bag, and helped Ineke pack hers. Papa had organised to collect our clothes that night to pack into suitcases. Aunty gave me one of her nighties to wear, and we only kept the clothes we would be wearing for our departure.

When I got to bed that night, I didn't sleep for a long time. I tried to imagine being on a big boat. The only boats I had ever been on were the ferries across the "IJ." I had seen barges and houseboats, so I imagined the boat would probably be three or four times bigger than them.

The next morning I woke up early, I couldn't contain my excitement. I woke Ineke up, and got her to get into bed with me. I cuddled her close, and talked to her about going on the big boat today. She wouldn't be five until August, and couldn't comprehend any of it. I just needed to talk to someone, and she was a good listener.

After about ten minutes Ineke fell asleep in my arms. I hugged her, holding her real tight. Today was going to be a very big day in our lives. Things would never be the same again.

When Papa arrived to pick us up, the rest of the family was with him.

"We're going to Mama's grave first," he said, "so we can all say goodbye to her."

He left the cases at the bottom of the stairs at Aunty Jo's, and we walked to the cemetery. I held tightly onto Lidy's hand. I hadn't seen the others for nearly a month, and although I had enjoyed my time with Aunty Jo, I had missed my brothers and sisters.

At Mama's grave, a deep sadness came over me. I started to cry. Ann came over and put her arm around my shoulders. She also had tears in her eyes. I hadn't thought about not being able to come to Mama's grave in the future. I bowed my head, and silently said a little prayer, "God, please look after Mama in heaven. Mama, please stay with me when we go to Australia. I love you. Amen."

As we left the cemetery, nobody talked for a while. But soon, the excitement of what was to come took over again. We went back to Aunty Jo's to pick up all our cases. As she was due to have her baby within the next couple of weeks, she wasn't coming to see us off. She cried as she said goodbye.

"This is hard," she said. "I love being around my sister's children, it brought her closer to me again." She gave me a real big hug and thanked me for helping her.

She waved from her front door until we were around the corner, where we caught a bus to the harbour. By the time we were all on the bus, along with our cases, there wasn't much room for anyone else.

It only took about ten minutes by bus, then onto the ferry, and then another bus. When we got off the bus I couldn't believe my eyes! This boat was enormous! It was about six stories high, with big chimneys. I had never seen anything like it in my life.

There were people milling around everywhere, and it took us a while to find a group of family members waiting to see us off. We lugged our suitcases over to them, and soon we were a very large group. Most of Papa's brothers and sisters and their families were there. Oma Wegman and most of my Mama's family as well as this Mama's family. All in all, more than one hundred people were there to say goodbye. It took a long time to get around all of them. Giving and receiving the traditional two kisses per person, by the time we got around them all, it was time to board the ship.

Oma Wegman was crying, as were some of the aunts and uncles. Walking up the gangplank we kept turning around to wave goodbye.

Once on board, we were led to some cabins on the lowest deck. As we were the largest family on board, we were given two four berth cabins, and one double. John was put into a dormitory type cabin, with eight bunks, for young single men. Mama and Papa had a double cabin.

We put our luggage down, and went up the steep narrow steps to the top deck. We found a spot where we could see the family on the wharf. We waved like mad until they spotted us. They all started to shout and wave, Oma waving a large white hankie.

Suddenly the ship's siren sounded loudly, and at the same time a big blast of black smoke escaped from the large funnel. It made me jump, it was so loud. A few minutes later, another siren, and more smoke. Then slowly the ship started to move away from the wharf.

The family on the wharf continued to wave, as did we. My arms were aching, but I kept waving, and yelling goodbye. They became smaller and smaller, until finally we could no longer distinguish them. We stood there for a while longer, until the ship went around a bend in the harbour.

"Come on everybody," Papa yelled above the noise, "go down to the cabins, and unpack your cases. You have about an hour before lunch is served in the dining room."

I shared my cabin with Willie, Trudy and Ineke. We had a wardrobe each, and a drawer each. When I unpacked I put my doll on my bed. I didn't argue about wanting to sleep in the top bunk, I was happy to sleep in the bottom bunk. I didn't realise then, but I suffered from claustrophobia, and the top bunk was too close to the ceiling of the cabin. Trudy and Willie each took a top bunk. It was exciting to have a separate single bed each.

It didn't take long for us to realise we were close to the engines, and it was going to be a noisy trip.

Papa knocked on the door, telling us we were scheduled to go to lunch. There were three sittings for each meal, and we had the first sitting for this lunch.

When we walked into the dining room, I went into shock. I had never seen such a feast of food. Some of the food I had never even seen before. The meal was a buffet, something new to our whole family. There were trays and trays of all kinds of food. No plain cheese or jam sandwich here. First there were two different soups to choose from. After that there was ham and chicken, with lots of different salads and a variety of hot vegetables. Not only that, there was another big table with all sorts of fruit. We could pick out what we wanted. There were waiters to serve up the meats, and then we could just dish up whatever we wanted. There was so much that it was actually scary. I wanted to try everything , but I knew I couldn't eat it all. How was I going to make a choice?

I am sure my eyes were as big as saucers, as were those of the whole family. We had never in all our lives seen such an abundance and variety of food. I ate until I could eat no more, and then I took an apple and a banana to our cabin to eat later. Whenever we had fruit at home, we would get a piece of something. If we had oranges, we would get one segment of orange each. An apple would be cut into quarters. Bananas and grapes were luxury fruits, and if we ever had them, the banana was shared by three, and we would get a maximum of five or six grapes.

In the afternoon there was a large meeting with the captain where we all got a free soft drink, another luxury we had never tasted before. At least I never had. A muster was held and onboard safety rules were explained.

By then, the ship had left the harbour and had entered the North Sea.

That night, we were scheduled for the second sitting for dinner. Another feast, but this time served at the table. Soup, then chicken or beef with vegetables, and ice cream and fruit salad.

After dinner, we all went into another big room, and we played games. There were lots of games to choose from. They had packs of cards, different board games and books to read.

As I lay in bed that night, the ship's engines were noisy and the ship itself was rolling, I went over the day in my mind.

If this is what the whole trip is going to be like, I think I'm going to enjoy this. So much food. And the Australian Government is paying for all this. Australia must be a very wealthy country, to give so much food to people they don't even know yet. I like Australia already!

Chapter 12

The next morning the first sitting for breakfast was at seven-thirty, and we went to that. There weren't too many people there, probably because it was so early, but also because quite a few people were sea-sick. Luckily I felt fine.

Again, we were amazed at the amount of food available. Different cereals, porridge and a variety of breads. There were thinly sliced cold meats, delicious cheeses, jams, peanut butter, many more spreads and fruit juices as well as tea or coffee. We had never in our lives seen so much food, or had so many choices.

"Just go and help yourselves," our waiter told us. A waiter, I never even knew they existed until this trip.

I felt like the princess Mama used to tell me I was named after. I didn't think there was anyone else in the world who could be so spoiled for choice. Again I snuck pieces of fruit back to our cabin, but soon learned I could have enough fruit every meal.

They also had morning and afternoon tea every day, usually on the top deck. Morning teas consisted of a variety of cakes and biscuits and afternoon tea usually another choice of various fruits, cheeses and some chocolates.

I was receiving quite some attention from a lot of the Indonesian crew, with promises of little gifts or some extra special treats. In my innocence, I was unaware these guys were flirting with me, and may have had some ulterior motives for their attention.

Mama and Papa were keeping an eye on my two older sisters, Willie and Ann, who were also receiving special attention from the crew. Willie was almost seventeen and Ann was fifteen. No doubt they were attractive to a ship full of virile young seamen.

We sailed past France, barely seeing the coastline. Then around Portugal and Spain, sailing close to the coast with the Rock of Gibraltar on the left side of the ship, and the Moroccan coast on the right. We continued to sail the Mediterranean Sea. Our first port of call was Malta, a small island just below Italy. We'd been sailing eight days, and had settled into a routine. The weather had been quite warm, and there were lots of activities onboard, catering for every age and taste.

I don't know why, but we weren't allowed to disembark in Malta. The ship anchored some distance out to sea. We were advised that approximately five hundred Maltese migrants would be joining us on the trip to Australia.

The island of Malta looked beautiful from where we were. High rising hills, with white buildings, some on steep inclines. The Maltese people were transported to the ship by ferries. Watching them board I felt quite intimidated. They looked wealthy, with exquisite jewellery, and fancy expensive looking clothes. The women dressed in lots of lace and colour, the men in suits and ties. The children were also dressed to the nines, girls in frilly and frothy dresses, the boys miniatures of their fathers, in suits and ties.

Before Malta, we'd been one of only a few families on the lower deck. Now the empty cabins filled up with Maltese families. I had been looking forward to meeting people from another country, but I soon found out communication was a problem. The Maltese language was as foreign to us as Dutch was to them. At least the Indonesian crew spoke Dutch, as they'd been a Dutch colony until recently.

We found out this was the last trip for most of the crew, as Indonesia had become independent. I befriended a young waiter, Hamil. He told me the crew weren't happy about being sent home.

"We like working on the ship, compared to Indonesia the pay is good," he said to me one night. He'd come off duty, joining us in the lounge. Mama and Papa didn't seem too concerned about his interest in me. I guess they believed I was too young to get into any shenanigans.

After leaving Malta, things on board changed very quickly. The Maltese took off their fancy clothes and put on their everyday clothes, looking more like us. As we sailed the Mediterranean Sea towards Port Said and the Suez Canal, the weather stayed warm, and overall, life on board was pleasant. I was lucky I wasn't a person who put on weight easily, because I certainly ate more than I ever had in my life, as I'm sure everyone did.

We had some problems on the lower deck, as some Maltese families decided their cabins were too crowded or too hot. They threw some mattresses on the floor in the passages and slept on them. The cabins didn't have toilets or bathrooms. To reach them during the night, we had to climb over sleeping bodies. Papa complained to the Captain after a couple of nights, telling him not only was it a nuisance, but he didn't like his daughters to have to step over the top of young men.

The Captain came down the following night, clearing the passageway.

Brother John complained that some of the young guys in the dormitory he was in drank and partied all night. I believe he joined in the first night, and became quite ill. He had never had alcohol before in his life. John had celebrated his fourteenth birthday on the twenty-sixth of May, the day after we set sail. He didn't tell Papa he had taken part the first night the Maltese boys came on-board.

Again Papa talked to the Captain, and each night, a check was made of the dormitories, curtailing a certain amount of these all night parties.

As we approached Port Said, a meeting was called by the Captain. All passengers were allowed to disembark for the afternoon.

"I must warn you to take care. Merchant boats will meet us as we approach Port Said. They sell many types of merchandise, especially leather goods. Tobacco products like cigarettes are very precious commodities, and if you plan to disembark, you must not take any cigarettes with you. The local police do not take kindly to anyone caught with cigarettes, and you could find yourself in trouble."

Papa and Mama decided we would all disembark and look around Port Said. I was so excited, my first time stepping onto foreign soil, although I had no idea what to expect.

As we approached Port Said, the ship slowed down, and as the Captain had predicted, small craft by the dozen came alongside the ship. The crew provided us with small baskets attached to large ropes. I watched fascinated with the goods being purchased. Papa said that everything was really cheap, but he said we should wait until we disembarked, and see what was on sale on shore .

As we left the ship for the first time in two weeks we were given special passes.

Walking down the gangplank, I spotted armed soldiers standing on either side, long rifles slung over their shoulders. They looked mean. I was really scared, and looked at Papa and Mama for reassurance.

"Why are they there?" I whispered to Papa, too scared to talk out loud.

"They are there to protect us," Papa said. But I could see in his face that he didn't like the look of these men either.

We walked past them, out onto the wharf. One of the ship's crew directed us towards the shopping area. As we followed his directions, we were quickly surrounded by children, dressed in rags, begging. Their dirty faces looking up, big eyes pleading, grubby hands cupped together. "Please, sir, a penny please." One after the other begged and pleaded. I felt so sorry for them, I almost cried. Of course, we had no money to give them. Papa told us to keep walking.

"If you stop, they will keep crowding us. If we don't take any notice, they will move to the next group of people," he said.

As we approached the shops, there were more soldiers walking around with rifles, making me rather nervous.

The buildings in Port Said were made of thick blocks of cement, painted white, the paint peeling in many places. The streets were narrow with small shop fronts and people sitting on little benches in front of them. As soon as we were close enough, they would rise and start gesturing, inviting us inside to view their wares.

We went inside several shops, but Papa and Mama didn't buy anything. When we went into a shop that had some beautiful hand-made leather goods, including bags and shoes, Papa told each of us to try on a pair of sandals.

I don't believe I had ever seen such lovely shoes, the leather soft and pliable. The pair I really wanted had a braided pattern across the instep, with a strap around the back of the heel. They were a light brown, beige colour, and felt really nice and comfortable to walk in.

Papa went towards the back of the shop, and there was some gesticulating taking place. Mama stood near the shop door, nonchalantly looking out. The other kids were all looking at all the things in the shop. I still wore the shoes I hoped Papa would buy, and walked over to where he was talking to the shop keeper. As I approached them, I saw Papa hand over a carton of cigarettes, which he pulled out from under his jacket. I caught my breath, remembering the Captain's warning.

Papa must have heard me, and turned around. He waved me away with his hand, and put a finger up to his mouth, warning me to be quiet. I was so scared. What if Papa was caught dealing with cigarettes? He would be put in jail! And then what would happen to us? Thank heavens he was soon finished, and told everyone to pick up their shoes. He had bought them for us with his cigarettes.

As we walked out of the shop, Papa put his hand on my shoulder, "Marijke, you didn't see anything, right?"

"No, Papa, I didn't see anything. I just saw you talking to the man in the shop." I was still shaking, and as we stepped back into the street, I looked around to see if any rifle-carrying soldiers were within view. It wasn't until we came to the corner that a couple of them walked past, smiling at us as we started our return trip to the ship. Whew, we had made it.

Papa delighted us all by buying an ice-cream for the whole family. They were soft and creamy, between two thick crunchy wafers. I enjoyed the ice-cream, but I didn't relax until we were back on board, scared we would be asked how we had bought all those shoes.

Once back on board, Papa started laughing. "So many beautiful shoes for the price of a carton of cigarettes," he said, wringing his hands with pleasure.

"Papa, I was really scared. What if you had been caught?" I asked.

"Well, I wasn't, was I?" he said. "Besides, we didn't steal or anything. The shopkeeper was happy and we made a good deal. I thought you'd like having such beautiful sandals. It was worth it to see all your happy faces!"

How could I possibly argue with him? And he was right, I loved my new sandals.

That evening, the ship started its slow trip through the Suez Canal. I stood at the rails of the top deck, fascinated. On the right side of the canal, there were two men in dark flowing robes, with long dark brown cloth over their head, tied to their heads with a band (burnous). They sat on two camels, real life camels. I had only ever seen camels in the zoo. They stayed with the ship for quite a while. They may have been border security, I don't know, but to me they looked majestic.

It took all that night, and most of the next day to get through the Suez Canal. By evening we left the canal, and we set sail across the Red Sea. The weather was getting hotter by the day as we were getting closer to the Equator.

One evening we were all sitting outside on the deck quite late into the evening. Papa wasn't as strict with bedtimes on the ship, and he was aware of the heat in the cabins, especially being so close to the engines.

I got up to go to the toilet, and on my way past the railing, some of the crew, obviously off duty, made some comments to me, which I didn't understand. I smiled at them, and kept walking. On my return they were still there, and a couple were standing in my way. I went to walk around them, but they moved, blocking my way.

"Come on, please let me past," I said shyly. I wasn't comfortable around boys unless I knew them well.

"What's it worth?" one of them said.

"Give us a kiss, and we'll let you past," the other one said. The guys still sitting down were laughing, and I started to feel uncomfortable.

"Come on then, give's a kiss." As he said this, he grabbed my arm, pulling me towards him. I had no idea how to handle this. I was scared, out of my depth.

"No, I don't want to kiss you, I don't like you," I said in my innocence.

"We not good enough for you, eh? You prefer the Maltese boys, eh? You don't like Indonesian boys?" He was still holding me, hurting my arm. I tried to pull away, but his grip tightened. I started to cry, when suddenly he let me go. I almost fell backwards.

"What are you boys doing?" Papa's voice sounded really angry.

I ran to him and stood behind him, shaking and crying.

"What were you doing to my daughter? Come on, you didn't seem to be short of words before when you were annoying her!" Papa was really angry, the veins on his forehead stood out.

"Come, Marijke, we're going to the Captain, to lodge a complaint," he said, and took my hand.

"We were only having some fun, sir. We didn't mean anything by it," the boy who had been holding my arm pleaded.

"It didn't look like fun to me. Look at her, she is frightened to death!" Papa glowered at them. "Nobody touches my daughters! Nobody!"

With that Papa turned around and marched me back to Mama and the others. He then disappeared. Mama asked Ann and Willie to take the younger kids to their cabins and get them settled for the night.

When they had all gone, Mama asked me what had happened. I told her the crew had been annoying me, and asked me to kiss them. She said "Yuk, I hope you didn't."

"No, Mama, I was scared. They wouldn't let me go past unless I kissed them. But I said I didn't like them, and then Papa came. He was really angry with them. I think he's gone to complain to the Captain." I cried again while I relived that nasty experience.

"Good for you, you did the right thing," Mama said. "Don't let boys bully you, ever. Be careful around them. Promise?"

"I promise. I will try not to go near them if I'm on my own again. I don't know why they did that, I didn't do anything to them."

"No. You will learn that some boys and men are like that. Just make sure you don't put yourself into that position again. If you ever need to go somewhere when it is getting darker, make sure someone else goes with you, okay?" I nodded. I sure had learnt a lesson that night.

This was the first time I had been accosted by boys, but there were many more experiences to deal with as I grew into a teenager.

When Papa came back, he said, "I told the Captain, and he asked if we want to have the boys suspended. I wanted to say yes, but decided that they're already under a lot of pressure, as they're going back to Indonesia at the end of this trip. So I told the Captain he should just talk to them and warn them not to do it again. The Captain agreed."

"Thank you, Papa, I was really pleased you came."

"I think you should go to bed now, okay? I will come with you and take you to your cabin, just to make sure they're not still there." Papa again took my hand, and walked me past the spot where the boys had been sitting, but they were gone.

When we got to our cabin, Papa gave me my goodnight kiss, and went back to Mama.

I lay in bed that evening, thinking about the boys wanting to kiss me. Although I had been scared, I also felt a thrill run through me. I wasn't sure why, but I thought that they must have thought I was nice to want to kiss me. There were young couples on-board, who strolled around holding hands, and kissing. Sometimes I watched them, and wondered how it would feel to have someone who liked you enough to kiss you like that. So I imagined that boy kissing me, feeling a shiver go up and down my spine. I fell asleep, hugging my pillow, somehow turning the event of the night around to make me feel good.

Above: 1954 - Class Photo: Fietje – front row, Marijke centre.

Above: 1954 – Papa and Mama Wedding Anniversary. Circled: Marijke front. Mama seated (Papa on her left) and Aunty Jos back right.

Above: 1958 – Last portrait of Mama before she went into hospital.

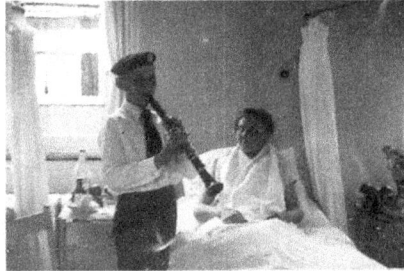

Above: 1958 – John plays clarinet for Mama in hospital.

Right: 1958 - Family photo Papa took for Mama. This photo sat on her bedside table during her hospital stay. From left: Lidy, Marijke, John (at back), Arnold, Willie, Ann, Margaret, Ineke and Trudy.

Above: 1958 – Going to Mama's funeral. John and Trudy on left, Marijke between nuns. Ann on right.

Above: 1959 – 30 April. Papa marries Aunty Jos.

Below: 1959 – All dressed up for the wedding: Left to right: Marijke, Willie (back), Margaret, Trudy, Ineke, Lidy and Ann.

Above: 1960 - Zuiderkruis

Right – 25 May 1960 – Family photo before boarding the Zuiderkruis for Australia

Above – 1960 – Weatherboard house in Wellington Street, Launceston, Tasmania.

Above – 1960 – Mama and Ineke outside one of our huts at Bonegilla.

Above – 1960 – Arrival in Launceston, Tasmania. Photo which appeared on front page of The Examiner newspaper.

Front to Back: Papa, Mama (Aunty Jos), John, Willie, Ann, Marijke, Arnold, Trudy, Margaret, Lidy and Ineke

Above – The Gorge and Basin Swimming Pool, Launceston.

Above – 1961 – Papa and Marijke checking for eggs in Wellington Street, Launceston.

Above – 1961 -. "Family Tree". Backyard Wellington Street, Launceston. From top: Marijke, Arnold, Trudy, Margaret, Lidy and Ineke.

Above – 1961 – Enjoying our first Australian summer. Backyard Launceston. From left: Ineke, Papa, Willie, Trudy, Lidy, Ann, John, Margaret, Marijke and Arnold.

Left – 1962 – Mama (Aunty Jos) serving dinner in our new house at St Leonards. From left: Margaret, Mama, Marijke, Trudy (in kitchen), Arnold and Ineke. (I'm wearing the dress I made at school.)

Right – 1962 – Margaret, Tiny and Marijke on front steps of our new house at St Leonards.

Above – 1962 - Happy family group at St Leonards. From left: Trudy, Arnold, Lidy, Tiny, Ineke, Marijke and Margaret.

Chapter 13

The next couple of days were scorchers. I didn't like the heat, and found it drained my energy. I tried to stay out of the sun as much as possible. We played card games and board games in the lounge with different people. We also drank lots of cold drinks to keep hydrated.

John became quite friendly with the Scheltinga family, another large Dutch family. They had several teenage boys, and John spent most of his time with them. These boys teased me at different times, but their teasing didn't worry me, it wasn't threatening.

Mama and Papa made friends with various Dutch adults, and seemed to be enjoying the trip. I didn't make friends with any girls; there was a definite lack of girls my age. There were quite a few older girls, over fifteen, like Ann and Willie, and lots of younger girls.

But I was included in lots of activities with all different age groups, from the over forties to the younger kids. The ship catered for those under twelve, with special supervised activities, giving the parents a break every day.

When we played games, some of the Maltese people played with us as well. Although we didn't understand each other too much, we managed to reach understanding. Some of the games were universal, so they didn't need too much conversation. Sometimes it became quite hysterical, as we used body language to try to come to an agreement, or understand how rules of the games were interpreted.

A problem became obvious as the heat increased. Many passengers on the lower deck again found it more comfortable to sleep in the passages, and some of them were sick during the night. Some of the younger guys used to drink alcohol until they were sick.

With the heat, this became unbearable; the smell of the sweating bodies, intermingled with the smell of vomit was awful. Papa spoke to some of them, but was simply laughed at.

Papa decided enough was enough, especially with Mama being pregnant, and her being so particular. She couldn't bear it, and it didn't make it easy when she tried to step over some of these sleeping bodies to try and go to the toilet during the night.

He went to the Captain and complained again. I'm not sure what the outcome was, but apparently Papa told the Captain if he didn't do anything about it, he would probably have diseases break out on-board. The Captain came down and spoke to the crew who were responsible for the cleanliness of the lower deck. He also spoke to all the passengers. "Unless you all want to get very ill, you are to sleep in your own beds and use the toilets if you need to be sick. If anyone is caught sleeping out here or not using the toilets, they will be removed from the ship in Aden."

A hollow statement because when we reached Aden, no passengers were allowed to disembark.

We anchored in the harbour, and the merchant ships with all their wares came to the ship. As in Port Said, people bartered over many of the goods, the likes of which we had never seen before. Tropical fruits, basket wares and leather ware, as well as jewellery made from large beads. I don't remember Papa buying anything this time.

Mama's pregnancy was becoming obvious, and I noticed she got upset easier than usual. I didn't understand this at the time, and thought she was just being a sook, looking for Papa's attention.

I was also becoming moodier, unaware that I was heading towards puberty. Sometimes I cried for no reason. I also became more conscious of the attention I was receiving from crew and other boys. I liked this attention, and received some small gifts, unaware I was probably expected to give something in return.

The heat in the ship, especially on the lower deck, was unbearable. The smell of sweat and blocked toilets did nothing to enhance the time spent down there. Papa and Mama, being so particular and clean, were angry that these conditions prevailed, and Papa complained to the captain again.

Early one morning I woke up as the ship was rolling and heaving. I was scared, and got off my bunk. I then saw the others were also awake. I opened the cabin door, but closed it quickly, as some passengers were vomiting in the passage way. My sisters also started to vomit, and I quickly grabbed some towels for them to be sick in.

I opened the door again, held my nose, and picked my way to Mama and Papa's cabin, trying to stay upright and not walk in anyone's vomit. I knocked, and Papa opened the door. Mama was vomiting and looked terrible. I told them the others were sick, but Papa said that he couldn't do anything about it.

Making my way back to our cabin, I decided to go up on deck to see what was happening. Walking up the narrow stairs was a challenge, and I almost fell down a couple of times.

Opening the door to the top deck, I was sprayed with salt water, and the door slammed shut, jamming my little finger. I screamed, and pushed the door open again, pulling my finger out. It was bleeding, and my nail had turned blue.

A crew member came down the passage, and asked me what I was doing.

"Don't even think of going out on deck, you silly girl. It's dangerous out there. The ship is rolling and the waves out there are higher than the ship. You will be washed overboard. Now go back to your cabin, and stay put until the storm passes."

"Yes, sir," I said, still holding my sore finger. *He could have asked if I was okay!*

Making my way back to our cabin was again a precarious proposition. People were still vomiting everywhere. All the bathrooms and toilets were taken up, and the stench was terrible. I finally made it back, and crawled into my bunk, putting my head under the blanket and my fingers in my ears. I didn't feel seasick, but the sound of the others vomiting wasn't doing me any good.

I slept spasmodically, and when I got up for breakfast, nobody wanted to join me. In the dining room only three passengers turned up. I enjoyed breakfast, and the storm settled down a little, although the ship was still rocking and rolling.

More people turned up for lunch, although most picked at their food. Mama and Papa, as well as the rest of the family were there. Trudy had just gone to the buffet bar when the ship was hit by a big wave. The ship rolled sideways, and as if in slow motion, furniture, passengers and crew started sliding. I hung onto my chair, and held the table, but to no avail.

It was then I watched a waiter, tray still on his hand, slide past us. Clinging on was Trudy, both arms wrapped around one of his legs. It looked very comical.

Through the glass windows we could see all the outdoor furniture flying around, and some of it going overboard.

I thought the ship was going to turn over, and so did many others. There was screaming and yelling, when suddenly the ship righted itself. Still heaving, but it was more stable, and we started picking ourselves up. I looked to where I had seen Trudy last. I couldn't believe my eyes. She was still holding on to the waiter's leg for dear life, and he still had his tray on his hand.

Just as we were picking up the furniture, a yell came from the kitchen. "Fire! Fire! Fire in the galley!"

I saw some smoke coming from the kitchen, and panic set in again. Passengers collected their kids and seemed to be running around in circles.

The fire was soon put out with fire-extinguishers. We certainly could not say that this trip was boring.

The storm calmed overnight, and the next morning the big clean-up began; repairs to damaged furniture and hosing down of passages and bathrooms.

As we sailed across the equator steaming towards Fremantle, the weather settled, although it was still very hot. It was a couple of days after the storm that the captain's voice came over the loudspeaker.

"We regret to announce that a crew-member has passed away. Our laundry man, Johan, was found in the laundry. The ship's doctor advised he had a heart attack. As is customary, and as was his wish, we'll be holding a service tomorrow morning at six o'clock, after which he will be buried at sea."

Being curious, I decided to get up early and watch the funeral. I was fascinated as to how that would happen. John also got up, and we stood back near a rail, as we watched the ritual. All crew lined up in full uniform, and some sombre music was played. The casket was covered with the Dutch flag, and was slowly lowered into the water.

Brother John said the crew told him they drilled holes in the bottom of the casket, so the water could enter, and take the casket to the bottom of the ocean.

I don't know why, but for some reason, the casket turned over when it hit the water, and didn't sink. It bobbed up and down. I had to giggle, but I did it behind my hand, as this was a sombre occasion. But it looked so funny, the crew trying to use the crane type thing they were using to turn the casket over.

After quite a while, it became obvious that poor Johan's casket would not be going under, and it was decided to pull it back on board. They then drilled bigger holes in the bottom, and started the whole procedure again. As the casket was lowered for the second time, the sun came up over the horizon, and the water glistened as the casket disappeared. A quiet serenity befitting the situation settled over us. Some prayers were said, and the ceremony finished.

Mama told me I should not laugh about the poor man's predicament when John and I were telling the family about the casket. But I couldn't help it, it was funny. I noticed Papa laughed along with me. I think Papa and I had a very similar, and sometimes, sick sense of humour.

A lot of the crew were young Indonesians, and had to return home, as Indonesia had become independent from Holland. However, most of them did not wish to return to their homeland.

And so it happened that a few days after the funeral, an announcement came over, "Man overboard, man overboard." The ship's funnel blew loudly, and the ship slowed down, and eventually stopped.

Curious, all passengers went to the ship's railings to see what was happening. I stared out, and imagined I saw something bobbing in the water, but couldn't be sure.

The ship slowly circled the area, and was soon joined by three other ships. As is custom when someone goes overboard, a call is made to ships in the near vicinity to help with the search.

We never did find the man, who was supposed to have jumped and committed suicide. Whilst we were searching we saw a couple of sharks circling, and the crew's verdict was that he couldn't have survived.

Running a day late to schedule now, the ship set sail again, and headed full steam ahead towards our first port of call in Australia: Fremantle, a suburb of Perth in Western Australia.

The rest of the journey was reasonably uneventful, and early morning on 21 June, 1960, we sailed into Fremantle. From the ship it looked beautiful, with one hill, and the city built around the harbour. Although this was the middle of winter in Australia, it was quite warm.

We stayed in Fremantle for the day, and were allowed on land, exploring the town. We climbed a hill and saw our first real life palm tree. Papa took photos of us under the palm tree, to send back to the family in Holland. How tropical was that?

We had climbed some uneven steps to the top of the hill. Papa was never comfortable with heights, and as we started to head down, he froze. He looked down and said he couldn't go down the steps. There were no rails. The only other way was to walk down on the grass, but as that was quite steep, he wouldn't go down that way either.

What to do? We had to be back on board in time for dinner, and our departure to Melbourne. In the end Papa sat on his bum and slid down each step, slowly and carefully. It looked so funny, and Mama was not happy, as the back of his good trousers was getting dirty, and by the time he finally made it down, it was torn and frayed.

Papa, being as particular about his clothes as he was, put his jacket on, and walked the rest of the way back to the ship with his hands held behind his back.

After dinner he spent the rest of the evening mending his trousers. He was very good at this, and used his craft to make them look new again.

"Invisible mending" he called it, where he would weave the fine fibre together, after cutting a small piece from inside the hem.

That night the ship was abuzz with excitement. We would reach our final destination, Melbourne, in the next few days. Our long and hot journey was nearly at an end, and our new life about to begin.

Chapter 14

The trip around the South coast of Australia was exciting. Not in the sense that we had any other problems on-board, but it was the anticipation of reaching our final destination. Although the trip had been an adventure, I wanted to see Australia. The movies shown in Holland had looked really beautiful; big houses, fancy cars, wild animals like kangaroos and koalas.

The trip from Fremantle to Melbourne took just over five days. Every so often we saw the coast-line. Whenever someone spotted anything on the horizon, the news quickly spread, and we'd hang over the rails pointing and staring at a little blob on the horizon.

The day before our expected arrival in Melbourne, we began packing. Not that it took us long; we didn't have a lot of clothes. We only had three reasonable sized suitcases between eleven of us.

I had brought my doll onboard when we left Holland, but I couldn't find her. Nobody had seen her, but I was sure I had put her in a drawer. I asked everybody, but she was gone. A medal I won in gymnastics in Amsterdam when I was eight was also gone, as well as the locket Fietje had given me. I knew my sisters didn't take them. I was devastated.

"Don't worry, Marijke, you are too old to play with dolls now anyway," Papa said. He didn't understand that my doll was my last physical link to Mama. She had given me that doll, and I treasured it.

"You don't care, do you?" I yelled at him, throwing myself on my bunk, crying my eyes out. *Mama, I'm sorry, I am so sorry.*

We expected to anchor in the Port of Melbourne late afternoon on 26 June, 1960. The last evening was celebrated with a special "Captain's Dinner" and live entertainment.

I didn't sleep much that night; the excitement intermingled with fear, made me restless. I got up early, and noticed the ship had slowed considerably. I dressed quickly and went to the top deck. Several dozen passengers were already there.

It was only 5.30am, and still dark. Ships of various shapes and sizes lined up to enter a narrow channel. I went back down, and packed my last few things. We had breakfast then I went outside again. The sun came up over the horizon. I stood in awe, I had never seen such a beautiful sunrise. I was sure the sun, as it came up, was much larger than it had ever been back in Holland. It had an orange-reddish tinge to it, and this reflected in the water.

Although there was a nip in the air, and a cool breeze blowing, I stayed on deck, eagerly awaiting our turn to head towards Melbourne. After a while it was obvious we were not moving, so I went inside and joined in a card game.

An hour after lunch the ship finally started its engines. Back up on deck I watched as we followed a cargo ship. We passed through "The Heads" and entered Port Phillip Bay. Going through this passage was choppy, but the water in Port Phillip Bay was calm.

Port Phillip Bay is, and was, Australia's busiest port, covering 1950 square kilometres. Nearly half the bay is less than eight metres deep. Its greatest depth is twenty-four metres.

We docked late afternoon. On shore, hundreds of people waved and shouted, obviously families or friends of people on board. I learned later that many Maltese people were sponsored by family groups already living in Australia.

I waved back, and smiled and yelled, pretending they were welcoming me to Australia. Mama stood beside me when we finally anchored, a big smile on her face. "Heh, heh," she said, in a relieved voice, "I thought we would never get here."

Several buses lined the wharf to transport passengers to a railway station in Melbourne. We were then catching a train to Bonegilla, a Migrant Camp. We learned this camp was situated on the border of Victoria and New South Wales, near Albury Wodonga. Looking at the map, it didn't look so far. We were used to looking at maps of Holland on a page. We innocently assumed by looking at a map of Australia on the same sized page, meant the distances were equivalent. Wrong! The distance was over four hundred miles!

It was another two hours before we finally disembarked and boarded one of the buses. It took a long time to have the paperwork and immigration clearances sorted out.

The buses left in convoy, ours the last one. That's what you get for having the surname "Wegman." W's always came last, or close to last. I thought someone should process people in reverse order. Even all the 'van' and 'van der' names came before the Ws. Not many Dutch surnames start with X, Y, or Z.

We were dropped off at Melbourne's Spencer Street Station, from where all interstate trains departed. It was another hour before our train was due to leave, so Papa decided we would have a look around Melbourne.

Papa carried one suitcase, and Willie and John the others. The sun was still warm, and the street wasn't very busy. It was late Sunday afternoon, and everything was closed. As we walked, I noticed the houses were nowhere near as flash as the ones we'd seen on the promotional movies shown back in Holland. Most looked small and run-down, with closed curtains or shutters.

"Mama, why do you think all these people have their curtains closed? It's only afternoon, and the sun is still shining." I couldn't work out why anyone would block out the sun.

"I don't know, it seems silly, doesn't it?" She smiled at me.

We received some strange looks from people walking past. I didn't realise that a family with nine children walking down the street was not a common sight.

When we arrived back at the station, the train was on the platform. We found a carriage with no other passengers, and got settled. We were soon joined by the Scheltinga family, who were also travelling to Bonegilla. Between the two families we filled the carriage. We spotted several other people from the boat boarding the train.

The train was old, with hard wooden benches. One window was jammed open, and no matter what we tried, it wouldn't close. I sat next to Trudy, and Ineke and Arnold sat opposite us. The train pulled out slowly, crossing other tracks before it was out of the station. It rattled and it groaned each time it crossed another track. I had been on trains in Holland, but they had never been this noisy!

We chugged along, and by the time we reached the outskirts of Melbourne, the sun was setting. As we travelled further in-land, the scenery changed from hilly to very flat country. Farms and huge gum-trees, the likes of which I had never seen before, flashed past.

As darkness fell the scenery disappeared except for when we travelled through small country towns. The trip became boring, and I became aware of my gnawing stomach. It had been some time since we last ate. Mama gave us a couple of lollies and a biscuit each, but I needed something more substantial.

The younger kids began whining. Papa started to sing a favourite children's song in Dutch, *"We zijn er bijna, we zijn er bijna, maar nog niet helemaal."* That was the extent of the song. The words literally meant, "We're nearly there, we're nearly there, but not quite there yet."

After about twenty repeats, even the kids no longer wanted to sing that song. "Tulips in Amsterdam," again in Dutch, was our next song. In typical Dutch tradition, everyone joined in, in full voice.

Eventually it quietened down and almost everyone fell asleep, including me. I woke up when the train pulled into a station. The wheels made a loud grinding sound. My back ached and my hand had gone to sleep, where my head had been resting on it. I tried to get more comfortable, but Trudy was asleep and leaning on me, so I couldn't move. I did think of waking her up, but thought that might be a bit mean.

Six long hours we were on that train. It was so slow, and stopped a few times. I dozed on and off, but the seats were too hard. *Gosh, I am so hungry. My stomach is growling!*

When we pulled into Albury, the train stopped with a jolt. The conductor, who had earlier checked our tickets, walked into our carriage.

"You need to get off here, there is a bus waiting to take you to Bonegilla," he said.

It took some time to wake the younger ones up. They sleepily stumbled off the train, holding on to each others' hands.

A big man with a fat round belly and no hair was holding a hand-written sign, with the word "Bonegilla" on it. Papa walked over to him and showed him some paperwork. The man nodded, which was really funny. He had a big nose, and was wearing thick glasses, which made his eyes look really big. When he nodded, the glasses sort of wobbled on his nose, which made it look like his eyes were bouncing up and down.

He indicated the first bus, and we followed Papa on. At least the seats were not made of wood. Once everyone was settled, we were on our way again. By now it was close to mid-night.

We turned left at the first intersection, and I thought we had come to the end of the earth. It was pitch black outside, except for the bus lights. Suddenly someone squealed. On the side of the road stood a big kangaroo; a real life kangaroo. The bus slowed down for us to have a closer look. The animal seemed as mesmerised with us as we were with him, or her, I really couldn't tell. As soon as we came to a stop on the side of the road, it jumped into the bush.

My heart was racing, not only in wonder, but also in fear. *I hope we don't see wild animals all the time.* I had never been brave around any animals, even cats and dogs. We never had any in

Amsterdam, and neither did our family or friends. I knew if I saw a kangaroo while walking, I would be terrified. The only animals I felt safe with were those behind enclosures in zoos.

For a while every vehicle coming the other way, and there were many, made me nervous. They drove on the left side of the road, whereas in Holland traffic drove on the right side. It took me a while to get used to this.

"Okay, everybody, we're here," the driver's booming voice startled me. I didn't know exactly what he had said, but "here" and *"hier"* are pronounced almost the same in English and Dutch, and have the same meaning. The bus pulled up outside a large hall of some sort. The lights were on, and the other bus pulled up behind us a minute later.

As I got off the bus, I shivered, as the temperature was very cold. We soon discovered the weather in winter in this inland part of Australia was quite warm during the day, but often frosty at night.

We were ushered into the hall, which was a large mess-hall. Bonegilla used to be an army barracks, and had been converted to a migrant camp after the war.

A group of smiling ladies greeted us, and asked us to sit down at long tables. A hot meal awaited us, and what a meal it was! An Australian baked dinner – yuk. We had never had anything like it. It didn't help that it had been cooked hours earlier and kept hot.

Roast lamb, baked potatoes, baked parsnips, baked pumpkin, and some watery peas and carrots, all covered in thick greasy gravy. It looked and smelled revolting. It had all been cooked in dripping (similar to a suet), and kept hot for a long time, which made it all the greasier.

Dutch people generally ate very basic food. Back in Holland we only ever had a small piece of meat on Sunday, with a light jus, with one vegetable and potatoes. Vegetables were always boiled, and the cheaper cuts of meat were braised, which created the jus. We had soup every evening, but always a light broth, like chicken noodle soup, with little meat-balls, or a thin tomato soup.

Mama started to gag, and we all played with our food, despite being so hungry. I didn't mind the roast lamb, but Mama said she didn't like the taste of lamb. To this day, most of my family members will not touch baked pumpkin or parsnips after this traumatic experience.

But, oh, the desserts! They were delicious! We learned that Australians love their desserts, or, as they call them, pudding.' We had apple crumble and custard, ice-cream and hot chocolate pudding with whipped cream. With this the kids got a hot chocolate, and the adults tea or coffee.

The puddings were put out in buffet style, so we went back and back until it was all gone. Mama also enjoyed this, and got the colour back in her face.

After dinner, someone spoke some words of welcome, but not many people in our group understood English. But we were polite, if nothing else, and clapped and smiled when the lady speaker beamed at us. Another lady then stepped forward and spoke in Dutch, explaining that tonight we would be shown to our huts. Breakfast would be served from seven to eight in the morning. She said that after breakfast we would receive information and rules of living in Bonegilla.

Outside, the cold air made me shiver, as we collected our suitcases. The first lady who had spoken inside indicated for us to follow her.

There were many huts lined up in rows. It was extremely dark, with only the lights coming through some of the windows guiding the way. It was quite creepy actually. The ground was dirt, not sealed, and huts looked like they were made out of corrugated sheets.

We finally reached our huts. Each block had four huts co-joined lengthways, and backed onto another four huts. We were given four huts in a row. Mama and Papa were given the first one. The two boys in the next one, and the girls shared the other two.

A wooden step led into the front door of each hut. Inside was barren, no toilets, wash-basins or bathrooms, not even a tap. As I'd been holding out to go to the toilet, I asked the lady, "Toilet?" and squatted to indicate what I meant.

"Ah, yes," she said, "follow me." Torch in hand, she stepped outside and led me past two long blocks of huts, then turned left. We walked past another stretch of huts before we reached the "ablutions block."

It was dark outside, but she showed me where the light switch was, and turned it on. She was about to walk away and I panicked and grabbed her arm. "No, no!" I pleaded. I tried to explain that this was really scary, and I would not find my way back to the huts. I wasn't good at finding my way around at the best of times, and she had the torch.

She seemed to understand, and I went in. On one side of the wall were six "long drop" toilets. On the other side three wash-basins and three shower cubicles. The floor was a slab of cold cement, and the partitions between the toilets and shower cubicles did not go to the ceiling. The block was reasonably clean, but I knew they wouldn't be up to Mama's standard.

I sat down, and whilst doing my business, heard a noise above my head. I looked up and my heart stopped beating. A pair of beady eyes stared down at me. I screamed so loud, I am sure the whole camp woke up. The lady came running in, which scared the animal. It started to run around, making a huge commotion. I pulled my feet up on the toilet seat, and curled myself into a ball, head between my knees. Maybe if I didn't look, it would disappear.

Finally the ruckus stopped, but I wasn't moving. Wild animals in the toilet! What had we come to? I cried and shook, and couldn't move. Finally the lady's pleas and the cold moved me. She walked me back to our huts, arm around my shoulders. She talked to me in a soft voice, but of course, I had no idea what she said.

Back in the huts it was busy. Everyone was unpacking and choosing beds. There was no heating, and it was cold, very cold. The walls were thin, the little curtains on the windows were almost see-through, and the floor was laid with linoleum which had seen better days.

The littlies now needed to go to the toilet. They also had to clean their teeth and have a wash before bed. Mama told me to take them to the ablutions block.

"No, I can't, I'm scared. It's too dark and there are wild animals in the toilet!" I objected.

"Don't be silly, you need to take some of the responsibilities while we are here," Papa said. "You take the kids to the toilet."

"I need to go too," Ann said.

"Me too." This time it was Willie. *Thank you, God, please make them come with me.*

The lady had left her torch with us. I led the way, torch in hand, and surprisingly found the toilet block. I made everyone promise they would wait for each other.

The animal, which we later found out was called a "possum," had gone back to the position where I first saw it. This time it was Trudy who screamed, and the commotion started again. The possum ran amuck, scaring all of us. I was sure if anyone had not needed to do a number two, they would need to now!

We finally returned to the huts together, and quickly climbed into our beds. The beds were prickly and cold and very, very hard. The blankets were a dark grey cotton army commission; very heavy. Having a single bed each, I didn't have my sisters to cuddle up to and warm myself. Eventually I fell asleep from sheer exhaustion. It had been a long day. Before dozing off, I wondered what tomorrow would bring.

Please, God, keep the animals away from me.

Chapter 15

Monday 27 June 1960

I woke up early the next morning, needing to go to the toilet. I tried to work out where I was. It felt strange to wake up and not feel the ship rolling.

I got up and remembered I had to go outside and walk to the toilet block. Peeking through the little window, I saw it was still dark. *I can't walk to that toilet block in my pyjamas, and there could be animals out there!*

I started to panic,. I'd never had good bladder control. I wrapped the itchy grey blanket around my shoulders and put my shoes on. Stepping outside, I couldn't see anyone, and more importantly, no animals. I walked around the corner between two sets of huts and squatted. It was awkward and a little bit splashed on my legs, but at least I didn't need to walk all the way to the toilet block.

Back inside I crawled back into bed. I lay there, looking around the room. The walls were a non-descript grey, and the ceiling off-white. There was a small round table and four chairs.

The cold morning air seeped through the window and from under the door. The others were still asleep and I wished I had my dolly to give me some security. I thought of my first Mama, and what she would have thought of this place. Suddenly I felt sad, knowing that if she hadn't died we would not be here.

When everyone was awake, we traipsed to the toilets and showers, teeth chattering. I kept looking around for animals. We must've looked a sight, eleven of us in our pyjamas and nighties, with overcoats and shoes.

"I don't want to have to walk this far every time I need to go to the toilet or have a wash," I complained.

Mama pulled a face. "I don't think we have a choice. I don't know what we'll do if we need to go during the night. I don't want to walk all that way, besides, with the baby, sometimes I need to go real urgent."

I didn't tell her I had peed outside next to the hut. "I don't like going out in the dark, with the animals. And it's so cold, why do they have toilets outside? It's not normal. In Amsterdam everybody has toilets inside," I said, "The films in Holland didn't show us outside toilets and little huts and dirt roads."

"It's not what I expected either. Papa and Willie are going to Tasmania to look for work and a house next week. We'll only be here for a couple of weeks, I hope!" Mama said.

"I'm sure it won't be too bad. Look at all the space and grass and there's even a playground over there." Papa's voice didn't reflect his optimistic statement.

At the ablutions block Papa and the boys headed into the "Men's" and we all went to the "Ladies." Other women and girls were already there, and we had to line up to use all the facilities.

The water was cold, like it had come from the snow, and the thought of removing my coat to wash myself was not appealing. But I had no choice, Mama was there and would have made me take it off anyway. Some of the women stripped completely naked to wash themselves. I couldn't believe it! We'd always been taught to be modest. These women were indecent; they didn't care that we could see everything.

I tried to divert my eyes, but I had never seen grown women naked before.

I hope I don't get that much hair down there! It looks awful. And they have lots of hair under their arms too. And their breasts, they are all different shapes and sizes. Big ones and little ones, and that lady's are hanging nearly to her waist. Some of the nipples are all brown and big and sticking out.

"Marijke," Mama whispered in my ear.

I jumped, I hadn't noticed her behind me.

"Stop staring, turn the other way. These women have no sense of decency. Now stop looking and finish washing yourself."

I blushed, knowing I'd been caught out. I didn't look at Mama, I just nodded my head and turned back to the wash-basin.

Only Mama had a shower. We shared two towels between all the girls, and by the time I used it the second time, it was quite wet and made me feel even colder.

I don't like this place. It's so cold, with outside toilets and bathrooms.

Back in the huts we made our beds and combed our hair. We headed to the mess-hall, which was busy and noisy. Inside one wall was a big fire, just open, not inside a heater. Big logs of wood burned in the big fireplace.

Skinny as I was, I ate like a horse, and I was starving. I couldn't make up my mind what to do first. *Should I have breakfast first? Or warm myself in front of that fire?*

I needn't have worried, there were no tables available for us, so we headed for the fire.

"Stand back a little bit," Papa said. "Let the littlies in front."

I don't want to be mean, but I really like this spot! Why should the littlies always get the best spots? I'm freezing!

The look on Papa's face told me to do as I was told. I grabbed Ineke, as she was the smallest, and put her in front of me. She smiled at me, like she thought I was wonderful. I felt a bit selfish then, because I only got her because she took up less of my heating space.

When our table was ready I felt much warmer, and we all had rosy glows on our faces from the fire. The breakfast items were lined up buffet style along the wall. Corn Flakes, Weet Bix and cooked porridge made with rolled oats, with hot or cold milk. There was toasted bread and different jams and spreads, as well as margarine. Fresh and stewed fruits were also lined up, as well as orange juice and hot drinks.

Apart from the hot tea, this was not breakfast as we knew it. Back home, we either had sandwiches (never heard of toasted bread before), with sugar or jam, and on special occasions, a thin slice of ham or cheese. Other mornings we had porridge, but not like the porridge in the big pot here. We had "griesmeel" which is semolina cooked in milk, with sugar.

Even though this wasn't what we were used to, it was a nice choice. I took one piece of toast, as well as porridge and orange juice and a cup of tea. Like on the ship, I put an apple in my pocket to eat later. We had no food in our huts, and I wasn't sure what our next meal would be.

We always said "Grace" before and after each meal, and Mama and Papa stuck with this ritual, no matter where they were. We had done so on the ship, and we continued that tradition here. We crossed ourselves, all together saying, "In the name of the Father, and the Son, and the Holy Ghost, Amen."

We then put out hands together, bowed our heads and closed our eyes. Papa said a short prayer, as the head of the house, followed by an "Our Father" where Papa said the first half by himself, and then we all joined him in prayer for the second half. This was followed with a "Hail Mary." Then Papa asked God to bless us and the food we were about to receive. We all said "Amen," crossed ourselves again, opened our eyes, and simultaneously said, *"Eet smakelijk,"* which loosely translated means, "Enjoy your food." It was then, and only then, that we ever touched our food or drinks. After each meal a similar ritual took place with slightly different prayers, asking for forgiveness of sins, and blessings for the whole family. Mama and Papa held to these rituals to the end.

One of the spreads which I took that first morning was called 'vegemite," which looked like a dark chocolate spread. After buttering the cold toast, I spread the vegemite on thick, and took a big bite. I spat it out as quickly as I had put it in my mouth. It wasn't chocolate, that was for sure!

"Marijke, don't spit food out, manners!" Mama admonished me.

"I'm sorry, Mama, but that was not chocolate. It is really terrible," I said, and pushed the plate with the toast aside. *Stop being so fussy! If you'd tasted it, you'd know why I had to spit it out. It's disgusting!*

Someone later told me that Vegemite is made of concentrated yeast extract, with salt and malt extract from barley. It is extremely salty, is supposed to be spread thinly, and is an Australian icon. Australians love it, most other people hate it.

During breakfast people walked around and introduced themselves to all the new-comers. We drew special attention because of the size of our family. We caught up with some people from the ship and the Scheltingas sat at the table next to ours. At least we knew some people, which made it friendly and social.

After breakfast we attended a meeting with other Dutch people who gave a run down on Bonegilla, what you could and couldn't do. We were told if we were there longer than three weeks, we would be enrolled in school. In the meantime, we all had to attend English classes.

By the time we went outside the weather had changed. The sun was out and it was quite warm. Bonegilla looked much bigger in the daylight. People were out and about, and it looked more inviting. Children played in front of their huts, many others played in the playground. Adults sat out in the sun, reading books or papers. Some others stood in groups talking.

We went back to our huts. Mama and Papa decided that as they had a hut to themselves, part of their hut would be our "family room." We carried chairs from the other huts near their door, and also put two of the small tables outside.

"What will we do now?" Mama asked. "Maybe we should make a list of things we need. Then we can ask if they have them here, or if we can buy some things."

We sat around and the first thing to go on the list was a kettle. Mama and Papa liked everything to run like clockwork. I suppose with nine children, it was the only way to survive. Two cups of tea each with breakfast; two cups of coffee at eleven o'clock;

tea or a glass of milk with lunch; tea at three; tea after dinner and coffee before bed. As there were no facilities in the huts, they wanted to make sure they did not miss out on their regular drinks.

Quite a lengthy list was made, including grocery items. Mama insisted we should get a potty to use at night. She didn't want to walk in the dark to the toilet block, and neither did any of us. And if the little ones needed to go, they'd have to wake someone up to take them.

Once we finished our list, Papa said, "Come on, Jos, we'll go to the office and find out what we can get, and if there are any shops nearby. Willie, you come with us, so we can ask about making arrangements to go to Tasmania. Ann and Marijke, you take the kids to the playground, and look after them. John and Arnold, you can be our scouts and look around the camp. Find out where things are, okay?"

We took off into different directions. Right then I thought that maybe this place might not be as bad as it looked last night. The sun was nice and the sky blue, and everything looked prettier.

We had a lot of fun in the playground, and met kids from many different countries. We were used to using body language and sign language to communicate with the Maltese passengers on the ship, so used these skills to communicate as best we could.

An Italian girl came up to me and I thought she asked where I was from, to which I replied "Nederland," the Dutch pronunciation of "The Netherlands." A little while later she tapped me on the shoulder and said, "Nederland." It took a while to get through to her that was NOT my name.

The rest of the morning went quickly, and before we knew it, we were back in the mess-hall, which we now called the dining-room. Our table, the longest one in the dining-room, was set for eleven. Lunch consisted of trays of sandwiches, with savoury fillings. Tomato sandwiches, egg and lettuce, cheese, and ham, all neatly cut into small triangles. My first mouthful of tomato sandwich came as a shock, and I spat it back on my plate again, much to Mama's disgust.

"Marijke, I told you this morning not to do that!" Mama scolded me, looking at the partly chewed sandwich on my plate.

If they gave us nice food, I wouldn't have to!

"It's horrible, I can't eat it," I said, pulling a face to indicate how bad it tasted.

"You don't spit food out, ever," she said quietly, "you know better than that."

"Mama, you try it." I passed the sandwich to her.

Hah! I'm sure she'll spit it out too. Then she can leave me alone. She's too picky!

"There's nothing wrong with this. It's nice, it's tomato with salt and pepper," she said after tasting it.

"But we always have sugar on tomato sandwiches, not salt! And we never use pepper, yuk!" I could still taste it, and quickly took a mouthful of egg and lettuce sandwich.

Oh, no, this is worse! This isn't egg? I can't spit it out; I'll probably be sent to bed without lunch.

I tried to swallow the mouthful, but started to gag. I didn't like wasting food, but these sandwiches were disgusting! Just then, Papa, who'd taken a mouthful of egg sandwich, started coughing and spluttering. He turned his head around, and I saw him spit the food into a serviette.

"What is that?" he said, quite loudly. "Yuk!"

While everyone's attention was now on Papa, I turned my head and spat my mouthful into a serviette too. *If Papa can spit it out, so can I!*

Mama glared at Papa. "Joop, how can we teach the children proper table manners, when you set this bad example?"

"That sandwich is inedible," Papa replied. "I don't know what it is, but I can't eat it."

Mama now tried a mouthful, and again, thought it was nice. "There's nothing wrong with this. It has curry in the egg, that's all. I think it's quite tasty."

"Well, you can have mine," Papa pushed his egg sandwich onto Mama's plate.

"Mama, do you want mine? I can't eat this either," I said. *If Papa doesn't have to eat it, why should I?*

Mama took both my and Papa's egg and tomato sandwiches, and he and I and the other kids decided to just eat ham and cheese sandwiches.

Fruit was once again available; this time really nice big bananas and apples. It seemed to me that the fruit here was bigger than any fruit I had ever seen in Holland, and it must be cheap, because there was so much of it. We used to only get a piece of fruit, like a quarter of an orange, or half an apple. Here we could have two pieces of fruit each, and nobody said anything. I ate one banana, and took an apple back and put it under my pillow.

After lunch we sat outside our hut, and John and Arnold said they'd found a large lake not far from the huts.

"The water is really cold," John said, "but it is real clean, not dirty like the canals. I reckon we could swim there."

"And, guess what? A man told me there are orange trees close to here, and you can go and pick your own oranges!" Arnold said excitedly. "Real oranges, they grow on trees!"

"I think someone is pulling your leg," Papa said.

"No, Papa, I am sure he was telling the truth. He was a really nice man. He said we only need to walk about fifteen minutes to get there."

"Well, maybe tomorrow we will go and have a look." Papa still looked doubtful.

"I think we'll also see if we can walk up that mountain there tomorrow. It doesn't look too far away and not real high." Papa pointed at the mountain. Of course, anything higher than a speed hump looked like a mountain to us. In reality it was a hill, and not a high one at that.

"You're joking, Joop," Mama said, "you couldn't even get down those steps in Fremantle. How are you going to walk down from that one?" Mama laughed, her growing belly shaking.

Just then a Dutchman walked over, and introduced himself as Jan. He said he was driving into Albury and asked if anyone needed to do any shopping. Mama and Papa jumped at the chance. We stayed behind, exploring our new home and surrounds. We met some of the friends we had made that morning, and had a pleasant afternoon.

Mama and Papa came back with a few bags and boxes. Mama couldn't wait to pull out an electric jug. We had always boiled water in a kettle on the stove in Holland. But, of course, we had no stove here, and only one power-point per hut.

One of the small tables was made into a substitute kitchen bench. The electric jug along with the coffee, tea, sugar and tinned milk for the coffee placed there.

Willie, Joop and I were sent to the large kitchen to ask if we could borrow cups and teaspoons. They were placed in a cardboard box for us, along with some glasses and plastic beakers. Proud of our booty, we took them back to Mama, who put the cups upside down on the table, so they wouldn't get covered with sand and dust.

Mama and Papa had also bought two oval plastic bowls; one for washing up, and the other to be used as a washbasin. We had found some taps sticking out of the ground next to some huts. John was sent to fill the bowls with water. I went with him and filled the jug.

We stood around to watch the electric jug boil water. Mama and Ann made everyone a drink (they had to boil the jug three times, as it only held four cups of water). I ran back and forth refilling the jug.

We sat outside in the fading sunlight with our first home-made cup of tea in six weeks. It tasted good, especially as Mama had also bought some biscuits. A packet of "Nice" biscuits, which were plain biscuits with sugar stuck on the top. While nobody was looking I dunked my biscuit in my tea. I always got into trouble if caught out doing it, but nobody saw me this time.

When the sun dipped over the horizon the temperature dropped dramatically. We quickly took the chairs and tables inside. So far it had been an interesting day.

I hope the food tonight will be better than what we got last night, I thought, as I lined up to wash my hands in the new "hand-basin."

"I wonder what delicacies will be dished up tonight," Papa said, as though he'd read my mind.

Chapter 16

Monday 27 June 1960

We walked into the dining-room together, and were surprised that the table we had for breakfast and lunch had been reserved for our large family.

We lined up for soup, which was being dished up from huge boilers.

"Which soup would you like?" a Dutch lady asked me. "There's pumpkin or vegetable soup. The pumpkin soup is thick and creamy, and the vegetable soup has different vegetables in it."

I took the vegetable soup, but was a bit hesitant, as it had lots of large pieces of vegetables. But it was quite nice, and very filling.

For main course, there was chicken, mashed potato, peas, carrots and thick gravy. I enjoyed the meal, as did the rest of the family. It was a vast improvement on the meal we'd had the night before.

That evening, after dinner, Mama and Papa said we should all go to the toilets and showers before it got too cold. I had a shower and enjoyed the strength of the water; it was like having a massage.

Back in our huts, we put our coats on over our nightwear to keep warm. Mama had requested heaters from the administration staff, but hadn't received any yet. She'd also requested a potty, as she had been unable to buy one on her shopping spree.

We played cards, and had some fun. It was nice that we could make hot drinks. Although it was crowded in Mama and Papa's hut, it didn't worry us. Our apartment in Amsterdam had been small; we were used to being cramped.

"Willie and I will be going to Tasmania next week. We have to catch a train back to Melbourne, and then catch a plane," Papa said, when we stopped to enjoy a hot drink.

Arnold's eyes widened. "A real plane?"

"Yes, a real plane. I think when you come to Tasmania, you'll also come by plane." Papa smiled nervously. I was sure that he wasn't looking forward to flying himself.

"We leave on Tuesday, and we'll be staying with Aunty Rie and Uncle Theo. We'll look for work and somewhere to live. As soon as we find a house, you can all come down. I hope it won't take too long."

On a plane! We'll be flying on a real plane! I don't know anyone in Holland who has ever been on a plane. I'll have to write all my friends about that. They won't believe it!

"Over the next few days, we'll look around Bonegilla and go for some walks. After all the time on the ship, it'll be nice to go for walks, like we used to at home."

The next afternoon we walked up the mountain. Like the previous day, it was cold in the early morning, but by the time we walked to the top it was quite hot.

At the top the view was unbelievable. It was a clear day, and we could see a long way. Most of the area around was flat, with a large lake on the other side of Bonegilla. Some isolated houses dotted the landscape, as did some smaller lakes. Although the farms were lush green, other areas were dry and arid.

We could see Albury on the horizon. The wide open spaces and the clear blue sky gave us the first indication of the sparsely populated area in comparison to Amsterdam. It was like we had moved to another world or another planet. It was all so big and there was nothing for miles and miles.

A Dutch boy had told me before we left the camp there were dangerous snakes in the bush. I was petrified, but we didn't see any, thank goodness. I didn't know what we would have done if we had come across one. I confronted the boy that evening, telling him there weren't any snakes. He said they hibernated in winter, and came out in summer. "You could've told me that before we went," I told him, annoyed.

That night wasn't as cold, and we played games again. Going to the toilet before heading off to bed, we found it was raining. It was only a light drizzle. We had our coats on, so it didn't bother us.

Sometime during the night I woke up with a start. It took me some time to realise the noise I could hear was that of heavy rain. I had never heard rain like that. I was scared the tin roof might fall in, it was so loud.

Margaret, Trudy and Willie also woke up. Then the sound of all that water hitting the hut, and the run-off from the roof, made me need to go to the toilet.

"Willie, I need to go to the toilet," I whispered.

"You'll have to wait till it stops raining."

"I can't. I have to go now!"

"Well, you can't, you have to hang on."

I started to cry, feeling like a cry baby. I couldn't hold it. Nobody ever understood that.

I put my coat and shoes on and opened the door, to be met by a curtain of rain coming straight down. I pulled my coat over my head and stepped outside. The ground was covered in water, and it seeped into my shoes.

I ran around the corner and squatted. Relief was more important than getting wet. When I got back to the hut, Willie was quite angry because I had left the door open, and the rain had made a puddle on the floor.

"You could at least be worried about me getting wet and cold," I said, annoyed.

I took my coat off, and put my wet shoes near the wall to dry. My feet were frozen.

The rain didn't hold up all the next day. "T'Jonge, jonge, jonge (Boy, oh boy, oh boy)," Papa said every now and then as he looked out. The streets were like rivers.

"They should've given us a potty by now," Mama said, as the huts became muddy from the comings and goings to the toilet by so many.

There was nothing to wipe our feet on. Mama looked close to tears. Papa yelled to shut the door every time someone came in. We had to take our shoes off as soon as we got inside.

Mama put a dark towel near the door, to use as a mat.

"When we can go to a shop again, we have to buy a mat. I can't stand this, look at all that mud being walked in."

"Oh, Jos, don't fuss too much, we can't do anything about it," Papa said.

That was not a smart thing to say, as I saw Mama turn around with tears in her eyes.

As we were so enclosed and the huts were cold, tempers frayed, and several times arguments broke out about silly things. Willie and Ann, who often fought, had a big argument. Ann ended up in tears, saying she was going to her own hut, and slamming the door behind her.

"This is not going to go on!" Papa yelled, as he thumped one of the small tables.

Ineke started to cry, and ran to Mama, who put her arms around her.

"This is not easy for any of us, and fighting is not going to help. I know it isn't what we expected, but it's only for a short time. We all need to get on while we're here," Papa said, a little calmer. "How am I going to know you will be all right when I go to Tasmania next week, eh?"

"Why are you and Willie going? Why do we have to stay here? I don't like it here!" I cried.

This is not how it was meant to be. I felt caged in. In Holland our apartment hadn't been big, but we had our own little spaces, and a lounge-room and dining-room. Here we only had these four huts. And we couldn't even go from one to the other without having to go out in that torrential rain. We didn't have many of our toys and games here, and there wasn't any room to play some of the games we did have. Everything was horrible.

"Why don't we go into our hut, Marijke, and plan to make a play? Then when I am in Tasmania, you can all practice it. We can stage it when we are all united again," Willie said, putting her arm around me.

I looked up at her. She was so grown up, almost an adult.

"Okay. Can I help make the play?"

"Yes, of course. We'll do it together. Come on, grab your coat and we'll go back to our hut."

"Can we come too?" Trudy asked.

"Yes, of course. We can all work on this together. Mama, do you have any paper for us to write on?"

Mama had composed herself, and gave Willie a pad. "Please don't waste it. There are so few things here. We'll need paper to write letters to the family in Holland."

"We're not coming, are we Arnold?" John said. "I'm too old to act in those silly plays."

"But I like being in the plays," Arnold said.

John, being the oldest of the two by three years, always bossed Arnold around. He would get him to do what he wanted. They'd always shared a bedroom, and Arnold seemed afraid to argue with him. John was very tall for his age, Arnold was not.

"But that is girl stuff. We'll do something else. Come on."

Willie, Trudy, Margaret, Lidy and I went back to our hut. We sat on the beds, and planned a play. It was going to be about Holland, and was going to be a musical. We would sing our favourite Dutch songs, and do little skits in between.

By the time we went for dinner that night, we had worked out all the songs, and written two little plays.

"Do we have to wash tonight?" Arnold asked after dinner. "We'll only get dirty and wet again walking back."

"Of course you have to. You know the old saying, "Cleanliness is next to Godliness," Papa said.

I didn't think Papa was right. How can that be, when God had made everything so dirty with all the rain? The paths were slushy and muddy. And like Arnold predicted, by the time we got back to the huts, we were wet and our feet were dirty again. I suppose our teeth were still clean!

In bed that night, I prayed, *"Please, God, stop the rain. This place is bad enough without rain."*

God didn't listen to me. It was still raining the next morning.

Chapter 17

After Papa and Willie left Bonegilla, I felt alone again. Although Papa was a disciplinarian, he was also what kept our family together. At least, to me he did.

The time at Bonegilla dragged on, especially on the days when the rain wouldn't let up. I couldn't remember ever seeing rain like this in Holland, where the rain was often sleety and accompanied by strong wind.

The Australian rain fell like heavy curtains; so heavy you couldn't even see the next-door huts. No wind, just sheets and sheets of water, which turned the streets into raging torrents. The misery of going to the toilets, bathrooms and dining mess was exaggerated, as the mud and slush ruined our shoes and socks. Walking the mud into our huts caused quite a few arguments, as Mama would burst into tears time and time again.

"I can't help it!" I yelled at her once. "This place is so awful, even the weather is terrible. Why did you have to make us come here?" In my mind, if

Papa had not married her, we would still be in Amsterdam. It might not have been much, but it was home.

I missed my friends, and had trouble making friends here. Apart from the language problems, there were no girls my age around. If there were, I didn't see them.

One sunny day I was playing in the playground with a couple of German boys. I didn't know their ages, but guessed them to be fourteen or fifteen. I got on one of the swings, and they took turns pushing me. I screamed when I went too high, as I was fearful of falling. They thought it was funny, and I got really angry with them. A lady made them stop, and I got off the swing, crying.

Not wanting to go back to the hut, as there wasn't anything to occupy me there, and I was sick of playing cards, I walked to the slide and climbed up. I was wearing a dress; as girls we never wore slacks.

On the boat, I'd overheard discussions between some of the adults, voicing their disgust that a young Dutch woman on-board was cheap because she wore jeans. "Real ladies do not wear jeans. Just look at her - she also wears red lipstick and bright red nail polish!"

I didn't comment, because I thought she looked really nice, with her hair up in a big bun, and she was very pretty. The jeans fitted her slim body well, and had lots of studs on them. She wore little boots with them.

As I slid down the slide, the two boys walked over and caught me before I landed. They laughed and smiled. I was so in need of friendship, I forgave them straight away for swinging me too high.

I walked around and climbed up the steps of the slide again, and heard the two boys below me, giggling. When I sat on the top of the slide, they ran around and placed themselves at the bottom of the slide again, both laughing.

I didn't understand what they were laughing at, but joined in. I hadn't done too much laughing since Papa left.

This time they didn't catch me, which took me by surprise, as I assumed they would. I landed rather heavily on my bum, with my legs up in the air.

They bent down, and before I knew what had happened, they had both put a hand inside my panties. Then I felt a finger scratch me. I jerked my dress down, shocked. They laughed and ran away. I sat there for a little while. I didn't understand what they had thought so funny, and I had no understanding of the severity of what had happened, but somehow, I knew what had happened was very wrong.

Yet, at the same time, my body had reacted in a way I didn't understand. It had sort of felt nice.

I got up slowly and straightened my clothes. I wasn't aware of anyone else around. When the boy's finger had partly gone inside me, it had scratched my skin, and I felt it sting.

"Are you okay?" a lady asked me in Dutch. I hadn't seen her, and she made me jump. I nodded, not sure what to say.

"Did those boys touch you where they shouldn't touch you?" she asked, her face concerned. "I thought I saw them touch you down there," she said, and pointed down below.

I nodded. "You go and tell your mother, and I will report it. Those boys will be dealt with." She gave me a hug, which reminded me of my mama, which made me burst into tears.

She took my hand, and walked part of the way back to the hut, gave me another hug, then walked in the direction of the administration block.

When I walked into Mama's hut, she saw I had been crying. "What's the matter, Marijke? Did you hurt yourself?" she asked.

I shook my head. *Should I tell her? I might get into trouble. Maybe I should not play with boys.*

"Sit down," Mama said, "I'll make you a cup of tea. I know sometimes it's difficult being here. But it is for all of us. I'm sure Papa will write us a letter soon to tell us we can go to Tasmania." She walked over to the kettle.

"The German boys touched me down here, Mama," I said softly.

"What? Which German boys? Did they hurt you?" Mama's shocked face told me this was bad. She didn't raise her voice, but her tone was very angry.

"I'm sorry, Mama. I don't know why they did that. A lady saw it and said she was going to report it." I started to cry again.

Mama handed me her handkerchief, followed by a hot cup of tea.

"You stay here, and drink that," she said, "I'm going to talk to someone. That can't happen." She stepped into her shoes and left the hut.

All my brothers and sisters were out, playing with friends, or exploring the area. Ann had taken the young ones for a walk. I sat and fidgeted with the hankie. I wasn't used to the quiet and felt desperately alone. I had finished my cup of tea when Mama walked back in. "I have lodged a complaint," she said. "They said the boys are in trouble and are not allowed near you again."

That was the end of the discussion, yet I had this awful feeling I had done something terribly wrong. I went to my own hut and lay down on my bed.

Mama, did I do something bad? I pulled the lumpy pillow to my chest and cradled it, pretending it was Mama cuddling me. I must have dozed off, as I woke up with a start when Ineke jumped on me, excitedly talking about some animals they had seen on their walk.

I put the pillow down and wrapped my arms around her. Her infectious excitement rubbed off on me, and I decided that I would forget about what had happened that afternoon. It was never mentioned again.

A couple of days after this incident we commenced school. As we had been at Bonegilla for three weeks, it was a requirement we receive formal education. I was placed in a combined class, due to my lack of English. Kids from all nationalities and aged from six to twelve were in the class.

To this day I can recite the alphabet we learned, day, after day, after day. A is for apple, b is for bear, c is for cat, d is for dog, e is for egg, and so forth.

Recitation of the words, plastered on a wall accompanied by pictures, became so boring, I completely lost myself in my misery, and the anger I had at being treated the same as the six-year-old kids in the class.

Early in August Papa came to visit for a weekend. It was Lidy's seventh birthday. Birthdays were such a big occasion in our family, and Papa had never missed any of our birthdays. He arrived very late Friday night, and left again Sunday afternoon. We had such fun that weekend, doing our plays and songs. We got quite an audience, as we performed outside. There was no room inside the huts. Papa smiled and laughed and clapped, and for the first time in weeks, Mama smiled, and looked happy.

Papa talked sternly to me about some of the things Mama had told him about. He said Mama had complained that I didn't help enough, and that I had yelled at her a few times. He said he expected more from me, and that it was very difficult for Mama, especially as she was pregnant. He threatened me with loss of pocket money if Mama had to speak to him again.

No mention was made of the incident with the German boys. I don't know if Mama ever mentioned it to him.

The rest of the weekend was fun, and I felt happier than I had since Papa had gone to Tasmania.

That was, until Sunday afternoon, when Papa got on a bus to go back . "It won't be long now, I promise," he said to us all.

"Papa, you said that weeks ago, and it is so awful here. Please make it soon," I said as I kissed him goodbye.

"I know. I'm trying my hardest, Marijke, but it is so hard to find a house. It seems Australians don't like the idea of renting a house to big families. As soon as I say there are nine children, their faces just drop. But, I'm sure it won't be too long. Now, don't forget what I told you and be good to Mama. This is very difficult for her." He kissed me and turned to the next in line.

Why is it so hard on her? This is hard on us. She's an adult. Papa, please, I want to go back to Amsterdam and see my friends. I knew I could not say those words out loud, but I couldn't be stopped from thinking them! *As soon as I'm old enough, I'm going back to Holland. Then no-one can stop me!*

The bus pulled away. Mama dabbed at her eyes as she waved with her other hand. The little ones jumped up and down and yelled, "Bye, Papa, bye!" until the bus disappeared.

"Come on, everyone, we'll go for a walk," Mama said. "I don't feel like going back to the huts yet."

"I don't want to. Can I stay here?" I asked. I didn't want to pretend to be happy, when I felt so miserable.

"No, I think you should join us. We're going to have a family walk. Much better than staying inside." Mama's voice was quietly firm. I decided not to argue. *I suppose anything is better than staying in this terrible place!*

Chapter 18

It was Saturday thirteenth of August, and another wet and miserable day. We were stuck inside all day, except for quick dashes to the toilet.

In the afternoon Mama sat down with Arnold, Trudy, Margaret, Lidy and Ineke and told them about her pregnancy. I sat back and watched, feeling very grown up, as I had known for some time.

I was pleased she was telling them, as I'd had trouble keeping the secret. I had told Trudy some time ago, but made her promise not to tell anyone else. Mama used a small book with pictures to demonstrate how the baby was growing inside her stomach. There was a lot of laughing and giggling and happy chatter going on.

"Mama, does the baby cry inside your stomach?" Arnold asked, which made everybody laugh.

We'd just arrived back in the hut after dinner, when there was a knock on the door.

"There's a letter here for you," a lady said, and handed Mama an envelope.

"I asked earlier if there was any mail, and I was told there wasn't," Mama said annoyed.

Every day she hoped to get a letter from Papa. When one arrived it always lifted her spirits, and ours. She would open it slowly, then read it, holding it close to her face. We'd wait around her, hoping she would share the contents with us.

Mama thanked the lady, closed the door, and sat down at the small table. We stood around her when suddenly Mama threw her hands in the air. "Thank God!" she said, then tears ran down her face.

I was a little confused. She was crying, but she had a big smile on her face.

"Are we going to Tasmania?" Arnold asked.

"Yes!" Mama's grin broadened. I jumped up, and spontaneously hugged Mama. The littlies jumped up and down, clapping.

"We're going to Tasmania, we're going to Tasmania," Trudy danced around, her skinny legs almost tripping over themselves.

Before we knew it, we were all dancing in a circle around Mama, chanting Trudy's words, "We're going to Tasmania, we're going to Tasmania."

I sang louder than anyone. I so hated Bonegilla.

"Shhh, shhh, that will do," Mama said after a while. "The neighbours will complain if we make too much noise." Although we usually did as we were told, it took a while for Mama to get us settled.

"When are we going, Mama? Tomorrow?" I couldn't wait to get out of there.

"Whoa! No, not that quickly. But it will only be a few more days. The government is organising our airfares ---"

More clapping and yelling!

"We're going on a plane to Tasmania," Trudy sang, and again, we all joined in. Singing, clapping, and not caring about any of the neighbours.

"Okay, everyone. Quiet!" Mama had trouble being heard.

Ann's voice was much louder. "Mama wants to talk. Come on, be quiet!" she shouted, laughing.

Mama still had the smile on her face as she looked around at all our excited faces. "Papa says we will be going on Tuesday. But, there is some bad news. He hasn't been able to find a house for us yet."

"Are we going to go to an orphanage again?" I asked. *Oh, please God, no. Although it would be better than to stay here!*

"No, some people from the Dutch Australian Association in Launceston have organised for families to home host us until we find a house.

Papa and I will stay with Aunty Tiny [pronounced *Teeny*] and Uncle Freek [pronounced *Frake*]." When we looked confused, she explained Uncle Freek was a cousin of hers, who had moved to Tasmania several years ago. "Aunty Rie and Uncle Theo, who visited us in Holland, will take in a couple of girls and the rest will stay with other Dutch families."

"But we don't know them," Margaret said shyly. "What if they're not nice?"

"I'm sure they're all nice. And the good thing is, they all speak Dutch and English, so it will be easier to understand what is happening. I am sure it will all work out. Papa wouldn't send you to any families he didn't think were nice."

"Mama, Mama, can we see you and Papa every day?" Lidy asked, a worried frown on her pretty little face.

"I'm not sure. But it won't be for long. As soon as we find a house we will all be together again."

Even the thought of going to stay with strangers didn't dampen my spirits. It couldn't be any worse than here.

It took some time for everyone to get settled that night, as we talked excitedly late into the night. Not only were we getting out of here, we would see Papa again, and Willie. We hadn't seen her for more than two months.

The next morning the rain had cleared, although it was still overcast. It was muddy outside, but Mama decided after we had been to Sunday Mass, that we should all go for a long walk together. The mood was happy and we sang as we walked hand in hand down the road.

John and Arnold acted as scouts and walked some distance in front of us. When the occasional car came down the road, we quickly let go of each others' hands and ran to the side of the road.

After a while, Ineke took my hand, and smiled at me with her big blue eyes; she was so cute. "I'm so 'cited to go fly on the plane. Are you?" she said, as she skipped alongside me.

"Yes. I think we'll go above the clouds. I'm a little bit scared, too, aren't you?" I looked at her, and it occurred to me that at her age, it wouldn't occur to her to be scared.

"No. I think we will see God, and Mama, and maybe some angels." Her innocence was contagious, and I wanted to tell her that maybe we would. But I knew we wouldn't, and I didn't want to get her hopes up.

"I don't think so. Heaven is way, way higher than the clouds. But I think they will be watching us," I said. "Come on, we will sing a song as we walk."

I skipped along with her, as we sang Papa's favourite Dutch song, "If I was a little duck swimming in the water."

As usual, everyone joined in, and our voices reverberated across the fields and hills. We sang with such gusto, when we passed a paddock with some sheep, I think our singing scared them. One started running away, and then all the others followed. The way their bottoms waddled as they ran, I imagined they were dancing to our singing. I giggled, unable to contain my happiness.

We returned to the camp just before lunch, and were still singing together when we walked into the mess. Some other Dutch people joined in, and lunch took on a party atmosphere.

After lunch it rained again, but it could not dampen our enthusiasm. We played games and sang songs, and decided to practice a little play for Papa and Wil when we got to Tasmania. It was all about kangaroos and koalas, and snakes and wombats. This was the happiest day in Bonegilla for me.

I took great delight in going to school the next day, as I could tell everybody it was my last day. No more A for apple, B for bear for me! I walked away feeling free. I knew I would never miss that school, not like I missed my school in Amsterdam.

Things were very busy when we got back to the huts. We all had to help pack and make sure everything was cleaned. We had to catch an early bus in the morning, then catch a train to Melbourne. We were falling over ourselves to help Mama clean. She would never consider leaving anything out of place, or a speck of dust. For once, I didn't mind how much she asked me to do.

At dinner that night some people came over to wish us good luck. There were no people left from our boat; they had all left within a few weeks of arriving here.

We were given breakfast before the bus picked us up, and the nice ladies in the mess hall gave us sandwiches and some fruit to have for lunch.

The long trip was uneventful. Getting off the train in Melbourne, we had a couple of hours before our flight. We had eaten our lunch on the train and Mama decided we would go for a walk. It was quite warm for a winter's day, the sun was out, although it disappeared behind some scattered clouds every now and then.

I was disappointed at the houses we walked past. They were all small cottages, made from big long wooden boards. Again, I couldn't understand that most of them had curtains and blinds completely covering the windows. Why would anyone block out the light and sun during the day? I didn't see any of those nice fancy houses they had shown us in the films in Holland. I didn't realise that this was the centre of Melbourne, and these were the first houses built there.

After about an hour, we got on the bus to go to the airport. No matter how much Mama tried, we could not be contained, much to the amusement of some passengers and the annoyance of others.

At the airport we were ushered to the First Class area, with comfortable chairs. There were some potato chips and nuts on the table, and we were offered drinks.

I felt soooooo important. We were being treated like we were very special people. A really pretty Air Hostess took us out onto the tarmac. There stood a big shiny silver plane. I couldn't contain my excitement. I almost wet myself. We crossed the tarmac single file. It started to rain, but nothing could dampen my excitement, nor that of my siblings.

Mama looked afraid. The doctor at Bonegilla had told her it was still safe for her to fly, but she was still very nervous.

"Can we see out when we get on the plane?" I asked Mama.

She shrugged her shoulders. "How would I know, I've never flown before, wait till we get on."

I only asked. She didn't have to get snappy. I won't let her ruin my day.

The Air Hostess stood aside as we climbed the metal stairs and into the plane. Once inside, I saw many eyes watching us, as we were given the first class seats at the front of the plane.

I got into a seat near the window and sat, mesmerised, as the rain increased and little streams ran down the glass.

"Can I sit near the window?" Ineke asked. She was seated next to me.

Mama leaned over from across the aisle. "No, Ineke, sorry. They said you are too little to sit near a window."

I gave Mama a big smile. *Thank you. I didn't want to give up my window seat.* I felt sorry for Ineke, but I really wanted to sit near the window myself. I put my arm around her shoulders and gave her a kiss.

When the plane lifted up, I was enchanted. The world grew smaller as we headed into the clouds. The plane started shaking, and I screamed. I cuddled Ineke tight, more for my own benefit than hers.

Then suddenly, we were above the clouds. The sun was bright, almost blinding, and the clouds looked like cotton wool, with some sticking up like mountains of fluff. I had never seen anything so beautiful in my life before.

Ineke was stretching her neck, and I leaned back so she could see. "Look, Marijke," she said, pointing her little finger to the bright sun, "there is heaven, it is shining like gold."

My eyes filled with tears. "Yes. And Mama is up there." I hugged her tight.

"Would you like a drink?" Another hostess asked. We were given orange juice and a packet of biscuits each. I sat back and closed my eyes, and sensed Mama's presence. I felt her smile down at me and knew that she was with me, no matter where in the world I was.

The flight was exciting and a bit bumpy. By the time we had finished our drinks and the hostesses had collected dishes and rubbish, the captain said we were preparing to land in Tasmania and we had to put our seat-belts on again.

Chapter 19

As the plane descended through the clouds, it shuddered for several seconds. One of the overhead lockers came open, and scared me. Nothing fell out and an air hostess quickly got up and closed it again.

"Marijke, I need to go to the toilet." Ineke tugged at my sleeve.

I'd seen some people use a toilet at the front of the plane during the flight, but we had been told to keep our seat-belts on. "I don't think you're allowed to go to the toilet now," I whispered. "Can you hang on?"

Her eyes filled with tears. "I'll try, but I need to go really bad."

"I know a little trick," I said. "I do this when I need to go really bad. I think about other things. It is only for a little while. Look, we aren't in the clouds anymore and it's raining." I noticed little rivulets running down the little window.

"It wasn't raining above the clouds. We were flying above the rain," Ineke said, in awe.

Phew, I must have taken her mind off needing the toilet.

As we descended I saw mountains and a long river, which twisted and turned, with houses and areas of forest on both sides of the river. It was almost six o'clock and quite dark. I was fascinated, peering through the window, trying to see everything.

Then the runway was below us, and we thumped down, which caused the overhead locker to fall open again. The plane made some loud noises, then slowed down quickly. I felt as if everything was happening in slow motion. I wanted to take it all in. The plane turned at the end of the runway and pulled up at an angle.

Because we were in first class, we got off the plane first. Compared to the airport at Melbourne, the Launceston Airport was small. Just a little building, and a ramp leading up to it, where people stood waving. I peered until I spotted Papa and Willie waving and smiling broadly. I waved back and started to run. I had missed them both more than I had realised. The rain had let up, but the tarmac was still wet with big puddles everywhere.

There were lots of kisses and hugs, and some tears, as our family was reunited. We walked inside the terminal and Papa introduced us to various other people waiting. They were all Dutch, and it was nice to be able to communicate with everyone. I met our new aunty and uncle, where Papa and Willie had been staying.

We were introduced to a man with a large camera. He was taking notes, and asked us all to go outside for a photo. Papa said he was from the newspaper, and he had interviewed Papa, with the help of some of the Dutch people as interpreters, for a story about our family. He lined us up; Papa and Mama in front, then from oldest to youngest. He stood back and then said he wanted John to move behind Mama, as he was too tall. John's chest came out, like he was proud to have been promoted in front of his older sisters. The photographer took several photos and left.

"Marijke, this is Mr van Maanenberg. You and Margaret will be staying with them until we get a house." Papa introduced me to a short, thin man, about Papa's age, who shook my hand. I had never before seen a face with so many freckles. He had reddish hair, which was partly grey.

"Hello, Marijke, it is nice to meet you," he said in a kind voice. I took to him straight away, he had such a nice friendly smile, and the palest blue eyes.

I was introduced to some other Dutch people, but couldn't remember their names by the time we walked out of the terminal. Carrying our cases, we walked to a large car park. Mama and Papa and the others all kissed us goodbye, and Mr van Maanenberg took some keys from his pocket and opened the door of a VW combi-van. Margaret and I clambered into the back and settled in. *Wow, they must be rich,* I thought, *I only knew two people in Holland who owned a car, and they were rich.*

Mr V drove slowly and told us about different things as we passed them. The road was quite narrow and winding. We came around a long sweeping bend, and in front of us were lights everywhere.

"Welcome to Launceston, girls," Mr V said.

I gasped; I had never seen such a beautiful sight. It was quite dark outside, and the city lights sparkled in front of us. I am sure my mouth was agape. There were hills all around, with a river reflecting the lights on the hills. Margaret and I just looked around. We drove through the centre of the city, then turned left and headed up a hill. The road zigzagged, with sharp hair-pin bends, which scared me. The van struggled to get up, but I didn't mind the slowness. The higher we went, the better the view became.

"We live right at the top of the hill in an old farmhouse," Mr V said. "We have five sons and a daughter. We also have chickens, a couple of dogs, and some cats.

Oh, God, I don't like dogs and cats. I hope they're not too big! I thought. Memories of sitting on a cat at a farmhouse when I was seven years old flashed through my mind. I had been placed at the farm for the summer holidays from the orphanage.

The family was lovely. They had a lot of hot houses and some pigs. I had walked into the traditional big farmhouse and was invited to sit down. I chose the chair with the fluffy black cushion on it. When I sat on the cushion, it jumped up and dug its claws into my thigh and buttock. I had never trusted cats since then. Not that I knew anyone in Amsterdam who had a cat.

And the memory of the last time a dog and I had come in contact was equally unpleasant. I had been to the shop with Mama when I was about six. A little dog had been on a leash, its owner a fat little lady. Suddenly the dog managed to free itself from the leash and ran, barking, towards us. It jumped up at me and nipped me on the arm and hand, before the owner reached us, profusely apologising. The dog hadn't broken the skin, but it sure scared the living daylights out of me. Mama offered to kiss it better, but I wasn't crying because it hurt. I cried from sheer fear; I had been petrified.

My attention was drawn back to the beautiful views outside. *This could be a really nice place to live,* I thought.

Finally, Mr V turned into a dirt-road, which led to an old weatherboard house. I couldn't make out the colour of the house. A small light hung near what I imagined was the front door, inside a small porch. Mr V turned off the engine. We clambered out of the van and a lady with blond wavy hair emerged from the door, followed by two red-headed boys. The drive-way was muddy from the day's rain, but it didn't seem to worry any of them. *Mama wouldn't like this. This is muddier than the roads in Bonegilla!*

We pulled our bags from the car, and headed indoors. We took our shoes off just inside the front door. The room was obviously a combined kitchen and dining room. It was small but cosy. It was very different to what I had ever been used to. The room was warm as toast. An old wood stove stood against the wall, a chimney lead to the ceiling. On the stove a kettle whistled loudly. The lady walked over and pushed it to the side. The whistle stopped immediately.

She then walked over and gave me a warm hug. "Welcome to Launceston. You must be Marijke, and that there must be Margaret," she said in a voice which reminded me of my late mama. It was gentle and compassionate. I felt I had found an ally. Mrs van Maanenberg had the same colour eyes as Mama had. She was pretty and had a buxom, homely figure.

I nodded, and returned her warm smile. "Girls, meet our sons, Denny here is thirteen and Tony is eleven. Over there in the high-chair is Andy, our youngest. Liske is in her room, a little shy, I'm afraid. Our two oldest sons, John and Rob are not home yet. Come, I'll show you girls your bedroom while you are here. I hope you don't mind sharing a bed, as we've had to squeeze our children together a little." Her bubbly, warm voice was soothing.

"We're used to sharing beds, thank you. We always sleep three to a double bed, so to share with Margaret is good. I like sharing beds, it keeps us warm," I said, not knowing what else to say.

We walked through a narrow hallway on a long carpet runner. There were doors on either side, and our room was the second door on the right. The room was small, with an old wooden wardrobe in one corner and a double bed in the other corner, with just enough space to walk between the two. The bed had what looked like a home-made hand-knitted patchwork quilt. I soon found out that Mrs V loved sewing and knitting, and made beautiful rugs and clothes. The quilt was bright and cheerful, as was a large cross-stitch picture above the bed. It was a Dutch scene with a windmill, and tulips. A single bed was against the far wall, on which sat a blond girl of about seven. The one window in the room was covered by a pull-down Holland Blind. I fell in love with the room. It wasn't big, but it, like the rest of the house, was homely and cosy.

"Liske, this is Marijke and this is Margaret."

Liske looked up shyly and acknowledged us with a smile.

"Now, let me show you where everything else is. We don't have town water here. We have a water tank outside, and the water is collected. It is filtered for drinking water, but we always like to boil water before using it for drinking. It is fine for showers and baths though," Mrs V said.

We followed her back into the hall. "Now, that room at the end of the hall is the bathroom. Next to that is the boys' bedroom. And here is the lounge-room," she said, as we followed her through the door next to the kitchen.

A welcoming wood fire burned in a large opening in the far wall. Logs at least two feet long, lay crosswise, and large flames flickered up into what I assumed was a chimney. A grate stood in front of the fire, stopping sparks from coming into the room. A big box with more logs stood on the hearth.

I felt we had been transported back a century. I had never been inside a place like this. But the biggest surprise was still to come. When I asked if I could use the toilet, Mr V asked the boys to show me where it was. Luckily I still had my coat on, because the toilet was outside! Next to the chook-house. I had thought I would never have to go outside to the toilet again when we left Bonegilla.

"This is a bucket and chuck-it toilet," Denny laughed, as he saw my horrified face.

"Twice a week we take turns to take the bucket out. We empty it into a big hole in the ground behind the chook-house and then we cover it up with dirt. It is the best manure for Papa to grow our vegetables."

There was a single light globe inside this toilet, with a wooden seat, and literally, a large bucket. The smell was not conducive to staying in there. I sat down with trepidation, not sure that I could use it. But necessity won out. When I stepped out, Margaret was waiting to use it next. "Oh, yuk, it stinks," she said, holding her nose.

"Get used to it, that's the only toilet we have," Denny said, a cheeky grin on his face. I was soon to find out that he was a fun-loving kid, and loved teasing people. He had a shock of red hair and his face had as many freckles as his father's. We waited for Margaret to come out, and quickly ran back inside.

Mrs V had set the table and she dished up some soup. We sat down and said Grace. After the food we had eaten at Bonegilla, I really enjoyed her cooking. The chicken noodle soup and little meat balls was just like what Mama used to make.

Over dinner Liske was quiet, but the rest of the family chatted happily about various things. They drew us into the conversation, but Margaret, like Liske, was shy and didn't say much. I, on the other hand, fit right in. Mr V was a very funny man, and had a terrific sense of humour. Mrs V obviously enjoyed his humour and laughed loudly at his jokes. The boys tried to outdo each other, teasing their little sister as well as Margaret and me.

After dinner I helped with the dishes, and Margaret got changed for bed. I asked her if she wanted to go to the toilet before she went to bed. "No. I don't want to go out there again," she whispered, afraid she may be overheard. "I don't like that toilet."

Liske came in and walked to her bed. "I have a potty under my bed. If you want to use it during the night, that is okay. But we have to make sure we empty and wash it in the morning."

Potty? They are for babies. I am twelve. But ... I guess it's better than going outside during the night.

Once the girls had settled down, I asked if I could go to bed too. I was tired, it had been a long day.

As I cuddled up to Margaret, who was already asleep, I tried to imagine living in an old house like this. Although I liked it so far, the idea of outdoor bucket toilets and cats and dogs had me a little worried. I fell asleep with the thought in my head that maybe all houses in Tasmania had outside toilets. *I hope not, I am sure Papa would have told us – or would he?*

Chapter 20

I opened my eyes; it was dark. I was confused as to where I was. Margaret rolled over and threw her left arm across my shoulders. The feel of her presence gave me comfort. Then I remembered I was at the Van Maanenberg's home in Launceston.

I put my arm over the blankets, but quickly returned it to the warmth and comfort of the bed. I had no idea what time it was, but it was obviously too early to get out of bed. I wrapped my arms around Margaret and wondered what lay in store for us. I knew I would enjoy being here with this family, but it would be strange. I had hoped we would be together again as a family once we arrived in Tasmania.

"Marijke?" Margaret's whisper surprised me. I hadn't realised she was awake.

"Yes?"

"I was just checking it was you. I wasn't sure where I was. But now I remember."

"Mmmm ... I was the same when I woke up. I wonder what time it is."

"This bed is comfortable. I felt like we were back in Amsterdam." I noticed the wistful tone in Margaret's voice.

"Do you wish we were back in Holland? I do. Well, sort of. I suppose when Papa finds a house and we are all together again, it will be better." I was talking to myself more than to Margaret.

"Yes, but I think it will be fun here. Liske is the same age as me, we might become friends. The boys are nice too. I like Denny and Tony, they are so funny." Her positive comments made me feel better.

We lay there, whispering, until the darkness lifted. A knock on the door interrupted our conversation. "Good morning, girls. Come on, Liske, time to get ready for school." Mrs V's voice was kind but firm.

"Do we have to go to school?" I asked.

"No, I believe your Papa and Mama are going to enrol you in school soon. But school holidays start at the end of next week. Your Papa said it would be easier if you start school after the holidays."

"How long are the holidays for?" I asked.

"Two weeks. The school year in Australia runs from February to December. You get a long holiday in December and January, for summer. When you go to school next month it will be for the final term of the year."

"Oh, it sounds funny to have summer for Christmas. Do you like it?"

"Well, sometimes I think it would be nice to have a traditional cold Christmas, but it's nice to be able to go to Midnight Mass in short sleeves and not freeze. And many people go away to the beach. Our boys always go swimming at the Basin. They will show you where that is. It's a lovely swimming pool, and it is free."

Swimming at Christmas? That sounds so strange.

In the kitchen the kettle was on the stove, as was a big iron pot.

"Porridge, girls?" Mrs V asked.

"What sort of porridge?" I asked, before I thought about it. *I hope she doesn't think I'm rude, but sometimes they had porridge at Bonegilla, and it was made from rolled oats with water. Mama used to make it with milk.*

"Rolled oats."

"Is it made with milk?"

"Yes, of course. What else would you cook porridge with?"

"Water," Margaret and I answered simultaneously, and burst out laughing.

We enjoyed a friendly family meal, much like our family at home. Everyone sat around the table, including the two eldest boys. Before the meal,

Grace was said, with Mr V leading the prayer, just like Papa always did. Mr V even said a special prayer to ask God to make Margaret and me happy in Tasmania.

The two oldest boys introduced themselves. Rob and John also had red hair and freckles, but Rob had a mischievous face, whereas John looked a more serious person. But they were both really nice to us. It was a nice friendly family.

After the boys and Liske had left for school, I helped Mrs V wash up and then I made our bed. I also made Liske's bed, and Mrs V thanked me. That's nice, to be thanked for something. I didn't remember Papa or Mama ever thanking us for things we did, as it was part of our role in the family. It felt nice to be appreciated.

I offered to help with some other housework, and Mrs V said, "Mmmm, I think you and I will get on really well, Marijke. It's nice to have a big girl around the house for a while. So many boys in our family, it is usually very noisy." She gave me a cuddle and a smile.

I know I'll love it here. At home I am one of seven girls. Here I am special. And Mrs V's cuddle is so much like Mama used to give me. Papa and our new Mama don't give spontaneous cuddles.

Spontaneously, I wrapped my arms around Mrs V's waist and hugged her, then pulled away, embarrassed. She smiled at me and turned to do something.

Margaret and I went outside and investigated the garden. Mr V had a lovely big vegetable garden. I had never seen a garden like it. And there were many trees, which I found out later were fruit trees. "You can come anytime and pick your own fruit. We have enough for everybody."

Wow! Pick our own fruit? How good is that? The only time I had such a luxury was when I was placed on the farm by the orphanage for summer holidays.

I used the outside toilet a couple of times during the day. Every time I went, Margaret went too. Neither of us was brave, especially since some spiders lived inside the wooden cubicle. They weren't very large, but Denny told us in the summer they got spiders as big as bread and butter plates, with big furry legs. I didn't know whether to believe him or not. I asked Mrs V about the spiders and she confirmed that sometimes there were very big spiders around in the warmer weather, as well as snakes. I shuddered at the thought.

Luckily their two dogs were behind a fence and we didn't have to worry about them.

This home was so far removed from anything I had ever experienced in Holland. But it was much nicer than Bonegilla, and the Van Maanenbergs were a really warm and friendly family, with a lot of love and laughter.

After lunch, while Andy had his afternoon nap, Mrs V sat down with us and showed us some cross-stitch she was doing. It was really beautiful. She also did a lot of knitting. I loved knitting, and before I knew it, she had given me a pair of knitting needles and some wool.

"Why don't you knit something for your new baby brother or sister? I think your mama said she is due to have her baby in about three months. I have lots of patterns, what would you like to make?"

I chose a simple little matinee jacket, while Margaret started knitting a blue scarf.

When Denny, Tony and Liske returned home from school, we played outside. Although it was cold, it wasn't as cold as Holland in the middle of winter. We played hide-and-seek among the fruit trees. Then the boys showed us a short-cut to walk to town.

A long set of steps, made from rock, at the base of their street. Denny said there were one-hundred and thirty-two steps altogether. There were no hand-rails, and the steps were uneven. When I looked down, I felt sick, and thought I was going to fall.

Denny grabbed my arm. "Whoa! Don't fall down. You're only skinny, but you'd be too heavy for me to carry back up," he said, half joking, half serious.

"Sorry, I'm not very good with heights. But I'll be right, once I get used to it," I said, feeling a bit silly.

I wanted to be the boys' friend, and I didn't want them to think I was a sook. Mama and Papa always said I was a tomboy, and I had a need to prove I could do anything boys could do.

"That's all right. Why don't we go down the steps, and then come up again? Once you've done it, you should be all right."

"Yes, of course. I'm just not used to high hills like this."

Margaret and I followed the boys down the steps. Tony ran ahead, but Denny was kind enough to walk slowly in front of me.

When we were down, I looked back. It didn't look half as bad from the bottom up.

"At the weekend, we will show you where the Basin is. We go swimming and rock climbing there in the summer. But we can go there in the winter too. There's a swinging bridge over the river. It's a really nice place, and it's just over the hill there."

Denny pointed to a street on our left.

"Are all the streets here steep?" I asked.

"In this part of town they are, but the streets in the city are on the flat. Most of Tasmania used to

be volcanoes many years ago, and it is very rocky.
Look over there. See those mountains? There is a
little bit of snow left on them. A few weeks ago they
were really white with snow."

Denny pointed to the other side of Launceston.
Behind the hills were some mountains, and I could
see the snow.

"That's Mount Barrow," Tony said, "and that
one over there is Mount Arthur and over there is
Ben Lomond."

"Are you okay to walk back up?" Denny asked.

"Oh, yes, I don't feel like I'm falling when I'm
going up." *I won't look back though!*

"We'd better go then. We help Mum with the
chores until Dad gets home. And it gets dark early
at this time of year, and we always have to be inside
when it's dark."

I was fit, but by the time we got to the top, I was
huffing and puffing.

"I don't want to walk up those steps too often!"
Margaret said with conviction.

"Well, the other way is to go on the streets. You
still need to get to the top. There are no buses way
up here. And if you walk up through all the streets,
it takes a lot longer," Denny told her. "When you
start school in September, it will take about twenty
minutes to walk to school using the steps, and if you
walk the other way, it will take nearly an hour."

"Oh," Margaret said. "I hope Papa finds a house not so high up as this one!"

When we arrived home, I helped Mrs V peel some potatoes and carrots. She was cooking some sausages. After dinner that night we played Monopoly, and I won! I beat the boys!

Chapter 21

We had been at the van Maanenbergs about a week when Mama and Papa came to visit. They had exciting news. "We've found a house," Papa said. "You can come home next week Saturday. We have to wait for the container to arrive with all our furniture. Then it will take a couple of days to have the house ready to move in."

"Yes! Oh, good! Where is it? Is it up on a hill, Papa? And does it have a toilet inside or outside?" I couldn't get my questions out fast enough.

"One question at the time, Marijke! I had forgotten you always want to know everything at once," Papa laughed.

"It is in Wellington Street, which is the main road into Launceston. It's about a fifteen minute walk into the city, and there are buses that go straight past our door," Mama said quietly.

"And to answer your other questions, no, it isn't on a hill and the toilet is inside. The house has three bedrooms, so it will be the same as in Amsterdam, share rooms and beds."

I looked at Papa's smiling face and realised I had missed him terribly. It had been so long since we had been together. I had to admit to myself that, even though I often got into trouble, it was better than not having Papa around.

As I had seen a lot of Mama while we lived at Bonegilla, I had missed her a little bit, but not too much. I was sure that if she wasn't there, Papa would cope just fine. I would help, and I knew Willie and Ann would too.

Mama and Papa stayed for a cup of coffee, and Mrs V had made a delicious Dutch *Appel Taart* (Apple Cake). We only ever had them in Holland on special occasions, like adult birthdays. I really enjoyed the treat, and once again, I thought Mrs V was so much like my late Mama, with her lovely cooking and her warm laugh. Mama used to laugh like that, and it always made the whole world seem bright.

Papa said that Mr V would drive us to our new home the following Saturday. Then the week after, we would be enrolled at the Catholic School. Papa had already spoken to the nuns, and they were willing to waive the fees for us. Papa had a real knack of getting things cheap, and for wheeling and dealing. We could have gone to the public school system, which was free, but Papa would not have been happy. In Holland there had been the

Catholic schools and the Protestant schools, and no good Catholic would ever go to a Protestant school. I am sure Papa thought the system here was the same.

Papa also told us we would get second-hand uniforms for school. I had seen Liske's uniform, and I didn't like it at all.

"Do we HAVE to wear a uniform? Those dresses are just awful!" I whined. "We didn't have to wear uniforms in Holland. They look so old-fashioned!"

"I'm afraid you have to wear a uniform. We're not in Holland now, and that is what they do here. I don't like the uniforms either, but you will just have to put up with them." Mama said.

I glared at her; I didn't want to wear that awful uniform. I was sure that if Mama had been alive, *she* wouldn't have made me wear it!

I didn't care about clothes being second-hand. Most of my life I had worn hand-me-downs. I only ever remembered having a new dress on a few very special occasions: one for my First Holy Communion, which had been lovingly crocheted for me by my Godmother; then a new velvet dress, which my late Mama made for me, when I attended my Godmother's wedding. And of course, the dress I had worn to Mama and Papa's wedding.

When Mama and Papa had gone, Margaret and I talked about the uniform. She didn't seem to care one way or the other. Margaret always fit in with everything.

The following week passed by quickly. The van Maanenberg children were home for the two week school holiday. The weather was still cold and it was usually quite windy on the hill. We got used to going to the outside toilet, and the knowledge that it was only for another week made it more bearable.

The week after Mama and Papa had been to visit, Denny and Tony and I went to the First Basin. Margaret stayed at home and played with Liske.

As we walked through the wide gate I couldn't believe my eyes. I never knew a place like this could exist anywhere in the world.

"Wow! This is beautiful. Look at that big swimming pool. And it doesn't cost anything to swim here?" I asked.

"No. It's all free. We often swim in the Basin itself instead of in the pool. The pool isn't heated, so the Council doesn't clean and fill it until the end of October when the weather warms up. See those rocks over there?" Denny pointed to a rocky outcrop on the left side.

I nodded.

"We often dive off them into the Basin. There is a diving board there too, but we like to dive off the rocks, it's more exciting. The water in there is real cold, as most of it runs from the Northern

Midlands. But it's really exciting to swim in there. There are often big logs floating just below the surface. We sit on them and float around. They say the Basin is so deep they haven't found the bottom yet. Some people have drowned in there, because sometimes there's a really cold underwater flow. You need to be a good swimmer to go in there!"

I felt that he was challenging me, or that he was implying that as a girl I wasn't strong enough.

"I'm a really strong swimmer," I said. "I'm sure I can swim in there."

Denny pointed out some other areas of interest, like the showers and change rooms, a playground and a barbeque area. He explained that barbeques are when people bring raw meat and then cook on a hot plate.

As he spoke I looked around in amazement. The whole area was surrounded by huge rocks and hills. A long swinging bridge hung over the river flowing into the Basin, and tall trees seemed to grow from between the rocks.

A large grassed area surrounded the largest swimming pool I had ever seen. The pool was divided into two sections; the Olympic size pool, and a shallow pool for toddlers.

Although it was still winter, there were quite a few people strolling around, but no one was swimming. I followed the boys to the rocky edge of the Basin, and climbed up to a good vantage point. I was wearing a full skirt, a jumper, my long grey coat and flat black patent shoes. I didn't let that stop me. The rocks were rugged; some very large, some smaller. Mostly solid, but some wobbled a bit when I stood on them. I felt a little afraid when I climbed them, but Denny stayed close to catch me in case I slipped. When we sat down I was awestruck with the beauty around me.

I took my shoes off and sat with my legs tucked under my skirt. I closed my eyes and listened to the rush of the water as it cascaded over some rocks below the swinging bridge, and slapped against the rocks.

I don't know how long I sat there, when a vision of Mama came to mind. *Oh, Mama, how you would have loved this place. It's so beautiful.* I sensed she knew I was thinking of her and I felt a peace and calm come over me.

"Come on, we can't stay here all day." Denny's voice brought me back to the present.

"Wow, you were really somewhere else, weren't you?" he said.

"Mmm, I was," I said, not willing to share my thoughts about Mama with him.

Every now and then I had a feeling that she was with me. That she had travelled from Holland with me and was experiencing the newness of this country with me.

I put my shoes back on, and we climbed down towards the flat grass. Going down wasn't as easy as climbing up had been and I was pleased that Denny offered me his hand. I enjoyed the warmth of his hand, it felt secure.

That night, over dinner, Mrs V said she would miss us when we went.

"But, Marijke, I don't think your Mama and Papa would be very happy if they knew you were climbing rocks. I noticed your skirt was quite dirty and your shoes were scuffed."

Both Mama and Papa were very particular about our clothes, which always had to be clean and in good repair. Papa always said, "We may not have much money, or many clothes, but if you look after your clothes, you can stand proud."

The tiniest little hole in a sock was darned, any button that was lose or came off had to be sewn back on, no hem cold hang out, and all clothes were meticulously pressed. Any spillages had to be cleaned up straight away. With Papa being a tailor and our new Mama an excellent dressmaker, neatness and tidiness were paramount.

Before I knew it, it was time to move to our new home. Saying goodbye to Mrs V brought a lump to my throat. I hadn't taken to anyone like that since Mama died. I wished she could have been our new Mama.

Mr V drove us down the hill, and within ten minutes he drove into a driveway next to a green weatherboard house. Papa came outside, and helped us out of the car. "Welcome home, girls," Papa said, as he playfully smacked us on the backside.

Mama walked from the back of the house. "Hello Marijke, hello Margaret, welcome home," she said. "Follow me, I will show you where everything is."

"I'll go then," Mr V said.

I had forgotten him in all the excitement. I gave him a kiss and thanked him for driving us down. He whispered in my ear, "You are always welcome at our house, Marijke. We really liked having you. Enjoy your new home."

He also whispered something in Margaret's ear before he shook hands with Papa and Mama. Then he climbed into his car and drove out.

We walked around the back of the house. The drive was made of cement which led to an old garage made of the same pale green weatherboards as the house. A large lawn, neatly cut, made up the bulk of the backyard, with a couple of trees and some bushes around the edges. A wooden fence separated the backyard from the properties on either side and at the back. We walked around the corner of the house and followed a slightly sloped path to the back door.

Inside the door was a small room with our old coat-rack from Amsterdam on one wall and a shoe-rack below it. On the right was a narrow kitchen. We walked through a door which led us into a long narrow hallway.

"Here's the boys' bedroom. They'll be sharing the room with Margaret, Lidy and Ineke. There aren't enough rooms for the boys to have a room for themselves," Papa explained as he opened a door on the left of the hall. A double bed and two single beds took up most of the space in the room.

Opposite this room was the dining room. Papa smiled as he showed the bench seats he had built around three of the four walls.

"This will save a lot of space instead of chairs, and as there isn't much storage space, the tops of the seats lift up, and we can put lots of things in there," he said, looking satisfied with his handy-work.

We went back into the hall and further on the left was Papa and Mama's bedroom. The door opposite their room led into what would be our bedroom. Our two double beds were almost side by side, with about a foot between them. Just enough space to get into and out of bed.

"Willie, Ann, you and Trudy will sleep here," Papa said. When Mama has had the baby we will see what happens."

Another door on the left led to the lounge-room. I sensed my late Mama watching when I saw the familiar furniture and other personal items. Papa had put a large photo of Mama, which had been taken a few months before she died, on the mantle-piece. A candle and her favourite statue of the Virgin Mary beside it.

I had just put my bag down on my bed when I heard a lot of voices in the hall. Then the bedroom door flung open and the rest of the family rushed in. I hadn't seen my sisters and brothers for nearly three weeks. There were kisses and hugs all around. I looked up to see Papa and Mama standing back, smiling.

At last I feel like I'm home; at last we're a family again. It's so nice for all of us to finally be together again. Please, God, let everything settle down now.

Chapter 22

The first night together in our new home was exciting. Papa and Mama didn't even complain too much when we all tried to talk at once around the dinner table. When Papa led us in prayer before our meal, he added a sentence, thanking Jesus for looking after his family, and for bringing us all together again. The resounding, "Amen" confirmed we all felt the same.

"I've cooked rice, as I haven't had time to get the kitchen in order yet," Mama said.

We hadn't had this rice for months, so I hoed into it.

"Marijke, slow down, you shouldn't eat so fast," Mama chastised me at one stage.

If I don't eat quickly, I might miss out when seconds come around!

I watched Papa eat his rice. He also relished this meal. It was funny that Papa always had two helpings of rice as well. When he was younger he'd had surgery for stomach ulcers, and he always told us that they had removed half his stomach. With lots of things which were milky or creamy he said he couldn't eat them, because they bloated him.

He seemed to forget that when it came to dishes he really enjoyed. Sometimes, if Mama reminded him that it might be too rich, he would get a bit snappy. "I know what I can and what I can't eat!" he'd growl.

This became a big secret joke amongst all of us. If we said we didn't like something, we still had to eat it. But when Papa didn't like something, he would say he couldn't eat it, and Mama would cook him something separate. We would all smile amongst ourselves, but didn't let him see us grin. If he caught you out, he would get really annoyed.

"One day you may have to have surgery and have half your stomach removed," he would say. "Then you wouldn't be laughing!"

That night, we finished unpacking our things and Mama showed which part of each wardrobe we could use. "Leave some room for your school uniforms," Mama said. "We're taking you to get enrolled at school on Monday, and we will get your uniforms while we are there. Arnold will be going to St Patricks College and the girls to Sacred Heart College. Both are next to the Church of Apostles, where we'll all be going to Mass tomorrow morning. Then we can show you the way. There's a Mass at half-past-eight and one at ten o'clock. We'll go to the earlier one, so we can have breakfast as soon as we get home."

Sunday breakfast had always been a big deal in our family, and I looked forward to getting back into our routine. We weren't allowed to eat or drink anything, except water, before Mass, otherwise we couldn't partake in Holy Communion.

When we came home we would have Dutch rusks with butter and sugar and a cup of tea. Then we had fresh bread with thinly sliced ham or paper thin sliced cheese. During the week we always had jam or peanut butter, or sugar or golden syrup on our bread.

"We are very lucky that Willie's working for Roelf Vos, a Dutchman who has just opened a grocery store in Launceston," Mama said. "He has Dutch rusks. Otherwise we wouldn't be able to have them."

I had missed our little Dutch treats, like the rusks and honey cake, which was another special breakfast treat. I hadn't had any of these things since we left Holland.

"We haven't been able to buy nice ham or cheese, I'm afraid." Mama pulled a face. "The ham is sliced really thick here, and cheese is in big blocks and tastes like soap!" She shook her head in disgust.

We all left home at ten-past-eight the next morning and walked into the reasonably large church just before Mass started. I can only imagine what the congregation thought as we walked in, blessing ourselves and genuflecting, before settling in a pew towards the front of the church. A pregnant woman, her husband and nine children.

A lady behind me put her hand on my shoulder. She scared me, and I spun around. She smiled and said, "Welcome." She said some other things, but I couldn't understand her.

I smiled back and turned around before I got into trouble for talking in church. That was a definite no-no!

The Mass started and a choir of nuns sat to the right of the altar. Although I didn't understand Latin, some prayers were familiar, and we could at least participate in those. The sermon went on a long time. As I couldn't understand a word, I was soon distracted and I started looking around. The church was about half full. Arnold sat on one side of me and he was also getting fidgety.

"Do you want a game of tic tack toe?" he asked.

I nodded.

"Ssshhhhhh!" Papa glared at us.

We didn't play. It always seemed to me that Papa had ears and eyes all around. We couldn't get away with anything!

When Mass finished, we moved out along with the rest of the congregation. Many people came to speak to us. Some were Dutch, which was nice, as it was difficult to respond to the English speaking people. I had no idea what they were saying, and by the look on Mama and Papa's faces, neither did they.

"Hello, Marijke. How are you?" a familiar voice said in Dutch.

"Mrs V!" I said excitedly. The whole van Maanenberg family was there.

They introduced us to some other Dutch people. Denny and Tony ran around, and I soon joined them. We played tag until Papa called me. "Come on, Marijke, we want to get home. I don't know about you, but I'm hungry."

I said goodbye to the Vs and we walked home. Although the weather was cool, it wasn't cold. The rest of the day was nice. We played a card game in the afternoon, and Mama cooked a meal of tomato soup with little meat balls, then the main course of boiled potatoes, our staple food, peas and carrots, and rissoles with jus.

We even had dessert of peach slices – from a tin - and custard. There was a happy atmosphere around the table, like it was someone's birthday.

"Now, there is still one week of school holidays," Papa said just before we said our prayer of thanks after the meal. "As Mama told you, tomorrow we'll get you enrolled at school. Ann is going back to the family where she was staying as they have employed her as their housekeeper. She'll come home at weekends. John will start looking for work. He won't be going back to school."

After all our chores were done, we played cards. When I went to bed I fell into a satisfied sleep. The familiarity of most of our furniture, our beds and even our old blankets had given me a sense of security.

A small sunroom at the front of the house had been set up as a workroom for Papa, where his old familiar sewing machine sat on a long bench. Papa had a job with the only hand-tailor in Launceston, and had agreed to take on some mending jobs to earn extra money. For some reason the sight of that sewing machine had brought tears to my eyes. It brought back memories of Mama sitting in the lounge-room or on her bed at night back in Amsterdam, telling us stories, while Papa sewed late into the night. I loved the familiar sound of that machine.

The next morning, after breakfast, we were given a list of chores, like we used to have in

Amsterdam. When all chores had been completed, Mama walked us to school, where Papa met us. "My boss said I could have some time off when I need it, to get things sorted," he said.

St Patrick's College was to the right of the church, and Sacred Heart College was a large complex behind the church. We stayed outside and waited while Mama and Papa went into St Patrick's College and enrolled Arnold. He came out carrying a bag with his uniform and some books.

A nun came down to meet us, and introduced herself as Mother Superior.

We were ushered into a large red brick house, which was obviously the convent. The front room was large and dark, and it reminded me immediately of that dark room in the orphanage where we had been told Mama was dying.

I didn't like the room, and wanted to run outside. As I was the oldest of the girls to be enrolled, I had to wait the longest. Papa and Mama filled in lots of papers, and Mama did most of the talking, as she had learned some English when she was younger.

When it was my turn, the nun read from the form Papa had filled out. She held out her hand and said, "Welcome, Maria."

I looked at Papa and Mama in confusion. No-one had ever called me by my baptismal name before. I had always been called Marijke.

"Marijke," Mama corrected the nun, "Marijke. Not Maria."

The nun pointed to the paper, and said again, "Maria."

I watched Mama try to explain that my call name was Marijke, not Maria.

The nun looked confused now. "Marikah?" she asked.

"Mah-rike-eh," Papa said this time.

Some more discussion took place, and after a while, some nodding indicated the adults had come to a consensus. As we walked out, Mother Superior nodded at me and said, "Goodbye, Maria."

I got really annoyed. She'd been told my name was Marijke.

Outside Mama said, "Marijke, Mother Superior said your name is too difficult to pronounce. She says Maria is such a beautiful name. She said it will make it easier to call you Maria, like your birth certificate shows."

"I don't want to be called Maria. It is such a holy name," I said almost in tears.

"Well, it's the name on your birth certificate, so it really is your name. We will still call you Marijke at home, of course. Mama loved the name Marijke, and I do too. You will have to get used to being called Maria in Australia." Papa gave me a lopsided look, as though to say there was nothing he could do about that.

I knew that Ann and John had already adopted Australian versions of their names, as had Margaret and Trudy. But I did not want to be called Maria. I wasn't Maria, I was Marijke.

We walked to the school building where another nun met us. A room full of maroon blazers, maroon tunics, maroon felt hats, striped ties and fawn shirts, all neatly sorted by size, greeted us. Then in another small room to the side, we were confronted with rows of fawn cotton dresses, with tiny maroon checks. Short sleeves, a little collar, and button up front, with a belt made of the same material. The skirt had three small pleats on each side.

"Summer uniform," the nun explained, slowly.

She then pulled a straw hat with a maroon ribbon around it from a shelf. "Summer hat," she said.

Oh, no! I have to wear that? They are so, so ... old fashioned! Like pictures I had seen of children in England before the war!

We spent the next half hour trying on the various pieces, until all of us had complete uniforms. I saw Papa hand over some money, and with the clothes neatly folded over our arms, we headed home.

My joy of the previous evening had dissipated. Not only did I have to wear these awful uniforms, I had also lost my name! And when I had tried on the winter uniform, the material was scratchy.

When we got home, Papa jokingly called out, "Maria, come and help Mama."

I burst into tears. "Don't call me that! I am Marijke, Papa. Mama named me after a princess in Holland. I don't want to be called Maria. And you promised you would still call me Marijke at home!" I stormed into my bedroom.

Papa came in after me. "I was joking. Don't be so touchy, and don't speak to me in that tone of voice!"

When he left the room I threw myself on the bed. *I hate it here. I don't want to go to that school and wear that uniform.*

"Come and have lunch, Marijke," Papa called out not much later. "I have to get back to work. Mama will walk into the city with you all after lunch, to buy some shoes and socks. And, oh, yes, you need to have fawn gloves too."

Oh, God! Fawn gloves! I'm pleased my friends in Amsterdam won't see me!

Chapter 23

In the city that afternoon, I was fitted out with a brown pair of lace-ups. "They are boy's shoes!" I exclaimed.

"Marijke, that is what the uniform is, I'm afraid," Mama said. "Now, stop complaining. Every other girl at the school will be wearing the same thing, so you won't look out of place."

"Did I tell you they are putting you in the senior college?" Mama asked.

"No, I thought I would go to grade 6, like I was in Amsterdam."

"Well, they looked at your grades, and they thought you could go to first year high school. As this will be the final semester, you can concentrate on learning English, and then you will stay in the same class next year, and be familiar with the teachers. At High School they have different teachers for different subjects." Mama explained.

"Oh. Wow. High School."

"Yes, and in High School you have to wear stockings, not socks, with the winter uniform. So we will have to go and buy some for you."

Suddenly I thought that maybe the uniform wouldn't be so bad. Stockings! They were so grown up. I was sure Mama wouldn't have let me wear stockings for at least another three years or more.

Although the stockings were thick, I loved the way they felt on my legs. And then we had to buy suspenders to go with them. I felt more grown up by the minute.

"Of course, you won't be able to climb rocks and do some of those other things you do in those. They are expensive, and once they ladder, they are ruined. We can't afford to keep buying these. Two pairs will have to last you a full semester."

When we finally got home, Mama said she was rather tired. I noticed that she had gotten quite big in the last few weeks. Although I knew the baby was growing inside her stomach, I didn't really relate to the discomfort she might be feeling.

Trudy, Margaret and I went into our bedroom and put our winter uniforms on. We had trouble tying our ties, and after some giggles, we had to ask Mama to help us. She showed us step by step how to get the best knot in a tie.

When we were all decked out, including blazers, hats and gloves, we walked into the lounge-room, where Mama sat with her feet on the old piano stool. She laughed when she saw us. "Well, I guess we'll all get used to these clothes," she said. "Marijke, I think your tunic needs to be lengthened a little. Come here and I will pin it for you. I will unpick the hem, but you can sew it back."

I loved sewing, so I didn't object, although I didn't think it was too short.

Half an hour later I sat in Papa's sewing room, carefully picking up one thread of the material for each stitch, like I had been taught. Not too tight, so as not to pull the material.

I was about half-way through when Mama came in to see how I was doing.

"Oh, Marijke, those stitches are too long!" She sighed. "I've shown you before how to do this properly."

Although I wouldn't admit it, I knew she was right. Not that my sewing was rough, but the stitches on the hem were about twice the size that Mama or Papa would have done.

"Why can't you say that I'm doing a good job for a change? You always find fault!" I shot back.

"If you do it properly I would say so. But you are making the stitches too long. The hem will come out too easy. And you know it looks terrible to walk around with a hem hanging down," she lectured.

"You always find fault," I repeated.

"I'm going to unpick the stitches, and then you can do it properly. There is no hurry. You don't have a train to catch, do you?"

I didn't answer her. My friends never had to do their own mending and sewing. Mama should be pleased that I was good at doing things. I glared as she undid my work. She then started the hem herself. After several stitches, she handed the tunic back to me.

"Now, see the size of my stitches? I expect you to do the rest the same. You might as well do it properly the first time." With that, she left the room.

"You might as well do it properly the first time," I mimicked her voice, as a tear rolled down my cheek.

When I finally finished, I hung the tunic up and went outside. I didn't know where John was, but the other kids were playing games. I felt too old to join in, so went back inside where I found Mama in the kitchen.

"Marijke, I need you to help me get tea ready," she said.

I still wasn't happy with her. "Why can't one of the others help you? I've just finished that hem. It took ages! And they're just playing."

"They are younger than you!" I hated it when she spoke so quietly when she was annoyed. If she yelled at me I could yell back. But she was so calm.

"Now that Willie and Ann are working and John will be too, we will expect you to take on more responsibility. Why, you're almost a teenager! Come on, don't make it more difficult for everybody. We're a family again. We're all here. I thought you were happy."

I didn't answer. I was confused as to why I was being so nasty to her. It must have been the uniform and the changing of my name, and then the hem.

"What do you want me to do?" I asked, none too kindly.

"Peel the potatoes. I have a new potato peeler, so you won't peel them too thick. Paper-thin, no wastage please."

As I stood at the sink peeling the potatoes, Mama fussed around in the kitchen, preparing the rest of the meal. There was a knock on the back door, and a male voice sang out in Dutch, "Hello, can you hear me?"

Mama looked at me and shrugged her shoulders. I peered around the corner while she opened the door.

"Leo! What are you doing here?" I heard Mama say.

"Can I come in?"

"Yes, of course."

I couldn't believe it. Our butcher from Amsterdam North walked through the door. Mr de Wit. He and his wife had been friends of my late Mama and Papa. I didn't know they were in Tasmania, and apparently neither did Mama.

"How did you get here?" Mama asked, still looking amazed.

"We moved here last year, after you guys moved to Amsterdam South. We heard you had arrived, or rather, we saw you all on the front page of the newspaper. So, I thought I would come and visit. How are things?"

They wandered off together into the lounge-room. I couldn't hear them anymore. I went back to the potatoes. How could our butcher be living in the same place?

At dinner that night, Mama told Papa about our visitor. Papa smiled and said he had met up with Mr de Wit while we were in Bonegilla.

"The Dutch Australian Association runs card evenings and dance nights. Oh, yes, they also have a dramatic society that puts on plays. Anyway, Leo was there. I couldn't believe it!" Papa said.

"Why didn't you tell me?" Mama admonished him.

"I thought you would get a pleasant surprise to see a familiar face," Papa said.

"Well, I thought I was dreaming," Mama said, smiling again.

The next day was sunny and I asked Mama if I could go to the Basin. Mama said if I took Margaret and Trudy, she would keep the two little ones at home. The boys had already gone off somewhere.

It took just over half an hour to walk there, but it was worth the look on my sisters' faces. "Oh, wow! Look at that swimming pool. We should have brought our bathers," Trudy said.

"It's too cold to swim, but we can go for a walk across the swinging bridge, if you want," I offered.

The paths to the bridge were made of gravel and steep in places. I almost slipped once. The bridge had wooden slats to walk on. We soon found out if you jumped up and down, it started swaying. Soon we were holding the side of the bridge and making it swing quite violently. Two ladies started to cross the bridge from the other side, but ran back, frightened by the sway. They tried again, and again, but each time they ran back. We saw one of them yelling something, but we couldn't hear her, as the water rushing below the bridge was quite noisy.

When we tired of this game, we walked to the other side where the two ladies were still waiting. As we passed them they said something, but I didn't understand them. I knew we probably should have stopped swinging the bridge, but it had been such fun.

When we walked further up the path there was a building and a rotunda. And there were several large birds with coloured tails. They were the most beautiful birds I had ever seen, and the biggest. Their shiny blue feathers were brilliant and they had beady eyes. They strutted, like they were the kings of the world.

We watched them for a while. When we came home that night I tried to describe the birds at the dinner table.

"I think they must be ostriches from the way you describe them," Mama said.

The following Monday I woke up early. It would be our first day at school in Tasmania. I was quite nervous going to High School. We all dressed in our school uniforms. Arnold had his as well. Grey woollen shorts, light grey shirt, green and grey striped tie and a dark green blazer. He had black shoes and grey socks. A green and deep yellow cap finished the picture. He actually looked cute. He always did with his curly blond hair and chubby face, but he didn't like me telling him so.

Mama walked with us to school. I held Ineke and Lidy's hands and Mama walked with Trudy and

Margaret. Arnold was close behind us, but didn't want to hold anyone's hand. We walked into St Patrick's College first, and once Mama was satisfied that Arnold was being looked after, we went into Sacred Heart College. We were met by two nuns; one from the primary school and one from the high school. "Hello, Maria," she said.

I almost burst into tears. I wanted to yell, "Marijke, I am Marijke!" but I managed to control myself.

She said something else, but I didn't understand her.

"She wants you to go with her, Marijke," Mama said. "I will take care of the others. Good luck on your first day." She gave me a kiss on the cheek and turned away.

With fear of the unknown in my heart and anger at my name change, I trudged up-hill after the nun.

Mama, please stay with me. I'm scared.

Chapter 24

As we entered the high school building, Theresa Dobber, a girl I'd met at the airport, walked over. Her dad and my late Mama and my new Mama were all cousins, so I guessed she was my second cousin. Mama and Papa had stayed with her family while I was at the van Maanenbergs.

Theresa asked me if I was okay. I told her I was, but I really wasn't. Lockers lined the full length of the long corridor and Theresa said she would share her locker with me until they gave me my own.

"In through that door is the assembly hall, and at the far end are the kitchen and the school's first aid room." She pointed to the doors. "Come on, we'll go upstairs to our classroom. Our first lesson today is Latin. Sister Lucy is nice, but strict. Have you studied Latin before?"

I shook my head. *I'll have enough trouble learning English without learning Latin.*

The classroom was large and noisy. About thirty girls stood around chatting and laughing. Some came over and spoke to Theresa. They all seemed to talk really fast, and I couldn't understand a single word. When Theresa said something, they laughed. I felt they were laughing at me.

One girl came over and said her name was Sophie van Galen. She spoke fluent Dutch. *Thank God, another person I can talk to!*

Sophie pointed to another girl on the other side of the room. "That girl is Dutch too. Her name is Maria."

Is her name really Maria or have they made her change her name too? I wondered.

Suddenly the class went quiet and everyone quickly found their desks. "You're sitting next to me so I can translate for you," Theresa whispered.

"Quiet please!" a stern voice said.

I looked up to see a nun standing in front of the blackboard. Her face was stern and I guessed her to be quite old. She said something else, and everybody headed towards the door.

"We have assembly every Monday morning," Theresa said.

"What is assembly?" I asked.

"We line up outside and Sister Xavier, she is the head teacher, tells us of any news, and also what is expected from us in the coming week. I see your uniform is the right length. Sister walks around and checks that our shoes are polished, and that our stockings don't have holes in them. If she thinks your hem is too short, she makes you kneel on the ground. She then measures how far from the ground the skirt is, and if the gap is more than one inch, she gives you a note to take home to your parents. She expects the skirt to be lengthened by the next day."

"Why?"

"These uniforms represent the school, and they are very proud of their reputation. They expect you to behave in a lady-like manner. When you wear your uniform between home and school you are not allowed to eat or drink in public, and you must wear your hat, gloves and blazer. You are considered to represent your school at all times."

She didn't have time to tell me anymore, as we'd reached the playground outside and we all lined up. The nun who'd enrolled us stood on the steps in front of us. When she crossed herself, we followed suit. We clasped our hands and bowed our heads, as she obviously said a prayer. After everyone said, "Amen," I lifted my head. Eight nuns, including Sister Lucy, stood behind Mother Superior.

Everyone sang the English National Anthem, as the English flag was raised.

Then came some kind of speech, and sure enough, like Theresa had said, Sister Xavier walked between the rows of girls. Three times she made a girl kneel down as she measured the skirt length with a ruler.

When she had completed her rounds Sister Xavier spoke again. We then filed up the steps to our classrooms in complete silence.

Back in class Sister Lucy wrote some Latin words on the blackboard. I looked around the room. Some girls looked much older than me and some younger. I was the tallest in the class, though.

My mind drifted back to Amsterdam and my best friend Fietje. I wondered if I would be able to make friends with anyone here.

I looked up to see Sister Lucy watching me. "Sister asked you to stand up so she can introduce you to the class," Theresa said.

I did as asked. The only word I understood was "Maria."

"Why is she calling you Maria?" Theresa whispered in Dutch.

"Because Mother Superior said Australians can't pronounce Marijke, and Maria is my baptismal name," I whispered back.

"Sister Lucy, her name is Marijke, not Maria," Theresa said firmly.

A conversation took place between the two of them. Theresa told me later that Sister Lucy wanted to know why I was called Marijke, not

Maria, when that was the name on my birth certificate.

After a while Theresa said Sister Lucy wanted me to write Marijke in big letters on the blackboard. I got up hesitantly, and in my best writing, wrote M A R I J K E.

She then asked me to read it aloud.

"Ma – ray – ke," I said slowly.

She pointed to my desk, so I assumed I had to sit down again.

I couldn't believe my ears. For the next few minutes, the whole class had to say my name.

"Ma – ray – ke, Ma – ray – ke, Ma – ray – ke," they all chanted, time and time again.

I think I had the biggest grin on my face. *Mama, can you hear that? I've got my special name back! Thank you, Sister Lucy!*

After the Latin lesson had finished, another nun entered the classroom. She was really pretty, and looked very young. Her face was round and friendly, and she had big grey eyes. Sister Lucy spoke to her and pointed at me. Then she winked at me and left the room.

I don't know what she said to the other nun, whose name was Sister Magdalene. But I do know that none of the other nuns ever called me Maria again, including Mother Superior.

At lunch time, as we sat outside, some girls came over to talk to me. I smiled at them and tried to understand what they were saying. The only words I understood were the words, "Ask her." Theresa would then turn around and ask me whatever question they had obviously asked her to relay.

Their questions were mostly about my family, and whether I liked Tasmania and Australia. Most of them said they had seen our photo in the newspaper, and asked about my brothers and sisters.

After school I collected Trudy, Margaret and Lidy from the primary school building. We met Arnold near the front of the church. We giggled when we noticed that Lidy had her hat on back to front. I straightened it for her and wished my hat looked as cute on me as it did on her.

When we arrived home we had to get changed into our everyday clothes straight away, and hang our uniforms up.

"You will need to polish your shoes every day, so you may as well do it as soon as you take them off. Then you won't have to rush in the morning," Mama said.

"How did it all go?" she asked us.

Everyone tried to talk at once. Mama asked the other kids some questions and when they had run outside, she turned to me, a questioning look on her face.

"It was difficult," I said. "We had lessons, but I couldn't understand what I was being taught. Sister Magdalene gave me an English book, and Theresa said that she will give me special English classes after school if I want them."

"That's nice of her. You've always been good at school. I'm sure you'll learn to speak English very quickly," Mama said.

She was right. It was amazing how quickly we learned to speak the language. Not perfectly, but within a few weeks we could all hold our own in a conversation.

I appreciated Theresa and her help, but she wasn't my type of person to be close friends with. As it was the last school term, the girls in my class had established friendships. Many of them had been at the school from kindergarten. I felt that I didn't quite belong. But everyone was nice to me, especially a couple of the school Prefects.

I soon learned that there was a pecking order in the school. Those in Matriculation (Fifth and Sixth Year) nominated and elected Prefects. The Prefects had special coloured edgings around their blazers.

Their role was to help younger students if needed. I soon learned they were also the nuns' eyes and ears outside of school.

They would report you if you were seen eating or drinking in public places while still in school uniform, or worse still, if you were not wearing your gloves or hat.

There was also one Head Prefect. The Prefects had regular meetings and reported back to Sister Xavier. It was an old English tradition, which had been brought to Australia with the first settlers.

One day I was summonsed outside. A nun from the primary school wanted me to come and speak to Trudy. Apparently something had happened and she was inconsolable. They had tried everything, but she wouldn't stop crying.

I went down and sure enough, Trudy was almost hysterical. She tried to tell me what happened between sobs, but she wasn't making any sense.

"Calm down and tell me. I can't help you if I can't understand you."

"She hit me!" she gulped.

"Who hit you?" I asked, shocked.

"My teacher," she cried, and pointed at the nun standing in front of the class.

"Why did she hit you?" I asked. I had never known a nun to hit anyone in Holland. I always thought of nuns as holy people.

"She told me to do something, and I didn't understand. Then she yelled and hit me with her ruler on the back of my legs." She started crying again.

I looked at her legs and sure enough, I could see the welts where the ruler had been. It took quite some doing to calm her down.

I told Papa and Mama what had happened that night.

"I believe smacking is allowed in schools here," Papa said. "In Holland it's illegal, but it isn't here."

"But she hadn't done anything wrong, Papa. Trudy just didn't understand what she was supposed to do." I stood up for my younger sister. *I wouldn't like it if I got hit by a nun!*

I did get hit at school, but not by a nun. I was smacked by my cooking teacher. We had cooking and arts and crafts classes once each week. Half the class went to cooking class in the morning, while the other half went to arts and crafts. Then in the afternoon we swapped around. I really enjoyed these classes, as I loved cooking, as well as sewing and knitting.

The cooking teacher, Mrs Dadson, told me to do something, but I had no idea what she said. She sounded grumpy, and I heard her snap at a couple of other girls. When she came to see how I was progressing, she shouted at me, and then hit my leg with a wooden spoon.

When Theresa came to my defence and told her that I didn't understand English, Mrs Dadson apologised. It was too late; I never liked her from that day on. I felt she could've asked me why I wasn't doing what I was supposed to be doing. Then I'm sure someone would have told her. She was extra nice to me after that, but I didn't trust her anymore.

About a week before my thirteenth birthday, I felt really bad. I wanted to cry, but didn't know why. I snapped at Mama for the tiniest little thing. Mama would tell Papa when he came home from work, and then I would get into trouble. I wished she didn't always tell Papa everything. I thought that was mean.

When I came home from school and went to the toilet one day, I found I had blood in my panties. I was terrified. I couldn't remember hurting myself at all, but I'd had pain in my stomach all day. I put some toilet paper inside my panties and hoped it would stop.

When I was getting changed that evening, Willie came into the bedroom. "Oh, Marijke, you've got your periods!" she said.

"My what? What are you talking about?" I asked, confused.

"Your periods. You're bleeding."

"Yes, I know. I don't know why. I can't remember hurting myself. But it won't stop."

Thank God for Willie. She sat me down and explained about periods. She gave me a pad and said I had to tell Mama so she could buy me some more pads and give me a belt to hold the pads in place.

Willie came with me to tell Mama; I was too embarrassed. After we told Mama, she gave me some more pads and a belt. "My word, you are growing up too soon," she said.

Later in the evening Papa passed me in the hallway, with a big smile on his face. "Ah, Marijke, congratulations. Mama told me you're a big girl now!"

I was so embarrassed. *She shouldn't have told Papa about this! This is so personal! Papa always makes jokes about things that are personal. Then he laughs and thinks he is really funny. Well, he isn't!*

I was hurt and angry with Mama and Papa and I cried myself to sleep.

Chapter 25

Willie's right arm lay across my chest when I woke up in the early hours of the morning. My stomach was cramping and I had a headache. I tried to roll out of bed without disturbing her.

"What's the matter, Marijke? Are you okay?"

"No, I feel awful. I have cramps and I feel awful."

"That's normal. I'm afraid you'll just have to get used to it," she said. "It does mean that you are growing up and your body is getting ready to be a woman and have babies."

"I don't want to have babies yet!"

"Oh, you won't have them yet. Not until after you're married. But your body needs to get ready for it." She said patiently.

After I had been to the toilet, I crawled back into bed, and Willie wrapped her arms protectively around me. We talked for a long time. It was the first and only sex education I ever received, but I was so grateful to her. At the same time, it scared me. I was horrified that a man would do things like that to a woman. It sounded revolting, and I shuddered at the thought.

Mama and Papa must have done that! Yuk! Yuk! Yuk!

If that's what it takes to become an adult, I'd rather not grow up!

"You'll get used to it," Willie reassured me again.

I don't think I ever will; it's messy and horrible. I wish I was a boy!

When I came home from school that day, Mama asked me to get the washing inside and fold it up while she went next door to get some milk.

To the right of our house was a Milk Bar and mixed shop. It was run by an English couple, Mr and Mrs Harker and their daughter, Bernadette. They also owned the house we were renting.

Apparently, when the newspaper ran our story on the front page when we arrived in Launceston, they mentioned that Papa had been looking for a house to rent, but had been unable to find one for our large family.

The Harkers had contacted the newspaper and told them they had an empty house. They had bought it to demolish and to build a large Milk Bar and shop on the double block. But that wouldn't happen for another eighteen months. So they offered it for rent.

When Mama came back from the shop I could see she was annoyed. "Every time I ask for something, they correct my pronunciation. But when they say it, it doesn't sound any different to what I said! I asked for flour, and they said "flour." I said that, and they said, "no, flour.""

I think Mama said "flower" instead of "flour", but she thought that was close enough. "They know what I mean. Every time I go into that shop it takes so long to get out again, because they insist on teaching me proper English." Mama's head was shaking, indicating she was really annoyed.

She calmed down after a while. "I know they're only trying to help. They're really nice people, and if it wasn't for them, we probably still wouldn't have a house. It's so different here. People assume when you have a large family, you're going to wreck their house. But, I tell you, Marijke, I don't want to go in there to be corrected on my English all the time. I want to learn, but they speak English English, not even the same as Australian English."

After that, Mama usually sent one of us kids to go to the shop if she needed something.

Late in October we had our School Sports Carnival. Everybody had to participate, and we all wore ribbons in the colour of our house (team). I was in Cotham, the colours being brown and blue.

Many parents turned up to watch. There were running races and three legged races. I had never seen anything like that before. The right leg of one girl was tied to the left leg of another girl at the ankle, and then they had to run together. They kept falling over. There was also a sack race. Big brown potato sacks were tied around our waists with a rope, and we had to run with the bag around our feet. It was really funny to watch, but more fun to participate. I was a pretty fast runner, and I won a couple of races. We were given coloured ribbons if we came first, second or third.

There were other sports, like long jump and high jump. Until we went into the orphanage in Amsterdam the last time, before Mama died, I used to go to gymnastics, and I was pretty good at it. Mama used to say I was double-jointed, because I could almost turn myself inside out.

Unfortunately, they didn't have any gymnastics as part of the sports day. I thought I would have been able to show off. I told one of the girls that I could put both my legs around my neck at the same time. She didn't believe me, so I showed her. I got quite some attention until Sister Lucy came over and told me it was unladylike to sit like that.

The barracking during the races was loud and the competition between the houses fierce. Each house had a different chant. It was fun, noisy, and I felt part of a larger community for the first time.

November was exam time, but because of my limited English, I didn't have to do the exams. I was being kept back in the same class the next year anyway. During exams the teachers let me read and improve my English. I did do the maths test, as I loved maths, and numbers are after all numbers, whichever language you speak.

My English was improving in leaps and bounds. During one exam, Sister Magdalene asked me to write an essay about my first days at Sacred Heart College.

I thought I did this reasonably well, and proudly handed it in to her when the other girls handed in their test papers. I called the essay, "Ask her, ask her."

At our next English class, Sister Magdalene asked me to come to the front of the class. I thought I was in trouble, but she then told the class I had written such a good essay, she wanted me to read it to the whole class.

With my strong accent, I proudly read my story. When I finished it, they all clapped. "Well done, Marijke. You write well, and the way you described your first few days here was really good," Sister said. "Would you mind if I keep this?"

I nodded.

Why does she want to keep it? I would like to keep it too. I could show Papa how good my English is getting. But I would never argue with a nun, so I never did get to show it to Papa.

"That was really good, and funny," Theresa whispered when I sat back down.

On the fifteenth of November I became a teenager. Mama and Papa gave me a little handbag. It was really nice and I liked the idea of having a pretty bag when I went into town or to church. It was big enough to put my prayer book in, as well as a hanky. I had seen other girls from my class with their bags, and I thought it looked posh.

Mama made my favourite mocha cake and I proudly blew out the thirteen candles. Willie had bought me a pretty necklace with her own money, and Ann gave me a box of nice hankies.

"Marijke, now that the pool at the Basin is open for swimming, do you want to swim before you go to school some mornings?" Willie asked me.

We both loved swimming. I asked Mama and she said it was okay, as long as we made sure our chores were done before we went. After that, two or three times each week Willie and I went to the

Basin. We'd swim for about half an hour, then we'd shower and dress and have our breakfast. Willie then walked to work and I headed in the other direction to school.

At the Basin, there would be birds singing and the peace and quiet was beautiful.

The pool was usually quite chilly, but I didn't care. I loved swimming. Willie and I would race each other, and sometimes I beat her. Usually there wasn't anyone else in the pool at that time of the morning.

One Sunday morning I decided to go to early Mass. I was always an early riser.

The rest of the family were still in bed when I left. As I walked through Bathurst Street, about two streets away from the church, a man got out of a car parked alongside the curb.

He walked over to me and asked, "Do you want a lift, little girl?" I said no, and kept walking.

He then grabbed my arm and snarled, "You think you're too good for us Aussies, little girl?" His breath was on my face, and it smelled awful.

"No!" I yelled, and tried to pull my arm away from him.

But he was too strong for me and dragged me towards his car. I looked around but couldn't see anyone. I screamed at the top of my voice. Just then a car came around the corner. He let go off my arm and ran back to his car. "I'll be waiting for you, little girl!" he shouted back at me.

I ran away as fast as I could. There was a small park which we cut through to walk to school and church, and I ran through that. I kept looking back to make sure he wasn't following me. I didn't stop running until I was inside the church, and then I sat down and cried. I tried to not make a noise, but a lady came over and asked if I was okay. I nodded, then wiped my eyes with the back of my hand. I looked around to make sure the man hadn't followed me. I couldn't see him, but I moved to the front of the church just the same. I felt safer surrounded by people.

After Mass I looked around furtively to see if I could see his car parked near the church. I didn't go home the same route, but walked a long way around in case he was waiting for me.

I don't know why I never told anyone what happened. But from that day I never walked to church on my own again.

The day after my birthday Mama went into labour. Mr Harker took Papa and Mama to the hospital. Our new little sister, Tiny (Christina Maria) was born the next day.

Mama had to stay in hospital for ten days. We took turns going to the hospital with Papa. It took us about half-an-hour to walk there.

Tiny was so pretty, and so little. She had fluffy blond hair and blue eyes. When our late Mama had babies in Holland I hadn't really noticed what any of them looked like. They were just cute babies. As it had been more than five years since our last baby, and maybe because I was older, I was really taken with Tiny.

I told everybody at school, and the nuns were really happy. "Oh, what a blessing. Another girl. How many girls is that now?"

"Eight girls and two boys." This response extracted a look of amazement every time.

When Mama brought Tiny home from hospital she allowed us to nurse her in turn. When I held her in my arms I felt an emotion I hadn't felt before. She was so tiny, and so pretty. For the first time in my life I saw this little baby as a human being. I guess I was growing up!

Chapter 26

School closed for the summer holidays a week before Christmas. The weather was warm as we prepared for the coming season. We celebrated the feast of Saint Nicholas on the sixth of December, as we always used to in Holland.

The Dutch Australian Association held a Saint Nicholas parade through the city streets. They'd done so for many years in Launceston, as many Dutch people had settled in and around the area. From the number of people who watched the parade, it was obviously popular with the non-Dutch population as well.

We shared gifts then, not at Christmas, as the Australians did. Christmas had always been a religious occasion for our family, and Papa saw no need to change that. Our gifts, as always, were frugal but well thought through. Mama and Papa bought us one gift each (from Saint Nicholas, of course), and we usually made each other small gifts.

A week before school broke up for the holiday, a newsletter was sent to all parents and families of students to attend a Speech and Presentation night.

The invitation stated that supper would be served at the end of the evening, with the request to bring your own plate.

Mama shrugged her shoulders. "They mustn't have enough plates at the school to go around. Maybe they don't have enough cutlery either. We'll take some, just in case."

The plates and cutlery were neatly wrapped in aluminium foil and handed over to the ladies busy in the school canteen.

I would have liked to have seen the looks on the faces of the ladies putting out the food when they unwrapped our plates, finding only knives and forks on them. Later we learned that in Australia, when you were asked to bring a plate to a function, it meant you brought a plate filled with food!

The school provided hot drinks and I must admit the variety of finger foods and cakes was delicious. It seemed that each family had tried to outdo each other. We could eat as much as we wanted. Just as well I never put on any weight! I think I ate enough to feed an army.

In our family you were always dished up one piece of cake or proffered one biscuit. It was the height of bad manners to just help yourself to more than one, unless a second was offered. It didn't seem to matter here. Everyone ate as much as they wanted. They just walked around, putting several things on their plate at a time, and then, when it was empty, they went back for more. Such gluttony!

When we arrived home that night we laughed at the fact that we had taken an empty plate each.

Papa said, "If we need to take one plate whenever we all go to a function, we're still going to do really well. I am sure between us we will eat much more than one plate full of food. Perhaps we shouldn't have a meal before we go. That will save a lot of money!"

After I got into bed I felt sick and had to rush to the bathroom. I couldn't eat my breakfast the next morning. Maybe eating that much last night hadn't been such a good idea!

Papa managed to buy a small Christmas tree and together we decorated the dining room and the lounge-room the Sunday before Christmas. Papa carefully clipped the small candle holders on the branches, as well as on the loose branches that had been hung on the walls. We oohed and aahed as the decorations from Holland were unwrapped, including the Angel Hair. I looked at them, and they reminded me of Mama, and the Christmases back in Amsterdam, and it made me feel a bit sad.

Papa took the longest time to set up the Nativity set. He and our late Mama had bought it in their first year of marriage, and it was very special to him. The little baby Jesus would not be put into His crib until after midnight Mass on Christmas Eve. Papa meticulously made the grotto from brown paper, and sprinkled powder on the top to represent snow.

Each night, after we said our prayers, we sang Christmas carols. I loved that time of day; the whole family singing together, in full voice. Yet, there was something missing this year. Papa had lit the candles, but of course, it was summer, and it was still light.

In Amsterdam, when we sang, Papa used to turn the lights off, and the glow of the candles gave a wonderful and flickering atmosphere. There would be candles in front of the grotto, and of course all the candles on the tree and on the branches on the walls.

It was like a full ceremony each night. Papa carefully lighting each candle, and when we'd finished our carols, we took turns to blow the candles out.

We held to this tradition in Australia. But it was warm, and it was light, and the atmosphere just wasn't the same.

The morning after we put up the decorations, I heard the mailman blow his whistle to let us know we had mail, I rushed outside, always eager to see if there was any mail from Holland. Not only were there a couple of letters addressed to Papa and Mama, but a pale blue airmail letter was addressed to me!

I knew the handwriting before I turned it over to see the return address. It was from Fietje, my best friend in Holland! How I missed her. I raced into the kitchen to grab a knife to cut the delicate and lightweight blue paper.

"Marijke, is that addressed to you?" Mama frowned at me.

"Yes, Mama, it is," I said indignantly, as I slid the knife through the side of the paper.

As if I would dare open mail that's not mine!

"It's from Fietje. I wrote her a letter a few weeks ago. She's sent hers by airmail. Look." I couldn't contain my excitement.

To send airmail letters was quite expensive. When letters were sent by boat they took several weeks to cross to the other side of the world. I'd sent mine by boat, as I couldn't afford an airmail letter.

"Dear Marijke. How I miss you and your family," Fietje started her letter. "Since you left, my life has been boring."

I felt tears well up.

"Is everything okay with Fietje and her family?" Mama asked.

"Yes, they're fine. She misses me," I said quietly. "I miss her too. I haven't made any good friends here."

"That'll take time. You grew up with Fietje, so of course, you will miss her. I miss my friends and family too. But I'm sure you'll find new friends here. We've already met some nice Dutch people, and of course we have some family here. What about the Dutch girls in your class?"

"No. I like them, but not as good friends. Besides, they're going to the next class, and I will stay in first year. It's no use making close friends when they won't be in my class."

"You always have all your sisters and brothers."

"Yes, but the boys are always doing boys' things. And because I'm stuck between the two boys in age, Willie and Ann are much older than me, and Trudy and Margaret are so much younger. Sometimes I feel left out."

"Oh, don't be so silly. You all do things together. And don't you and Willie go swimming at the Basin together?"

"Yes, but it isn't the same as having a friend," I said, finishing the conversation. *I don't think she understands that I miss Fietje.*

* * * *

On Christmas Eve, we dressed in our Sunday clothes to go to Midnight Mass at the Church of Apostles. It felt so strange, dressing in summer clothes instead of the warmest winter woollies; it was still quite warm.

Mama even dressed Tiny up in a sweet little dress and jacket she had made for her. She looked so cute.

We set the table for our traditional Christmas breakfast before we left. When we walked outside it was quite dark, although the moon was high in the sky surrounded by the most beautiful star filled night I had ever seen. I was never up at midnight, so hadn't seen the Milky Way in all its splendour.

"Look, Papa, over there. Is that the star that the three wise men followed?" Lidy asked, as she pointed to the brightest star in the sky.

"Maybe," Papa said, with a big smile. "Let's see if it leads us to the church."

When we arrived at the church, Lidy pointed up again. "Yes, it has, see? The star is now here!" We all laughed.

Many families had congregated outside the church, and we saw some we knew. Some girls from my class spoke to me and a few of the Dutch families we had met were also there, including the van Maanenbergs. After some chatting we all piled inside.

A choir was singing Christmas Carols. Some of the tunes were familiar, but the words were in English. As we loved singing as a family, we blended in by singing in Dutch. Some of the people sitting in front of us turned around and smiled.

After Mass the priest stood outside and wished everyone a Merry Christmas as they filed past. He shook Papa's hand and placed a little cross on Tiny's little head, blessing her.

We walked home, and had to be reminded by Papa several times not to make too much noise, as many houses were in darkness, and people were obviously asleep. It was almost two o'clock when we walked in the door. Papa lit all the candles, while Ann helped Mama make hot drinks.

When we were ready, Papa gave the statue of the baby Jesus to Ineke to place in the crib. We said a prayer, had our Dutch rusks and hot drinks, then sang a couple of Christmas carols in Dutch; *Stille Nacht* (Silent Night) and *Wij Komen Te Zaamen* (Oh Come Let Us Adore Him).

As always, it didn't matter what time I went to bed, I always woke up early. I stayed in bed for a while, but became restless. I dressed and went to the kitchen. I might as well get breakfast ready.

We always had brunch (breakfast and lunch together) on Sundays and special days like Christmas day. Then we had coffee and cake or biscuits at about lunchtime; afternoon tea at about half-past-three in the afternoon and dinner at six. Mama was very set on routines!

"Marijke, you've got everything ready," Mama said, as she walked into the kitchen about an hour after I got up.

She had Tiny in her arms and looked tired.

"Yes, I woke early."

"Thank you. Tiny has been rather restless, and didn't settle down too well. So I haven't had much sleep. Do you want to nurse her for a little while so I can get dressed?"

She didn't have to ask me twice.

Chapter 27

Christmas day was surreal; it was so warm. We sat outside in our big back yard in the afternoon. We'd carried out the laminate table and some chairs. When we sang some Christmas carols, our neighbours from the house behind us looked over the fence and wished us a Merry Christmas.

They introduced themselves as Mr and Mrs Elton. They had two children, Helen and Peter. Helen was about ten and Peter eight. Mama and Papa invited them to join us for a drink. The adults enjoyed a cup of tea, while we chatted to the children. They soon joined the younger kids in a game of tag. It was pleasant, and they were the first Australians we had befriended away from school.

What we knew as the second day of Christmas in Holland was called Boxing Day in Australia. We went to Mass in the morning, and later in the day walked to the Basin. It was a warm day, and we had a wonderful day in the crowded pool. Mama and Papa sat on a blanket on the ground while Tiny slept in her pram.

Ineke and Lidy played around in the shallow pool, while the rest of us jumped into the large pool. I couldn't remember ever having had such a long time in a swimming pool. I couldn't get enough. We played games and held swimming races, which were rather hazardous, as we had to dodge and dive between so many other swimmers.

When we arrived home, Ann and Willie helped Mama prepare dinner, and after I set the table, I nursed Tiny. There wasn't much chatter at the dinner table that night, as we were all exhausted from all the fresh air and swimming.

New Year's Eve, like Christmas, didn't feel real because of the heat. As we did in Holland, we were allowed to stay up to see in the New Year. Papa cooked our traditional Olie Bollen and Appel Flappen, and Mama had made a Dutch salmon and potato salad.

She had written "Happy New Year for 1961" with thin slithers of red beet. This salad was one of my favourite dishes, and I looked forward to it every year.

We sang Christmas carols and other songs. At midnight we wished each other happy new year. Papa had bought some fireworks and sparklers, and except for Tiny, who was fast asleep, we all went outside. One of the crackers went sideways instead of into the air, and we all laughed as Papa had to jump up and down to avoid it hitting him on the legs. It then seemed to chase Trudy around the yard, and she screamed and ran into the back door.

* * * *

The rest of the holidays passed quickly. Although I clashed with Mama at times, most of the time was spent outdoors and enjoyable. After Papa, Willie, Ann and John went to work, Mama and I would cut some sandwiches and make cordial, and we'd head to the Basin or to City Park in the centre of Launceston. In the park was an enclosure with monkeys and another enclosure with kangaroos and wallabies, which kept us entertained for hours. We were amazed that our favourite places were free to enjoy, and we made the most of it.

There were also some swings and a slide and a rotunda in the park. Sometimes bands or singers performed in the rotunda. While Mama sat on a seat, we'd dance to the music. The large trees in the park were mainly European, which had been brought from Europe with earlier settlers. They provided lovely shade and also made us feel nostalgic, reminding us of parks in Amsterdam.

It was just as well we were encouraged to entertain ourselves from a young age, as we didn't have television reception in Tasmania. We had a TV that Papa had bought for our late Mama when she was sick; it had been a real luxury at the time, but the wiring was for Dutch television stations.

Papa had put the television in the lounge-room. He'd paid so much money for it when he bought it, he couldn't bear to leave it packed in a box.

Saturdays were busy days, as we all had to pitch in to help with the housework. We had our individual chores, and one of my favourites was baking. We rarely bought prepared biscuits. It was much cheaper to bake them. As these biscuits had to last a week, we made them by the dozens. We used to get one biscuit with morning coffee (or in our lunch box when we went to school), and one with our bed-time drink. We always made some extra biscuits in case we had visitors.

Thus the biscuits were carefully counted by Mama, to make sure there were enough to go around. Two biscuits per person per day, for seven days, meant we had to cook at least one hundred and fifty-four biscuits. For special occasions, like birthdays, Christmas and Easter, we also baked cakes.

It used to take quite some time to mix the batter for the biscuits. One day I decided to roll them into little balls in my hands, rather than roll the mixture out with the rolling-pin on a floured board. Then I put them on the greased trays and pressed them down with a fork. This made a wonderful crisscross effect and was much quicker. Mama thought this was a wonderful idea, and we never rolled biscuit mixture with the rolling pin again.

Mama also bought lollies to have with our afternoon cup of tea or cold drink. We also had one lolly or a small piece of chocolate with our after-dinner cup of tea.

* * * *

Papa used to say that I was the naughtiest of his children. The main reason was that I was dishonest. I thought nothing of lying about something, if it meant I may not get caught out. I also used to steal things. Nothing big, but I did have a feeling of entitlement.

If I'd spent the whole Saturday morning baking biscuits, why shouldn't I be entitled to more than the others? Or if I was hungry, what would it matter if I snuck one or two lollies from Mama's special jar?

When asked if I had taken some lollies or biscuit, I would deny it. Usually it was me, but some of my brothers and sisters knew that if something went missing and if everyone denied any knowledge, inevitably, Marijke would get the blame.

This caused me to do it more often. *If I'm going to get blamed for everything, I may as well do it!* would be my reasoning.

After one episode of being caught out, having pinched a sausage that was left over from a meal, and then for lying about it, Papa said sternly, "Marijke, your Mama was always worried about your dishonesty. It was only because she got sick and died that you didn't go to a psychiatrist to see what caused you to be so dishonest. Mama had made the appointment, but had to cancel it when she became ill!"

I was devastated. *Mama wouldn't have sent me to a psychiatrist! She wouldn't have! Papa just wants me to feel guilty. I am not that dishonest. I only take a biscuit or a lolly sometimes and perhaps a few coins. And what is a sausage? I was still hungry. And I don't tell really big lies, just ones that get me out of trouble. Besides, some of the others pinch stuff and tell lies too, and then I get the blame for everything. Why am I the only one who gets into trouble?*

I didn't speak to Papa for the rest of the day, I was so angry with him.

That evening Mama made a comment about the sausage, and how upset she was with me.

I felt all my frustrations and anger boil over. "Papa's been different since he married you. He always listens to you, and he isn't the same as he was when my Mama was alive!" I sobbed. Tears trickled down my face.

I saw the hurt in her eyes, but I didn't care. *I'm only in trouble because she tells Papa everything*, I reasoned.

Later that evening, Papa called me into his sewing room.

"I'm very disappointed in you, Marijke. Mama's really hurt by what you said to her. She had every right to be upset with you for stealing that sausage. What you said to her was cruel, and I expect you to apologise to her. I won't speak to you until you have done so." His eyes were blazing and I could see he was controlling his urge to hit me.

Well, I was angry too. I was expected to do many things like an adult, like the cooking, and darning everybody's socks, and other things. Yet, they still treated me like a child!

Papa kept his word; he didn't speak to me at all. No good mornings or good nights. I was just as stubborn and didn't apologise to Mama. In my mind, this was all her fault.

Mama talked to me, but she was very cool. In the end, I gave in. It took a lot of pride, but after a week of silence from Papa, I couldn't take any more. I waited for Mama to be on her own in the kitchen. I didn't look up when I said quietly, "I'm sorry."

She didn't say anything, and I wasn't sure she'd heard me. I looked up and saw her eyes well up with tears. She nodded and turned away.

That night, when Papa walked in from work, he walked straight past me. When he came from the kitchen, where Mama was, he gave me a lopsided smile and said, "Hello, Marijke." That was it; we were on speaking terms again.

* * * *

The first week in February Mama took us to school to get our books for the coming school year. We had to stand in a special line, because we'd been put on the free list. I felt embarrassed, because I thought everybody was watching us, as they knew that only poor people received free books.

Ineke would be going to school for the first time and was fitted out for her uniform. We then went into town where she got her school shoes. She was so excited that she danced around in the shoe shop singing, "I'm going to schooooool, I'm going to schooooool," making up her own little tune as she sang.

First day back at school, and I was as nervous as I had been the previous semester. Even though I had a reasonable grasp of the English language by now, I hadn't met any of the girls in my class before. They had been in grade six in primary school the previous year.

What a surprise to find out there were three other Dutch girls in my class. Doreen van Galen, Marianne Post, and Josie van Riel.

Each of them came and said hello after assembly. Josie offered to sit next to me in class and I was more than happy to accept. She was a very attractive and tall blond girl. She was actually taller then I was, making me the second tallest girl in the class.

After school Josie offered to walk part of the way home with me, and I found out she lived less than five minutes walk from our house.

"Why don't you come and meet my mum," she invited.

We walked into a white weatherboard house, similar in size and layout to our house. A blond lady smiled at me as Josie introduced me as her new friend from school. Those words sounded so wonderful! A friend, a real friend.

Mrs van Riel had a nice smile and I could see where Josie got her looks and her pretty long blond hair from, although Josie obviously didn't get her height from her mother.

I was offered a drink of cordial which I accepted eagerly. It had been a hot day at school, and wearing gloves, my blazer and the straw hat walking home had been almost unbearable.

"Hi, Mum," a boy's voice shouted from the back door.

"Hello, Robbie," Mrs van Riel called back.

"This is our oldest son, Robbie. Robbie, this is Marijke Wegman."

"Hi, I saw your photo in the paper last year." He smiled, and I think I fell a little bit in love. He was about fifteen, and he was cute and tall!

"We've met your parents, of course," Mrs van Riel said. "I didn't realise you would be in Josie's class at school. We met your parents at a Dutch Australian Association card night, but I didn't get to speak to them too much. They're related to the Dobbers and the de Roos aren't they?"

It was more a statement than a question, so I nodded. "My late Mama and this Mama were cousins and Mrs de Roos and Mr Dobber are also cousins. I guess that makes them all some sort of cousins," I explained. "It's a bit complicated, because my Mama's mother and my new Mama's mother and my Mama's father and my new Mama's father were two brothers and two sisters who married each other."

Mrs van Riel laughed. "Well, that's keeping it in the family!"

"Do you want me to walk with you?" Josie asked, when I said I should go home.

"Yes, that'd be nice. You can meet some of my family."

My heart sang as we walked down the street. I walked more sedately than I usually did, because

Josie was very elegant and she seemed very grown up, even though I was a few months older than her. *I think Mama and Papa will approve of my new friend. Not only is she Dutch, but she seems very nice. Papa always likes to tease pretty girls. I hope Josie doesn't mind, because she is the only friend I have.*

That night I went to bed happy. I'd made a new best friend on my first day back at school.

Chapter 28

I settled into the school year with vigour. I loved to learn, and now that I understood most of what was being said, I enjoyed the challenges of the subjects. As in Holland, maths was my first love, now closely followed by English. I wanted to learn, and I wanted to be like the Australian girls.

Josie and I continued our friendship, and she helped me whenever I struggled with the language. In our lunchbreaks we were often joined by Doreen van Galen. At times we also met up with a group of three; twins Rose and Rita Woodfield and Carol Swinton. I found out they all lived in Riverside, a western suburb of Launceston. The Woodfield twins were also from a large family, whereas Carol only had one brother.

I took an immediate liking to all these girls, and they all seemed to like me. Sometimes we sat in a circle on the lawn and talked about our families. They were very interested in my history. I told them my Mama had died, but I didn't go into any more detail. We had never been encouraged to discuss Mama's death and how it affected us. By now I thought that it wasn't appropriate to discuss her loss.

Within a few weeks, Carol asked me if I would like to come and visit her house. Her parents had said I could stay for the weekend, if my parents allowed me to come.

I was so excited I ran all the way home. I forgot I'd told Josie we would walk home together.

"Mama, Mama, where are you?" I yelled as soon as I ran through the back door.

"Here, in the dining room. What's wrong?" She looked up from feeding Tiny.

"Nothing's wrong. Can I go to a friend's house this weekend? Please? Carol's parents have invited me to go to her house. Please, can I go?"

"Slow down, girl. Who is Carol? And where do they live?"

"She's a girl in my class. She is really nice, and she asked her mother if I could sleep there this weekend."

"I'll have to talk to Papa about that. We'll probably have to meet her family. Leave it with me and I will talk to Papa." She went back to feeding Tiny.

Oh, please, God. Tell Papa I can go to Carol's. I've never been asked to sleep at a girlfriend's house before.

The following morning Mama said that Papa thought it would be a good idea. He wanted a note from Carol's parents to say it would be okay for me to go there. And he said he wanted me to be home before dinner on Sunday night.

On the way to school I saw Josie walking ahead of me. I ran to her and as I fell into step beside her, she didn't say anything.

"Hello," I said.

"Hello," she replied. Then silence.

"What's the matter?" I asked, perplexed.

"You didn't wait for me yesterday, like you said you would," she answered. She didn't look at me.

"Oh, I'm sorry, I had to go home in a hurry. I forgot to tell you," I lied. I didn't want to tell her I had been invited to Carol's house, in case she got jealous.

We continued walking, but she didn't say anything else. I felt a little guilty, because I had promised her I would walk with her.

"I promise I will walk home with you today. Then if you want to, you can come to our house and we can play a game," I said.

"All right. I didn't mind that you didn't wait for me, but I thought you could've told me."

"Yes, I should've. I'm sorry." I tried to sound remorseful.

By the time we had lunch, Josie was back to herself. As soon as I got to school I sought Carol out and told her that Mama and Papa wanted a letter from her parents about the weekend. She said she would bring one the next day. Excitement gripped me, but also a little fear. What would it be like to stay with an Australian family? I would have to speak English all weekend.

The next day, Carol gave me an envelope, which had the letter from her parents. She said they could ring Mama and Papa, but I told her we didn't have a telephone.

Mama and Papa agreed that I could go after they read the letter. They wrote some words on the letter, and told me to give it to Carol to give to her parents.

That Friday I had trouble concentrating in class. I'd carried a bag to school with nearly every item of clothing I owned. As I was only allowed to wear my Sunday best on Sundays, I'd also brought the skirt and blouse I usually wore after school.

I walked into the city with Carol to catch the bus to Riverside. Rose and Rita Woodfield caught the same bus, as did another half-a-dozen girls from my class. The bus drove along the West Tamar Highway, which ran adjacent to the Tamar River.

Carol's home was made of the same weatherboards as our house, but it was painted a pale yellow colour. Once inside, Mrs Swinton welcomed me and gave me a hug. Carol's bedroom was the same size as my bedroom at home, but instead of two double beds, it had two single beds; one on either side of the room, with a large wooden wardrobe and dressing table combination between the two beds.

Carol threw her schoolbag on her bed; I put mine on the floor. We were not allowed to put things on our beds at home, as the blankets might get dirty. And once our beds were made, they had to be nice and smooth. Mama disliked rumpled beds.

"Come on, we'll see what Mum's got to eat. Are you hungry?" Carol asked.

"Yes." *I'm always hungry!*

"Well, come on then. Mum might have some ice-cream or something for us." She headed towards the bedroom door.

"Don't we have to get changed first?" I asked.

"Why?"

"So our uniforms don't get dirty," I said.

"Oh, that's all right. If it gets dirty, Mum will wash it for you. Come on."

I followed her into the kitchen, where her mother sat at the table, peeling some green beans. "What would you like, girls?" she asked.

We settled for a bowl of ice-cream and a drink of pineapple juice. Mrs Swinton asked some questions about my family and if I liked Tasmania, and after telling her I did, Carol suggested we go across the road to the twins' house to play.

In bed that evening we talked for hours, until finally Mr Swinton knocked on the door and told us to go to sleep.

The next day we went to the Basin to swim, but instead of having to walk there, Mrs Swinton gave us money to buy bus tickets and also some extra money in case we needed it. We had a fun day, meeting up with some other girls from school. Some boys followed us around for a while, and Carol told me to ignore them. Yet I sensed that we were flirting a little, giving them little glances and giggling between ourselves, discussing which one looked nice.

On Sunday Mrs Swinton told us we were going on a picnic. Carol said they often had family picnics. Some of her aunts and uncles also came with their children, and they all played together.

Mr Swinton drove his car to an area near a stream. A big willow tree provided the shade and the car was parked beneath another large tree. Soon another two cars arrived and after hugs and kisses, I was introduced as Carol's friend from Holland.

They spread large blankets on the grass, and carried some boxes and large baskets from the cars. I had brought my bathers, and Carol and I paddled in the shallow stream. There were several children of varying ages. They had a cricket set as well as an Australian football. I was not familiar with either of these sports, but had great fun participating.

I didn't understand the cricket rules, but understood when they gave me a wooden bat that I was meant to hit the ball that someone else threw. Others stood around and tried to catch the ball. Three sticks were put in the ground, with little sticks balanced on top of them. "These are the stumps!" Carol told me.

The first ball was bowled to me by a teenage boy, who took great delight in the fact that I missed it altogether, and it then hit the sticks behind me, knocking them over.

"Yeah! Clean bowled, you're out!" he yelled, with a finger up in the air.

I was then sent behind the stumps to try and catch the ball when others batted.

After a while some people argued about whether or not someone was out. I couldn't understand what they were arguing about, but decided not to ask. I was already confused enough by this game.

"Lunch is ready," someone yelled from under the weeping willow.

All arguments were forgotten as adults and children alike rushed towards the food. I was again surprised how everybody just took what they wanted. There were plastic knives, forks, and plates and a packet of paper serviettes. Two whole roast chickens were being pulled apart into small pieces. Several bowls of salad, some boiled eggs, already peeled, and two loafs of bread, sliced and buttered, finished the spread.

I piled my plate high and Carol and I sat up against the tree trunk while we ate, mostly with our fingers. *I'm pleased Mama can't see this, I'm sure she would have a fit!*

When everybody had sufficient, the left-overs were packed up. The adults had flasks of hot water and made hot drinks and the kids had cordial.

"Anyone for cake?" Mrs Swinton asked, passing around a large metal tin which held a variety of small home-made slices.

After lunch we played Aussie Rules football. The ball itself was oval, with two pointy ends. We split into two teams; some long sticks were put in the ground on either side.

"They are the goal posts," Carol's father explained. "If you kick the ball between the two in the middle, you get six points, and if you kick them between the side sticks, you get one point."

They all started running around. But they threw the ball more than they kicked it. *They should call this hand ball!* The game was nothing like the football (soccer) I was familiar with. Somehow I got hold of the ball and kicked it really hard, and it went between the centre goal posts. I jumped up all excited until Carol said, "That is their goal, not ours!"

Carol and I burst into fits of giggles until we were both in tears. I didn't really know why I was laughing so much, but it felt good. In the end the adults were laughing too. For the second time since coming to Tasmania I knew I had made a real friend. I was also learning so much Australian culture: Aussie Rules and Cricket, and being able to eat as much as you want!

The Swintons dropped me off at our house on the way back from the picnic. I thanked them for having me.

"It was a pleasure, Marijke. You're welcome any time," Mrs Swinton said, as she hugged me goodbye.

"Yes, we need to put some meat on your bones, you're too thin," Mr Swinton added, a smile on his face. "And we need to teach you how to play cricket and football. You can't live in Australia and not know about our national sports!"

I watched their car drive down the road. Not until the car disappeared from sight did I turn to go inside.

What a lovely relaxed and friendly lifestyle they have, I can get used to this.

I walked around the back of the house. The table was outside and Mama was pouring a cup of tea. "Hello, Marijke. Did you have a good time?" Mama asked.

"Yes, it was really fun," I said. But I was distracted by the sight of Papa at the back of the garden. He was putting up some wire fencing. Dressed in his good trousers, he had his shirt sleeves rolled up. He hammered a nail into a wooden post, which was being held by John.

"Papa is building a chicken run," Mama said. "We have so much room here, and Papa thought we could have some chickens so we can get fresh eggs. Chicken food is really cheap and we can take turns feeding them."

Sure enough, within a week, we had half-a-dozen female chickens. They were so cute; we didn't need to be told twice when it was our turn to feed them. When they got bigger we realised that one of them was a rooster, not a hen. The rooster grew at twice the rate of the hens, and soon became the boss of the chicken run, attacking anyone who dared enter his domain. One day he jumped on the back of my legs, scratching them and pecking with his beak. I screamed and ran out.

"I'm not feeding the chooks again. That rooster is dangerous," I told Papa when he came home.

"I agree, he attacked me the other day too," Papa said. "I have asked Mr de Wit to come and kill him."

The following Saturday, it took Mr de Wit and Papa some time to catch the vicious animal. When they finally did Mr de Wit broke the rooster's neck. We had roast chicken that Sunday night for dinner. I didn't want to think about what we were eating, but the taste of the meal soon overcame my concern. I justified it by remembering that he had attacked me; I still had the marks on my legs.

Chapter 29

Summer turned into autumn. Willie and I walked to the Basin most weekday mornings. We enjoyed a swim before school and work, and we usually had the pool to ourselves.

Uncle Theo and Aunty Rie had a little car. They visited regularly to play cards with Mama and Papa. They were a fun couple, and there was always much laughter in the house when they were around. I especially loved it when they came, because uncle was a patisserie baker and he made the most delicious cakes. They had a cake shop in Launceston, and always brought left-overs for supper.

One day they told us they'd purchased a large block of land at Dilston, a small village about ten miles from Launceston, on the East Tamar Highway. They planned to clear some of the trees and build a house in a few years.

One Friday evening they said they planned to go to their block to do some clearing. Willie and I asked if we could go too. "We won't have any room in the car when we go there," Aunty said. "We need to take a wheelbarrow and some other tools. But we will be leaving them there, so there will be room for the return journey."

"We'll walk, won't we Willie?" I said. Both Willie and I enjoyed walking, and it didn't sound that far away.

"It will take a few hours to walk there," Uncle said. "It's a long way. We plan to be there by about ten o'clock, and we'll leave again after lunch. We'll bring a picnic lunch and something to drink. Are you sure you want to walk that far?"

Willie and I said we would. We decided we'd start really early, to give us plenty of time to get there. We couldn't get lost as we just needed to follow the main road.

The alarm went off at five o'clock. We had a big bowl of Weet Bix and milk, and a cup of tea each. Willie said she'd bought some lollies to eat on the way.

We set off at five-thirty. I wore a cardigan as it was quite chilly that early. We'd walked about fifteen minutes when a police car pulled up alongside us.

A policeman on the passenger side opened his window. "Where are you young ladies going this early in the morning?" he asked.

Willie explained what we were doing, but he didn't seem convinced. "Why would you walk all the way to Dilston at this hour of the morning? Do your parents know where you are going?"

Willie got a little upset. "I'm old enough to go to Dilston. We're meeting our aunt and uncle there, and they will bring us back to Launceston in their car. Marijke is my little sister, and I'll look after her. Our parents gave us permission to walk," she said in a firm voice.

Now it was my turn to get upset. *I am not your little sister. I might be a few years younger, but I am not little!*

Willie must have convinced them that we would be okay. "Be careful, girls. Make sure you don't take any lifts from anyone, and stay on the right side of the road when there are no footpaths, so you can see the traffic coming towards you."

We nodded and watched them drive away. Willie looked at me and started laughing. "I think they thought we were running away from home," she said, and laughed again.

She gave me a boiled lolly and we took off again. By seven o'clock we were at Newnham, the last Launceston suburb before we were on the East Tamar Highway. I was quite warm by then, and I took my cardigan off. Willie handed me another lolly, when another police car pulled up beside us.

"Are you two all right?" the policeman behind the wheel called through the window.

"Yes, thank you," Willie answered, "we're going to Dilston."

"I can give you a lift and drop you off," he offered.

"No thanks, we like walking," she replied politely.

"Are you sure? It's a long way. Why are two pretty young ladies walking at this hour of the morning? Do your parents know where you're going?"

After further explanations, they too drove off.

The East Tamar Highway was a narrow two-lane road, with no footpaths on either side. We decided to walk on the right side as we had been advised. There wasn't a lot of room, and whenever a car came our way we walked on the rough terrain at the side of the road.

Twice we were whistled at by boys in cars. One car turned around and pulled up in front of us. "Hey, hop in the car, we'll give you a lift," the driver said.

"No, thank you," Willie said. "Keep walking," she whispered, "and don't look back." She took my hand and began walking real fast.

The car took off with a screech of tyres. We walked a couple more minutes before I dared look around to see if they had actually gone. "You mustn't accept lifts with strangers," Willie advised. "Those boys are only after one thing, and it's dangerous to get in the car with any of them."

It was nearly ten when we reached our destination. I looked at the land and knew why they would need to clear it to build a house. It was dense with trees and shrubbery and tall dry grass. We walked through a gap in the wire fencing and followed a narrow path. It wasn't really a path, but it looked like some shrubs had been cut to be able to walk through. I felt branches and thorns scratch my legs.

We found a small clearing after a couple of minutes. I looked at my hands, which were swollen, and my right foot was quite sore. My black slip-ons probably weren't made for walking.

Willie pointed to what looked like the top of a wooden crate; several planks nailed to two cross planks. It reminded me of a raft.

"Why don't we pick that up and put it over those two stumps?" she suggested.

We got on either side of the raft and lifted it up onto its side. As we held it up I spotted a huge hairy spider stuck beneath the planks. I screamed and dropped my side. Willie too let go and it landed on the ground with a thud. Still screaming, I jumped back, and almost fell.

Within a few seconds what seemed like thousands of tiny little baby spiders crept through the gaps between the planks. No bigger than small ants, they scuttled along at amazing speed.

"It must have been a girl spider," Willie said. "It looks like she was pregnant."

I'd stopped screaming and looked in amazement at these tiny little creatures. I shuddered and felt sick. "I don't want to stay here. This is giving me the creeps!"

"Aunty and Uncle won't be far away. Come on, I'm sure we killed the spider when we dropped it."

"But she wouldn't be the only spider here, would she? There are probably lots of them, hiding under everything." Again I shuddered.

I sensed gigantic spiders hiding behind the trees and in the branches. My skin crawled. *Why did I want to come here? That spider was bigger than my hand! Yuk!*

Although Willie tried to make light of it, her face had taken on a definite shade of white.

When Aunty and Uncle arrived we told them what had happened. They laughed and said we'd better get used to spiders, as they were quite common in Tasmania. "Wait until you see the size of the snakes we've seen on this land. We've seen brown snakes and tiger snakes. I believe they are both highly poisonous. But don't worry, they're more scared of people than we are of them." Uncle laughed when he saw our faces.

Nothing could be more scared of me than I am of snakes and spiders. What am I doing here?

"Come on, girls, we came to clear some scrub from around here. If we clear a patch we can bring a tent and camp out here some times. Maybe you'd like to come camping too?" Uncle handed me a rake.

"No, thank you. I don't think I'd like that. What if the snakes come into the tent?"

"I don't think they would."

"Well, I'm sure the spiders could come into a tent. And where would we sleep? On the ground?"

"We'll bring some foam mattresses. Nearly everyone in Australia goes camping, and not too many people die from snake or spider bites," Uncle reassured me.

No matter what you say, I will never go camping in the bush. NEVER! In Holland I'd only ever seen tiny spiders, and I didn't even like them!

As I raked away leaves and some small branches and sticks, I was petrified. Everything that moved made me jump. When Aunty gave me some sandwiches for lunch, I gagged on them. I kept seeing that big hairy spider, and still my skin crawled.

After lunch Aunty said that it was too warm to do any more work, and we'd better pack up the car and head home. I couldn't get away quick enough, and I kept my word. I never ever visited that block of land again.

I was exhausted when we arrived home and I told Mama I wasn't hungry and that I felt sick. I crawled into bed, but it took a long time for me to get to sleep.

It was only a couple of weeks later that we had a big hairy spider inside the bathroom. I heard a scream and ran in to find Trudy pressed against the wall, pointing at the spider on the ceiling. We found out that these spiders usually came into the house when it was going to rain. I wasn't the only one afraid of the spiders, and it took Papa all his time to calm us down.

"They don't hurt you," Arnold said another time when one was spotted on the ceiling in the dining room. "Look, I'll pick it up." He climbed up on the seat and grabbed the spider by one leg as we all screamed and ran away. He ran after us, spider dangling from his fingers. I slammed the bedroom door shut, and Trudy and I pushed against it, making sure he couldn't get in.

We heard a yelp, but stayed where we were. Whatever was happening could not possible be more important than keeping ourselves out of harm's way!

"Come on, girls, you can come out now," Papa said, some time later. "Arnold killed the spider, but not before it bit him on his finger."

Serves him right! That'll teach him to chase us with a spider! I hope it hurts.

Chapter 30

"Marijke, let me cut your hair for you. The way your father cuts it makes it look like you have a bowl on your head." Josie's words echoed what I thought too. Quite a few people had commented on my hairstyle, and I became increasingly aware that many girls at school took a lot of pride in themselves, especially Josie.

Her blond hair was shoulder-length, and it was always perfectly groomed. At school it was tied back into a ponytail, with a fawn ribbon around it. The school was strict as to what hairstyles were and were not permitted. Only fawn coloured bands and ribbons were allowed, and pins had to be neutral. There was no teasing of hair, and long hair had to be tied back.

I had been thinking of letting my hair grow. My hair was thin, fine and straight. The way Papa cut it wasn't flattering, nor did I think it was suitable for a teenager.

Josie threw a white sheet around my shoulders and started trimming and shaping. I was a little nervous, as I wasn't sure she had done anything like this before. I wasn't fond of my bowl cut, but it would be better than if it was hacked all over the place.

I shouldn't have worried; the end result was really nice. She had shaped my fringe, without it looking straight. She had then flicked the side of my hair back from my face with two small pins, and all in all, I thought I looked much more mature.

I was a bit concerned that the nuns may not like it, and asked Sister Magenta if it was acceptable.

"Marijke, your hair looks lovely. It is clean and shiny and neat. That's all we ask."

Mama and Papa also liked the new haircut. I told Papa he had been sacked as my hairdresser. "No more Papa cuts for me," I said jokingly, although I meant it.

After a few weeks, of course, my hair had grown to a stage where it was no longer manageable. I decided if Josie could cut my hair, I should be able to do so myself. I found Papa's sharp scissors and took a small mirror on a stand into the bathroom. First I cut the fringe and the top, then the sides. *Now comes the difficult part – the back!*

I placed the small mirror on top of the window-sill, so that I could see the small mirror above the hand-basin, and I could see what I was doing.

Nervously I started trimming the back of my hair. I remembered how Josie had thinned the hair, so it fell towards my neck. When I was finished I was proud as punch. I thought it looked as good as Josie had done. When I showed Mama she said it looked nice. "There are a couple of little pieces that need tidying up. Come here, and I will do that." She made a couple of little snips.

At dinner that night, Mama told Papa I had cut my own hair. "I always said you were a bijdehante ka (clever girl/know all)," Papa said. "Seeing you're so good at cutting hair, you may as well cut all your younger sisters' hair for me. That will save me some time and money."

That weekend I set up in the bathroom and cut the hair of my four younger sisters. Of course, Tiny was too young, and she didn't have much hair yet. John wouldn't let me touch his hair. I told Papa I couldn't cut boys' hair, because they had to be short back and sides, and that was too hard for me.

Arnold and John weren't brave enough to let me cut their hair anyway, but they didn't like Papa's haircuts either. *They're boys, they can sort it out with Papa.*

* * * *

The Dutch Australian Association held regular card evenings in Launceston and Mama and Papa enjoyed the interaction with their countrymen.

"The Dutch Australian Association's Dramatic Society is looking for younger members," Papa said one Sunday morning. He and Mama had been to a card night the evening before.

"They're looking for someone to play Anna Frank and her sister Margot. There's a small theatre near the City Park where they'll rehearse. At Easter they will perform to the public. It will be in Dutch for the Dutch community here."

Willie and I decided we'd go to the auditions. I visualised myself looking a bit like Anna Frank, and being thirteen, felt I was the right age. I had never acted before, except for the plays we put on at home for family members.

Papa and our late Mama had met through a dramatic society in Amsterdam. Papa used to tell us he saw an angel when he first met Mama. He said he walked into a theatre and Mama was on stage in a long white gown, singing like an angel. Mama used to smile sweetly whenever he told us this story.

When Willie and I arrived at the Little Theatre we were met by about a dozen people. One girl walked over and introduced herself as Bernadine. She was really pretty, with blond hair and blue eyes, and her skin was like porcelain. Willie told me

Bernadine was eighteen, but she looked much younger.

We were given scripts and auditioned by reading lines from different parts of the play. At the end of the auditions I was quite peeved when Bernadine got the role of Anna and I got the role of Margot, Anna's older sister. *Bernadine is too old to play Anna! She is five years older than me, and I have to play her older sister!*

"At least you got a part, and one of the major parts," Papa said that night when I complained.

"But Margot only has one line! And Bernadine is too old, she's eighteen."

"When people are good actors they can play any age," Mama said. "Stop being so childish. Accept that Bernadine is more suited to play Anna than you!"

Why is it you never stick up for me? I would have been good as Anna! I walked off in a huff.

"Come back here and don't be so rude and selfish!" Papa called me back. "You might as well go to bed. This just goes to show you're not mature enough to take on a big role. You need to accept that some people are better at some things than others. Stop being a sook!"

I glared at him and Mama. *Why couldn't they tell me they thought I'd be better suited to play Anna?*

I went to all the rehearsals and sat on the stage for hours. Margot was in every scene, but she said nothing, except for that one line. For the most part I sat in a chair, reading a book or doing some sewing. Or I had to look like I was talking to someone else on the stage. I wasn't allowed to make any noise, just move my mouth and hands. *How much rehearsal do you need to be on stage doing nothing!* I thought time and time again. It was rather boring.

On the night of the performance I was surprised that I was terrified. The Little Theatre filled up with people and was abuzz. Just before I had to go on stage, I ran to the toilet, where I threw up. *I can't go up there. Everybody's looking at me!*

"Come on, Marijke, we're waiting for you," a voice called through the toilet door. I wiped my mouth and made my way to the stage.

When the curtain opened I froze. The theatre had been darkened, but I could make out all these dark heads. I felt someone prod my leg, and the man who played Mr Frank whispered, "You're supposed to look like you're talking to me, remember?"

I looked at him and made my mouth move. Several times during the play I forgot what I had to do. Then came the most embarrassing moment of all. I forgot my line. My one line. It had removed itself from my brain, and my mouth wouldn't move. I stared at the audience and heard another voice say the words that I should have said. I had blown it! *Maybe they were right! I couldn't have done the role of Anna. I couldn't even remember one single line!*

After the play, supper was served. I felt so embarrassed, I didn't want to see or speak to anyone. All the comments I heard about the play were complimentary. Not one person said anything about me forgetting my line. Even the other cast members didn't mention it. When we walked home I waited for Mama or Papa to say I hadn't even deserved that role, but they didn't. I began to realise that nobody had even noticed I had forgotten my line.

I'll never audition for anything again!

* * * *

Just after Easter, Papa said he had some important news to give us.

"You know we're only able to stay in this house for a total of eighteen months, until Mr and Mrs Harker start building their big new shop." Papa looked around his large brood, waiting for a reaction.

When no one spoke, I asked, "Will we need to stay with the other Dutch families again then?"

"No. That's our big news. Today I signed a contract to buy a block of land. We're going to build a house, and we should be able to move into it before this house gets pulled down." Papa had a look of pure joy on his face.

"You're going to build a house, Papa? Can you do that?" I asked in amazement. I always knew Papa was clever with his hands, but I didn't think he was able to build a house.

He burst out laughing. "No, Marijke, a builder will build it for us. We'll have to pay them a lot of money to do that. But we have a loan from the bank, and we know some Dutch builders who will build the house. They will draw up the plans for the house."

Wait till I write Fietje and our all family in Holland about this, they will be so envious! A house! Nobody I know in Holland has ever built a house. Our own house, just like they showed us in those movies in Holland.

"Where is the land? Is it in Launceston? It isn't like Aunty and Uncle's land is it, with trees and spiders and snakes?

"No. The land is about the same size as this block of land here. It has some trees on it, but they're fruit trees, and some of them will have to be cut down. The rest is grass. It's in St Leonards, which is about ten miles from Launceston. It is about half-way up a hill, but the block itself is quite flat. Why don't you wait until this weekend, and we'll go and see it."

I couldn't get to sleep that night. *Our own brand new house!* In my mind I visualised a big double story house, with lots of bedrooms, like I'd seen in the movies. *I think this is the most exciting thing that's ever happened to us. Who would have thought when we left Holland we would have our own house built!*

Chapter 31

I woke up early the following Saturday. I got up quietly and went to the kitchen. Mama and Papa had told us we'd all go to our new block of land when all the chores were done. One of my jobs on that Saturday was to bake the biscuits for the week.

By the time Mama came into the kitchen to warm a bottle for Tiny, I'd finished about half the biscuits.

"Mmm, it smells nice in here. What time did you get up?" Mama looked sleepy.

"I don't know, about two hours ago. I was too excited to sleep."

"Why, what are you excited about?" She looked puzzled.

"The land! We're going to see the block of land where we're going to build a house!" *How could she forget?*

"Oh, yes. Sorry, I'm still half asleep. Well, it looks like you'll be ready early, the way you're going." She poured some boiling water in a jug and put the baby bottle in it.

It wasn't long before everyone was up. After breakfast I helped Mama cut and pack sandwiches and packed some biscuits for morning tea. We left the house before ten o'clock. Tiny was in the pram, and we took turns pushing it. "If we go over the hill we'll get there quicker," Papa said. "We could also go through Kings Meadows or through town, but that would take longer."

When we got to Howick Street, which was about five minutes walk from our house, we turned left. Howick Street was really steep, and I guessed the top of the hill was as high as where the Van Maanenberg's lived. But there were no steps here, just a narrow footpath.

Just as well we were fit, because it took some effort to push the pram up the hill. Not only was Tiny in the pram, but Mama had put all the bags with our lunches and drinks at the bottom of the pram; it was quite heavy. We took turns pushing, two of us at a time. When we got to the top we had to cross High Street, and then walk down David Street. David Street was as steep as Howick Street, and now we had to pull the pram back to keep it from taking off down the steep hill.

It wasn't a hot day, but we were all red in the face by the time we reached Newstead at the bottom of the hill.

"We go around that corner, and then it's about four miles. I think we'll need a drink when we get there."

Once we left Newstead, we crossed a bridge over a narrow river which had large trees on either side. A terrible smell hung around there. "I don't know what's in that river, but it stinks!" Mama said, gagging. We all held our hankies over our noses until the river was out of sight.

The road to St Leonards was poorly sealed, and there were no footpaths. The first couple of miles was an industrial area with factories and warehouses. After a while a sign indicated we'd arrived in St Leonards. My excitement mounted. The buildings were now residential houses. Not quite up to the standard we had seen on the movies in Holland, but most of them looked nice.

Obviously most people took pride in their gardens which looked well tended. We saw men mowing lawns; some with hand mowers, others with motorised mowers.

Every now and then we'd see a house which looked untidy. The wood needed paint, and some gardens were just a mess, with overgrown grass.

"You'd think if you were lucky enough to have your own house and garden, you'd look after it," Papa said, shaking his head in disgust.

At last we arrived in the centre of the village. There was a hotel on one corner, a couple of empty shops on another, a small supermarket on the third, and a service station opposite. "We're nearly there," Papa said, as he pointed to the road between the hotel and the service station.

A sign said Benvenue Road. The road was unsealed and a passing car created a cloud of dust as we started up the hill. Mama held her hands over Tiny's little face to stop the dust from making her dirty.

The pram felt extraordinarily heavy by now, and it took three of us to push it uphill. On the right side of the road, behind the hotel, was vacant bushland. On the left were some houses, and a few vacant blocks of land.

"See that brick house on the left? The land in front of that is our block," Papa said.

Ineke, Lidy, Margaret and Trudy got a new lease of life and ran to where Papa had pointed. I would have joined them, except I was helping push the pram.

"Apparently this land was all part of a fruit orchard before the owners decided to break it into blocks and sell it off. That's why the fruit trees are on there. The fruit is finished for this year. We'll need to cut some of them down, but we'll try to keep what we can." Papa looked around as he spoke. He looked like a king overseeing his kingdom.

Mama had pulled a couple of blankets from under the pram and spread them beneath one of the trees. She poured the drinks while I shared the Eggless Brownie cake. For a while we sat and enjoyed the rest. It had taken us nearly two hours to walk there.

The view from the block was lovely. We could almost see all the way back to Launceston. "Hello, how are you?" A lady walked over from a weatherboard house behind our block. "I'm Mrs Loney. I guess we'll be neighbours when you build a house here?" She shook Mama and Papa's hands.

While the adults talked, we explored the block and were soon playing tag with the little ones. When we left to walk home, Papa surprised us all by buying ice-blocks. That was really a special treat! Some people in the shop stared as we gathered around him. I guessed they weren't used to seeing a family with ten children too often.

* * * *

I became quite self-conscious as my breasts kept growing. For a skinny girl, they were quite big. At school I noticed most other girls in my class wore bras. Even girls whose breasts were much smaller, and some didn't even seem to have any yet.

I waited until Mama and I were alone in the lounge-room one evening, and I shyly broached the subject. "Mama, I need some bras. My breasts hurt when I run, and all the other girls in my class have bras."

"You're too young to have bras, Marijke. Ann's only just started wearing them, and she's sixteen."

"But my breasts hurt when I run!" I repeated.

"I guess I can give you a couple of my old bras. Now that I'm not breast feeding Tiny, they are too big for me. Mama had little breasts compared to mine.

She left the room and gave me two bras; one white pair and one skin-tone. I took them into my bedroom and tried to put them on. They kept getting tangled up, and I couldn't do them up. Later that evening I asked Willie to help me. She patiently showed me how to put them on.

"When you have them on, make sure you bend down and shake your breasts into place in the cup, that way they will be more comfortable," she said with authority.

They felt uncomfortable, and didn't fit well, but they made me feel mature. I'd begun to feel a sense of femininity, and noticed boys looked at me and sometimes gave me wolf-whistles.

I hated that the school uniforms weren't made for big breasted girls. The bigger the breasts, the more they pulled up at the front, making them look uneven. *As if these clothes aren't ugly enough!*

The weather was cooler now, and we were back in our winter uniform.

There was great excitement in the class when I arrived at school one day. "Look at the little puppy! Isn't she cute?" Carol came over and showed me a little bundle of fluff in a cardboard box.

"Are you allowed to have puppies at school?" I asked, worried she might get into trouble.

"Oh, it isn't my puppy. Someone's raffling it and raising money for the school. Wouldn't you just love a puppy?"

I'd never considered having a dog. I stroked its soft black and white fur. She had the cutest eyes.

"Why don't you hold her for a minute? She's so cuddly." Carol lifted her from the box and put her in my arms. She gingerly licked my hand, and I felt little puffs of breath from her nose. *Oh, she's so cute!*

I'd always been afraid of dogs, but this puppy was so small, it didn't scare me. After a while some other girls wanted a cuddle, and I reluctantly gave her up.

Carol told me the raffle tickets cost one penny each. I had two pennies left over from my pocket money that week. I bought one ticket. *What would*

Mama and Papa say if I brought home a puppy? I don't think they would like it. It would probably make a mess, and Mama doesn't like any mess at all. Oh, well, I probably won't win it anyway.

During the morning different girls were nominated by the teachers to puppy sit. I was surprised when I was selected to puppy sit for the last lesson. When the bell went for lunch, Sister Magdalene told everyone to remain seated. "We will draw the raffle for the puppy now. Whoever wins it, whether it is someone from this class or from another grade, they can look after the puppy for the afternoon before they take it home. Marijke, seeing you have the puppy now, come here, and you can draw the winner."

Feeling important, I walked to the front of the class, the box with the puppy in my arms, which I placed on Sister's desk. She held up a shoe box with the raffle tickets in it. I swished the tickets around and pulled one out. Sister took it from me and opened it up.

"Oh! It is someone from this class." Excited gasps filled the room.

Sister looked around the room, from one girl to another. She took her time, keeping everyone in suspense.

"Marijke, take the puppy from the box and let everyone see her." I obeyed the instructions.

Silence fell over the room.

"Okay, I won't keep you waiting any longer. Marijke, can you believe you pulled your own name from the box?" She said smiling broadly.

"Me? I've won the puppy? Really?" I couldn't believe it. My heart was pounding and I felt my eyes tear up.

"Yes, see? Here is the ticket with your name on it. I don't think there are any other Marijkes in this school, do you?"

I shook my head, I was in shock. The other girls gathered around me, congratulating me and asking what I was going to call it.

I have no idea. What am I going to tell Mama and Papa? "Guess what, we have another member in our family. Here she is – a dog!

I felt sick all afternoon as I looked after her. The girl who'd raffled her gave me a packet of food for her and told me to make sure she always had clean water to drink. "And you'll have to bath her and brush her fur," she said. "Take good care of her, won't you?" I said I would.

Oh, God, what if Mama and Papa won't let me keep her? What will I do then? I can't take her back to school. I think Mama will be so angry! I can already hear her say, "Don't you think we have enough mouths to feed?"

Chapter 32

I picked up the box with the puppy and headed home. My four younger sisters met me, excitement in their eyes. They'd heard I had a puppy, and couldn't wait to see it.

"Marijke, can I cuddle her, please?" Trudy caught up with me first. "Can I?"

"If you're very careful, she's very little," I said, feeling protective towards this little ball of fluff.

I lifted her from the box and placed her in Trudy's arms. The other three reached across to pat her. The puppy tried to lick each hand, her little tail wagging so much, I thought it might drop off.

"What's her name?" Trudy asked.

"I don't think she's got one. Everybody just called her Puppy," I said. It hadn't occurred to me to give an animal a name.

"She has to have a name," Trudy insisted. "We can't just call her Puppy all her life. That would be like calling you Girl all your life."

"Let's put her back in the box and go home. I hope Mama's going to let us keep her."

Trudy gently placed her back in the box. "I think we should call her Pukkie," she said. "That is a nice name for a dog."

"That's a Dutch name. Australians don't like Dutch names." I remembered the problems I'd had keeping my name, and Trudy and Margaret had adopted English names.

"I don't care. She'll live at our house, and we can call her what we want. I like Pukkie, it's cute, just like she is." Trudy could be quite obstinate at times.

"We like Pukkie too, Marijke," Margaret said. "Don't you like it?"

I nodded; I wasn't worried too much about a name, I was concerned about what Mama and Papa would say.

"Good! You like it and we like it, so we'll call her Pukkie?" Trudy said, the matter settled.

"Okay. Maybe Mama will like a puppy better if she has a Dutch name," I said.

After crossing the last intersection before our house, the girls ran ahead of me. *At least I don't have to break the news to Mama; they'll have told her already.*

Walking in the back door, I heard a commotion as four excited voices tried to talk to Mama at once.

"Whoa! One at the time," I heard Mama say. "What is this about a dog? What dog?"

Should I wait until the girls have explained it all, or go in and give the box to Mama?

I decided I might as well bite the bullet. I walked into the dining room and placed the box on one of the benches. "This puppy, Mama. I won her in a raffle. Trudy's called her Pukkie. She's so cute, Mama, come and have a look at her."

"Come and stroke her, Mama, she's so soft," Ineke said, her blue eyes shining.

I tentatively opened the box, lifted Pukkie out, and handed her to Mama. I expected her to pull back, but she didn't. She held her against her chest and gently stroked her.

"She's lovely. Did you say you won her in a raffle? She's your dog?"

I told her what had happened and that I'd drawn my own name from the tickets.

"Well, that was lucky then, wasn't it? But we know nothing about looking after a dog. Do you know how big she will grow?"

It hadn't occurred to me that Pukkie would grow; she was a puppy! I shook my head. "The girl who raffled her gave me some food for her, and said I have to make sure I always have clean water in a bowl. And she said I have to bath her and brush her fur every week. She also said that she has been inoculated, whatever that means," I said, gaining confidence by the minute. *Mama hasn't said we can't keep her, and she's still holding her!*

"First, I think you should take her outside and show her the lawn and where she can go to the toilet. You'll be responsible to clean up any messes she makes. We can't have anyone walking in poo. I'll give you a small plastic bowl to put water in. You'll fill it every morning before school, and again when you get home. She'll sleep in the small shed out the back. Use this box as a bed. I'll give you some rags for her to sleep on. Oh, I love her name. Pukkie, who thought of that?"

"I did!" Trudy was obviously pleased Mama approved.

I stared at Mama. *She's letting me keep Pukkie! I thought I'd be in trouble, and look at her, she likes her!*

"Yes, Mama, I'll do that, I promise," I said seriously. I felt like hugging her, but I wasn't sure how she would react to that, so I didn't.

"Can I help you look after Pukkie too?" Trudy pleaded.

"And me too," Margaret, Lidy and Ineke chimed in.

"Okay, we'll set up a roster. You can all help me look after Pukkie." *I'll make sure they pick up the poo, I don't want to do that!*

I took the puppy outside, and as soon as I put her on the lawn she did a wee and a little poo. *Mama must've known she needed to go!*

I cut one side from the box and placed it in the shed. Mama came outside with a white plastic bowl filled with water. She placed it near the door to the shed. When Arnold came home, he too was smitten.

Papa didn't stand a chance. If he'd objected to keeping Pukkie he would have had the whole family in uproar. It was the first time I'd known Mama make a decision without consulting Papa first. If he was upset, he didn't show it.

"Now, you do have to remember, she's a dog. She has to stay outside or in the shed. You'll have to make sure she doesn't get out on the road," Papa said, then picked her up and stroked her.

When I went to put Pukkie to bed that night, I was assisted by many pairs of hands. Everyone, except Mama and Papa, came out to make sure she was comfortable. She'd won everyone's heart, and within a few hours, had become an integral part of our family.

* * * *

Mama was very protective of her personal property. I guessed, as she had been single all her life until she married Papa, she was used to having things to herself. She got angry if we used her scissors, for example, or her comb or hairbrush. It annoyed me no end. We were always told to share things, but what was Mama's was Mama's, and no one was allowed to touch.

I got into trouble time and time again for using something that belonged to her, even something as simple as a nail file. It never occurred to me that some of these things may have had sentimental value for her, as they related to her previous life, and some were gifts from the family she'd left behind.

One Saturday morning, Mama and Papa had taken Tiny and the younger kids shopping. I was home alone and set about dusting the bedrooms, one of my chores that day.

Papa had built a wall cabinet for Mama. The front folded down, and was used as a change-table, and Tiny's baby clothes and toys were kept in the cabinet. As it didn't fit into Mama and Papa's bedroom, it was in the boys' bedroom, which they shared with Margaret, Lidy and Ineke.

I pulled the front down to dust inside. Mama was very particular, and would run her finger over dusted areas. If there was any dust left, it had to be done again.

Inside the cabinet were some soft fluffy animals that had been gifts to Tiny when she was born. I pulled them out and dusted that shelf. Instead of putting the animals back on the shelf, I put then on top of the cabinet. *Why hide them? They make the room look nice lined up against the wall.*

When I'd finished dusting the bedroom, I continued with my other chores and promptly forgot about the stuffed toys.

It was mid-afternoon when Mama came into the dining room where we were playing a game. The weather was miserable and cold and the dining room was warm.

"Who's been playing with Tiny's toys?" Mama asked, looking from one to the other. She pointed to the three girls who shared that bedroom with John and Arnold. "Who's been playing with Tiny's toys?" she asked again.

They all shook their heads and denied it was any of them. It didn't occur to me that Mama was talking about the stuffed animals, which I had lined up on the cabinet.

"I'm very angry. They're Tiny's toys, not yours. She's only little and the toys need to stay clean. If any of you have touched things outside and then touched the toys, they may have germs on them and make Tiny sick. Why, you could even have touched Pukkie and then not washed your hands. If no one owns up, I will talk to Papa about punishment. You will all be punished until we know who did this."

After dinner that night Papa told the three girls they wouldn't get any pocket money until the culprit owned up. "Even though no one should have touched Tiny's toys, the punishment is because someone is lying. You can own up now, and you won't be punished for what you've done." He looked sternly at the three, but all shook their heads.

The following day I received my pocket money, as did Arnold and Trudy. Arnold hadn't been home the previous day. Because Trudy and I shared the bedroom with Ann and Willie, Papa didn't believe we would have done it.

Later that day I walked down the hall and overheard part of a conversation between Mama and Papa. They were in the lounge-room, and the door was ajar.

"They were all on top of the cabinet instead of inside it," Mama said. "Why doesn't one of them own up instead of punishing the others?"

My heart pounded as I rushed into my bedroom. *Mama was talking about those stuffed animals! I thought she meant someone had played with some other toys and hadn't put them back. It was me! And I am not being punished! Oh, God, they will never believe me when I tell them I didn't realise what they were talking about!*

I sat on the side of the bed feeling terribly guilty.

You have to tell them.

But they won't believe me.

They will say it was just another one of my lies.

You must tell them, you can't let the others lose their pocket money for something you did.

I got up with a heavy heart and headed towards the lounge-room. I couldn't do it. I'd be in trouble again. *Surely they will give them their pocket money next week?*

I tossed and turned that night, my conscience pricking me. Yet, I justified not telling them it was me. *Mama's too fussy! I'm sure Tiny wouldn't get any germs from us! And they shouldn't punish the girls for something they didn't do. They didn't know who did it, so why punish all three?* I was able to put the blame back on Mama.

By the third weekend the girls still hadn't received any pocket money, I realised Papa wasn't going to give in. I should have known. Papa was strict and always followed up on his threats. I saw the hurt and confusion in my sisters' eyes as he passed them by again. Suddenly the guilt was too much. *I can't do this to them. I have to own up, even though I know Papa and Mama won't believe I hadn't set out to lie originally.*

I waited until Mama was in the kitchen on her own later that evening.

"Mama, I did it. I didn't understand what you said, and I did it," I said, tears rolling down my cheek.

"You did what? What didn't you understand?"

It was such a big deal to me, it was all I had been thinking and worrying about all day. *She's just pretending she doesn't understand, to make it harder for me!*

"What are you talking about, Marijke?" she asked again, exasperated.

"The toys. I didn't play with them, so when you asked who played with Tiny's toys, I didn't realise you meant the soft fluffy animals. I'd put them on top of the cabinet when I dusted! I didn't mean to lie."

For a moment Mama looked confused, then her face darkened.

"You did that? You did that to your sisters? Oh, Marijke, how could you? You and your lies! Always telling lies! Don't tell me you didn't realise. Even if you didn't realise at first, you must have known later, otherwise you wouldn't be telling me this now!" Her voice shook with anger as she spoke.

"I didn't realise until the next day, and then I knew you and Papa wouldn't believe me. See, you don't believe me now!"

"No, I don't believe you. You've let your sisters go without their pocket money for three weeks, while you still took yours. How could you?" She walked past me and left the kitchen.

I stayed where I was. *She's gone to tell Papa and he'll be furious. I may as well get it over with now.*

I didn't have to wait long. Papa walked in, eyes blazing.

"You make me so angry, you draw the blood out from under my nails," he shouted, shaking his finger in my face. He then lifted his hand as though he was about to strike me.

I cowered, but he dropped his hand. Papa didn't smack often, but when he did, he smacked hard. He didn't need an implement; his hands left big red welts when he was done. When we were younger he'd put us over his knee, and the number of smacks depended on how naughty we'd been.

"You're too old to smack, and I thought you were too old to have played with those toys!"

"I didn't play ..."

"I don't care what you did with the toys. You lied! You let your sisters take the blame for something you did. I guess I shouldn't be surprised, but I'm very disappointed in you. I'm not sure what other punishment you will receive yet, but you will not get any pocket money for two months. That money will go to your sisters, to make up for what they lost. I don't know what we're going to do about your dishonesty! It's bad enough when you lie about stealing things, but when you make your sisters suffer, that's inexcusable!" He slammed the door as he stormed off.

I don't deserve my sisters to forgive me. I don't blame them if they never speak to me again. Why didn't I tell the truth when I realised what had happened?

I'd never felt so guilty in my entire life.

Chapter 33

Papa shamed me at breakfast the next morning by telling everyone what I had done. I received some well deserved glares. I hadn't had much sleep and the guilt was still deep.

"Marijke, what do you think would be a suitable punishment for you?" Papa asked me that evening.

I shrugged my shoulders. *I don't know. You're taking my pocket money away, isn't that enough?*

"I hope this will teach you not to lie. I suppose your sisters will forget soon enough, but I won't. I will watch you closely, and if I catch you lying or cheating again ..."

"I'm sorry, Papa, I was scared." Right then I decided I would not be dishonest ever again, as long as I lived.

"Mama and I've talked, and for now we believe you're too immature to go to any of the teenage dances that are run by the Dutch Australian Association."

"But you'd promised I could ..."

"Yes, but that was before this last episode. For the time being, no dances. Don't ask for how long, that will depend on your behaviour. I will tell you when I think I can trust you again. Until then, you are grounded."

I knew better than to argue. I'd looked forward to going to the dance with my older sisters. Willie, who had recently turned seventeen, had met a Dutch boy at the last dance, and was now dating him regularly. She'd told me there was a really good rock and roll band with some cute guys at the dance. I'd been thrilled when Papa said I could go as well next time. Now I'd ruined my chance at being treated as a mature person in the family.

On the way to school Ineke told me I had been naughty. Then she promptly took my hand and skipped all the way to school. All seemed to have been forgiven. *I wish Papa could forgive me as quickly as she has.*

* * * * *

We made several more trips to the block of land at St Leonards. Papa was given a small tent by a Dutch family. When the weather picked up early spring, we pitched the tent on the block. Mama would put Tiny inside the tent to keep her out of direct sunlight. Tiny was crawling by then. She was a sweet baby. She didn't cry much and was often the centre of our attention.

Papa said it would take quite some time to pay off the block of land, before we could get our house built. On one of our trips to the block in early spring, Papa said he wanted to turn the first bit of soil. He'd brought a small spade with him and did his hardest to dig into the unyielding ground. It was as hard as rock. We willed him to succeed, but at the same time laughed at his efforts. Finally, with sweat pouring down his red face, he moved the tiniest bit of grass, and we clapped and cheered.

* * * *

I'd settled into school well and managed to stay friends with both Carol and her group of friends, as well as with Josie. I envied the freedom my Australian friends had as opposed to the regimented and strict rules we lived under at home.

Even Josie, although her parents were Dutch, had more freedom and seemed to have so much more than I did.

She had lovely clothes, and always looked beautiful. I felt gangly and awkward around her. Yet she took lots of time to show me how to wear my hair stylish. My clothes, like those of my sisters, were pretty, but I only had three outfits. My Sunday best, which I was allowed to wear each Sunday; my school uniform, and my weekday clothes.

Due to the amount of washing in our large family, we had to make our clothes last a week. If we spilled something, we'd get growled at, and had to go to the bathroom to remove the stain straight away. I noticed that my friends just threw their dirty clothes in the laundry bag or basket at their homes, and they had several outfits to choose from.

Willie and Ann didn't seem too fussed about fashion. Both had Papa's dark wavy hair. Ann had let her hair grow since we arrived in Australia, and liked to wear it in a pony-tail. Willie's hair was short, which suited her. My straight, mousy-brown hair had a mind of its own, and it took some special brushing techniques after I washed it, to make it go into a neat bob.

As we were only allowed two showers each week, I had to wet my hair every morning to stop it from sticking up all over the place. I wished my hair was more manageable.

* * * *

Willie's relationship with the Dutch boy she'd met seemed to be getting serious. Bill had a car and picked her up most nights, but she had to be home by ten o'clock.

One night Papa invited Bill inside to have a chat. Papa was concerned that Bill wasn't Catholic, as he had never seen him attend a Dutch Mass, which was held once each month in a small church in Trevallyn, a suburb of Launceston.

Papa took Bill into the lounge-room and my curiosity got the better of me. Bill was a short, stocky man. His surname was of French origin, which probably accounted for him not looking like a Dutchman.

I stood close to the door and heard Papa ask Bill what his intentions were in relation to Willie. Bill said he hoped to marry her.

"Well, you can't!" Papa said. "She has to get married in the Catholic Church. You not being a Catholic will cause all sorts of problems."

"Who the bloody hell said I'm not Catholic?" Bill's voice raised a notch or two.

"I've never seen you attend the Dutch Mass since we've been here, and I haven't seen you in the Church of Apostles." Papa also raised his voice.

"They are not the only bloody churches in Launceston," Bill was shouting now.

I was shocked by his swearing. I'd heard one or two girls at school use those words, and they were punished by the nuns. I wasn't sure if Papa understood the swear words.

"Are you Catholic or not?" Papa said, his voice now calmer.

"Yes, I bloody well am!" came the response. "I go to another church near where I live."

Their voices dropped so I could no longer hear. I went into the bedroom before I'd get caught eves-dropping. I'd never heard someone stand up to Papa like that, and I didn't think he would like it.

It had been some months since I was punished for my dishonesty. Although I'd planned never to lie again, I'd found it difficult to implement. It didn't matter what I did wrong. Whether I pinched something or tried to wriggle out of something I'd done, I was always caught out.

I wanted to go to the dance so badly, I tried extra hard to be honest, and obviously it had worked, because Papa told me I could go to the dance with Willie and Bill and Ann that Saturday night. As Bill was picking Willie up, we could go with them in Bill's car.

I soon found out that perhaps this wasn't due to Papa considering I was now honest and mature enough to attend the dance. Papa wanted Ann and I to be Willie's chaperones. I sensed he didn't trust Bill. We were told we were not allowed to leave them alone, and Willie was told she had to come inside as soon as we arrived home.

Bill wasn't overly impressed with this arrangement, but he was stuck with us. I hadn't made up my mind whether I liked him or not yet, but Willie glowed in his presence. He swore too much for my liking. He was a builder and Willie said that all builders talked like that. When Bill arrived in Australia, he'd been taught the swear words by his work-mates.

After dinner on Saturday, I put on my good dress and we piled into Bill's car, Willie in the front passenger seat and Ann and I in the back.

The dance was in a hall in the centre of town. I had a wonderful time, but spent most of my time watching others dance. Bill danced close to Willie, and his large hand was firmly placed on her buttock. I was shocked, but Willie seemed to enjoy this closeness.

I felt shy and awkward. Josie was there with her older brother, and Robbie asked me to dance. I'd never danced with a boy in my life and I declined quickly. *I don't think I can dance like that. I'll probably fall or make a fool of myself.*

Josie danced with a couple of other boys and tried to encourage me to do the same, to no avail. I enjoyed listening to the band play rock and roll music as well as slow songs. The lead singer was good and he seemed to be able to imitate the voices of some of the popular singers like Elvis Presley and Cliff Richard. Josie had a couple of their records which she had played over and over again when we were at her house.

When we got home Papa and Mama asked if I had enjoyed myself. "Yes, I did. I loved the music and the band. I was too scared to dance with anyone though," I said.

"You? Shy? Marijke, I didn't think you would be shy. You're certainly not shy at home!" Mama remarked.

That night I dreamt I was a good dancer and that all the boys in the hall wanted to dance with me. I danced and twirled and had a wonderful time. Suddenly my dress changed into a white gown, like my late Mama had worn on the stage on the night she met Papa. Then I became her and she sang and danced, a soft smile on her face. I was mesmerised. Then she turned into me again.

I awoke feeling warm and calm. I didn't share this dream with anyone. Usually if I remembered a dream, I shared it with someone. But I felt this dream had been just for me. I thought Mama had watched me the night before and had shown me that I could dance. I decided I would ask Josie to teach me to dance.

As the day was sunny, we sat in the back yard for morning coffee. Papa had his camera out and took some photos to send to our family in Holland.

The tree stump in the garden made an excellent prop for a photo.

"Come on kids, climb on the tree and make a pyramid," Papa called out.

I climbed to the top of the tree, as I was the oldest to participate. Arnold was on the branch below me, and then the other kids were in order of their age, with Ineke and Lidy at the base of the tree. Tiny wasn't walking yet, she was too young to join in.

When Papa told us to smile, I remembered the dream I'd had. I threw my arms in the air, like I was dancing. Usually, I didn't deal with heights well. If I was off the ground more than an inch, I felt I was falling, unless I had something solid to hang on to. For whatever reason, I felt no fear that day.

Chapter 34

Pukkie had settled into our family well, and her growth rate was amazing. Her fur turned a darker colour black with the occasional tuft of white. The rules of the house meant nothing to her. Whenever she could, she'd sneak inside, and she became an expert at hiding when Papa walked in. Not that he didn't like her, but he felt a dog should be outside.

Mama, however, had really taken to Pukkie, and as house proud and fussy as she was, she made concessions for Pukkie which weren't even granted us kids. I'd see Pukkie beside the fridge eating some little morsels Mama had given her.

I was almost fourteen by now, and although I loved Pukkie, I also had other things to occupy me, like my friends and school work and doing my hair.

Trudy, three years my junior, was the one who was besotted by Pukkie. She scooped her up as soon as she walked into the back yard after school. I didn't have to worry about filling the dog's water bowl or to clean up her messes. Trudy did it all, with love. Nothing was too much, rain, hail or shine.

Trudy was different to all the other kids in the family. Of course, we were all different, but in some ways we had many similarities. Not only in looks, but in mannerisms. Trudy was the dreamer in the family. A talented artist, her drawings and paintings were unique. Already the nuns recognised her ability with pen and brush, and some of her works of art adorned the classrooms and corridors of the school.

With that artistic ability came her dreaminess. Her thought processes often astounded us. They were seldom practical, but very ethereal and romantic. Of course, many of her paintings reflected these qualities. She was a philosopher well before any of us knew what a philosopher was. She also looked different. Willie, Ann and John all had Papa's dark wavy hair. The rest of us had blond or a mousy coloured hair; some straight and thin, some with curls. But Trudy had thick auburn hair, which she wore in a short bob. It fell naturally into place. No bits sticking up like mine first thing in the morning, nor did it fly away with the first breeze.

We were overall tall compared to the Australian population, but Trudy was shorter than any of us.

Her hazel eyes misted over whenever she went into one of her dream worlds, and when she was upset, she sobbed. No silent tears for her. Deep, heart-wrenching and agonising sobs, which could be heard throughout the house.

Trudy's love for Pukkie was a delight to see, although sometimes she'd get into trouble for playing with her instead of doing her chores. To Trudy there was no question of priority; Pukkie always came first, even if it meant she'd get into trouble.

It was early spring, and I'd been to Josie's on the way home from school. As I came around the corner I saw Trudy running towards me, her arms flailing. "Marijke, Marijke, she's dead!" she sobbed as she reached me.

My heart stopped. *Who's dead?* I felt tears well up without knowing who Trudy was talking about. Her tear-stained face and red eyes told me she wasn't joking. She grabbed my hand and dragged me towards our house.

Visions of Mama dead on the kitchen floor flashed before me. This Mama's face then changed to my late Mama's face.

"They did it on purpose. I saw them," she sobbed, pulling me along.

"Who did?" I asked. I didn't want to know, but I had to know.

"The people in the car. Pukkie was on the footpath barking at the cars, and they swerved and hit her." She let go of my hand and, still sobbing, pointed towards a patch of blood on the curb.

She took hold of my hand again and pulled me into the back yard. There I saw Mama. She had her back to us, but I could see she was crying. Near her feet lay a bloodied and matted Pukkie whose eyes stared vacantly, her hind legs twisted. Mama came over to me and tried to hold me back, but it was too late. I heard myself scream. I knelt down on the lawn next to Pukkie's body. My sweet little Pukkie. Dead!

Yet it was Trudy who broke my heart. She was inconsolable. She knelt next to me. I put my arms around her and tried to turn her away from the gruesome sight.

"Marijke, I'm so sorry," Mama said. Her eyes too, were red and swollen.

"When did it happen?" I whispered.

"A few minutes ago. She ran into the back yard yelping, dragging her hind legs. I tried to get her, but she snapped and snarled. I guess she was in too much pain. And then she lay down and stopped breathing." Mama tried to keep it together for our sakes, but without success.

I should've come straight home from school, maybe I could have stopped her barking at the cars. Then she'd still be alive.

"We have to bury her." Trudy's voice penetrated my thoughts. "We have to give her a special spot in the garden, and then she'll be with us forever."

"Are you sure she's dead?" I asked. Her eyes were open. I'd always thought when anything was dead, their eyes would be closed.

"She's dead, Marijke," Mama said, "and Trudy is right. We can't leave her here like this. I'd rather the little ones didn't see her like this. It's too upsetting. They're all playing next door. Let's get this done before they come home. Get Papa's spade from the shed and we'll bury her now."

She gently pushed me towards the shed. I felt like a zombie. The last funeral I went to was my late Mama's. I tried to recall what had taken place, but for some reason my mind still blocked the memories.

Mama took the spade from me and pointed to a spot behind Papa's chook pen, near a small bush. "I think we'll bury her there," she said.

We had to take turns to dig the hole, as the ground was quite hard. When I was digging, Mama wrapped Pukkie in an old towel. It was Trudy who picked her up, there was no way in the world I could have done so. The thought of touching something that was dead made me feel sick.

Now sobbing quietly, Trudy carried Pukkie's broken body over and placed her in the hole. Mama, still crying, began covering her with soil. I stood and watched. I wondered whether we should say a prayer for her, but I didn't think dogs went to heaven or hell.

Trudy had walked away when Mama started filling the hole, and now came back with two sticks tied together with a piece of string. She had painted Pukkie's name on the horizontal stick. "Here, I made this cross for her. Mama, can I pick a couple of flowers to put on her grave?"

Mama nodded agreement. Trudy and I went to the front yard and picked some pretty flowers and carried them to where Mama had now levelled the ground with the back of the spade.

Together we bent down and placed the flowers on her grave. Trudy then stuck the cross into the soil. We stood there for some time. My mind had gone blank; I was unable to absorb what had happened. I hadn't even been inside since I'd arrived home.

"Come on, girls, let's go inside and have a drink. I think that is enough sadness for one day," Mama said.

We didn't speak as we walked inside. For once my appetite had gone. I went to the bedroom to get changed. Once there my emotions exploded. I flung myself on the bed and cried. I don't know how long I'd been there when I felt a hand on my shoulder.

"Marijke, Pukkie is all right. She won't hurt anymore." Trudy's voice sounded wise beyond her years. I rolled over and threw my arms around her. We lay there, holding each other for a long time.

Dinner that night was a sombre occasion. The whole family mourned the loss of our beautiful Pukkie. She'd only been with us for a few months, but she had been as much a part of our family as any one of us.

I slept fitfully that night, seeing Pukkie's body every time I closed my eyes.

When I arrived in class the next day, the girl who had raffled Pukkie came over to me. "Marijke, I heard your dog was killed yesterday. Trudy told Sister. I'm so sorry." I nodded acceptance of her sympathy.

After the last class she walked through the school-ground with me. "Would you like another puppy? Next time my dog has another litter, you can come and pick one, if you want," she offered.

I tried not to show her I was horrified with this suggestion. *That's the same as when Mama died, and then Papa replaced her with our new Mama. You can't replace one person with another when they die! And you can't replace Pukkie with another puppy!*

"No thank you," I said, trying not to cry.

"All right. You tell me if you change your mind. Okay? Maybe when the puppies come you'll want another one," she said. "See you tomorrow." She waved and headed down the street.

As soon as she'd gone I burst into tears. I wasn't sure if I was crying because Pukkie was dead or because I missed Mama. Sometimes I felt guilty that I didn't think of her for long times. But when bad or sad things happened I still missed her terribly.

Chapter 35

"Marijke, it's your turn to darn the socks today," Mama reminded me one Saturday morning.

As if I could forget! Oh, how I hated darning socks! Everybody had two pairs of school socks each week, and then their normal socks, which were worn when not at school. Ann and Willie didn't wear socks anymore, and I wore the compulsory thick stockings to school. But they also suffered from wear and tear and needed darning at times. The two boys were really hard on socks, and of course, Papa wore socks too.

Not only did I have to mend the holes, if there was just a hint of a worn spot, I had to fix them before they became a hole. I had to place my fist inside each sock and slowly and carefully withdraw my hand, fingers outstretched, keeping the sock tight so any holes or thin patches could be identified.

Mama had a box of darning wool in a variety of colours. I selected the colour closest to that of the sock I had to darn. If the sock had any thin patches,

I had to weave forwards and backwards, first vertically then horizontally. With the holes I had to put a cup inside the sock, pull the hole over the cup opening, and weave a neat patch. Some socks had been darned so many times before that the toes and heels looked like a patchwork quilt. Mama always checked to see it was done neatly and smoothly, and if not, I would have to unpick it and do it again.

I loathed this job with a passion, and would much prefer do the dusting, or the baking or ironing, or even to clean the toilet! But, as with all the other chores, we had to take turns darning the socks, except for the boys. That really annoyed me. *They wear socks, and they usually have more holes in their socks than any of us girls. Why shouldn't they darn socks too? Papa sews! Darning is no different!*

Sometimes the line-up of holy socks seemed never-ending. It was a slow and tedious task, and patience was never one of my virtues. "When I get married I will never, ever, ever, darn another sock!" I said to Mama, as she checked my handiwork. "I'll make my husband darn his own socks, or he will just have to buy new ones or walk around with holes. And I will never, ever, ever, make my children darn socks!"

"That will waste a lot of money, Marijke. Just imagine if we had to buy new socks every time someone had a hole. Besides, it teaches you to look after things and use money for more important things."

What could be more important than new socks when they have holes in them? They hurt and chafe with all the patches, and sometimes they cause blisters!

When Mama walked away I counted how many more socks I had to darn. *Another thirteen! I'll be here all afternoon. I want to go to Josie's house; she doesn't have to darn socks!*

Josie had to help her mother a little bit, but she never had to do as much as me. Josie said she thought Papa and Mama used us as slaves, and sometimes I agreed with her. We had so many chores every day. Washing the dishes; drying the dishes; or putting the dishes away. Then there was setting the table for each meal, cutting lunches, making beds, and helping with the little ones. And that was during the week. On Saturday the whole house had to be dusted and vacuumed, and linoleum floors scrubbed. The bathroom and toilet had to be cleaned each day, and the sink was never allowed to have dirty dishes on it.

We all shared these chores, but Papa often said that he got me to help more because I did things quicker. Sometimes I tried to do them slower, so I wouldn't have to do so much. But it wasn't in my nature to do things slowly.

I loved cooking the best, and part of my curriculum at school was a cooking class. Whatever we cooked we were allowed to take home. The school had a strong emphasis on preparing us to be good wives and mothers. Being an all-girls school, we not only had cooking classes, but also handicrafts, which included sewing, knitting and crochet.

Sometimes, when we'd cooked something really nice, I would eat some of it on the way home from school. It gave me a great feeling of exultation that I could eat something without getting into trouble for it. Mama never knew how many biscuits or slices we'd cooked.

Large cakes were different. I could hardly take a bite out of a cake without it being obvious; unless I had one which had broken or got stuck to the side of the cake tin. I figured Mama wouldn't expect me to bring home all those broken bits and crumbs!

A lot of the recipes we made at school were different to anything we cooked at home. Our meals didn't vary from what we had eaten back in Amsterdam, and the biscuits we made each Saturday were the same standard recipe.

* * * *

Willie's involvement with Bill became serious, and Papa insisted that they always have a chaperone with them. I didn't like going out with them, as they were so engrossed in each other, I felt like a third wheel. Bill was shorter than Willie, had broad shoulders and big hands. His language was rough, whether he spoke Dutch or English. Yet, at times, he showed a real soft side. Sometimes we'd go to the Basin, and I'd leave them alone and go for a swim. Then, when I came out from the water, they'd be kissing; their bodies really close together, oblivious to the crowds around them. Bill was a noisy kisser, and I didn't know what I was supposed to do. Interrupt them? *I think not!*

I'd just walk away and leave them to it. Whatever they weren't supposed to be doing, I was sure they wouldn't do it while in this public place. I was really embarrassed by their behaviour, although I saw other couples equally engrossed in each other. I wondered what it would be like to have a boy so close, almost on top of me, kissing and moaning, and hands groping.

In one of our religious classes, we'd been shown a film of boys and girls kissing. Very sedate compared to what these couples were engaged in.

Then we were shown discreet drawings of the male and female anatomies.

"Now girls, you have to make sure you treat your body with the respect it deserves. Our bodies are our temples. They should not be used for pleasure. Don't let boys kiss you, because that could lead to mortal sin. When you let a boy kiss you, he will want you to do more." Some girls in the class giggled, which made Sister Majella blush profusely.

"Remember to stay pure. Pure in mind and pure in body. Do not give into temptation. Don't let others of lesser commitment convince you that it's all right. It is not! So, don't forget, if you let a boy kiss you, it could lead you to moral corruption, which will see you be condemned. Not only in eternity, but here on earth. Other men do not want a tainted wife. You will no longer be pure." The more some girls giggled, the more Sister Majella blushed. It was obviously not a topic she was comfortable with.

I won't let any boys kiss me. I don't want to commit a mortal sin, I vowed to myself.

After class I waited until Sister was on her own. Shyly I asked her what it was that kissing could lead to. She blushed and dropped her eyes. "I think perhaps you should ask your mother that question, Marijke. I would have thought you would have had that discussion at home. It's up to your mother to talk to you about the birds and the bees." She smiled and left it at that.

*God... I can't talk to Mama about things. She's so prim and proper, and besides, she isn't my real Mama. I think she'd be worse than the nuns, she gets embarrassed really easy! Why did Sister say something about birds and bees? I thought we were talking about boys and kissing...*I was more confused than ever.

Maybe I should ask Willie what they were talking about. She'd talked to me when I got my periods. But then... maybe she'll think I'm trying to find out when she and Bill do... I guess I'll find out one day.

* * * *

A few days after my fourteenth birthday (November 1961) Papa announced that our new house would be built in the new year. Proudly he spread some big sheets of paper over the dining-room table, which had various drawings of house plans. It all looked very fancy. I had hoped we'd all get a room of our own, but of course, that wasn't to be. Papa pointed to a very long room, almost the full length of the house. "That will be the girls' bedroom. There will be partitions between the beds," he said, a big smile on his face. "The room is big enough to sleep all the girls."

We'd picnicked on our block several times over the past months, and the thought of finally having our new house built there was really exciting. *This is what we dreamt of when we left Holland. A beautiful big brick house, all our own. How envious our family and friends in Holland will be!*

Our second Christmas in summer still felt unreal. However, it didn't take any getting used to the long summer holidays, which found me at the Basin almost every day.

Although the pool wasn't heated, the warmth of the sun made it pleasant to swim in. Over the long school holiday period I often met up with friends from school or with the van Maanenberg boys.

Some days Mama and my siblings also came. Although Mama didn't like water, she was happy to spread a blanket on the ground and watch us have fun. Tiny was a toddler, and I took great delight in walking in the wading pool with her; her giggles and squeals not only delighting me, but others around us. Or I'd race Arnold and the younger girls in the fifty-meter pool.

Bikinis had become popular, but even if I had been game to wear them, there was no way Mama and Papa would have approved. I had developed a lot over the past twelve months, and attracted quite some attention from the boys. Taller than the average girl, I had long slim legs and what could be described as an hour-glass figure. Well, not quite hour-glass, as my breasts were somewhat large for my slim body. I felt gangly and awkward compared to most of the Australian girls, who were short and petite.

Papa had a sick sense of humour and used to tease me about my big breasts. I hated it when he did that, but any sign that I was embarrassed would encourage him to tease me some more. Sometimes Mama would say, "Joop, that's enough."

"Oh, she's got to liven up. I'm only having some fun," he'd respond.

Yet, despite Papa's ability to make fun of us, he did not appreciate anyone else saying things that were inappropriate, or what he considered inappropriate. He used to make me laugh when we were out somewhere as a family. If some boys made eyes at me, Papa would watch from a distance; a proud look on his face. It seemed to me that he thought, *they can admire my daughter; but they'd better not get close!*

Chapter 36

The new school year came around all too quickly. In mid-February I commenced Second Year High School. My First Year results had been good, considering I was still learning the English language, although I had become quite proficient and had passed my English exam.

As in Holland, I didn't do so well in History, although I had found it more interesting. The history of Australia only went back two-hundred years, as opposed to going back to the days of the Huns and beyond. Not as many dates to remember, and it also gave me a better perspective about the country we now called home. I passed the exam, but only just!

But I still refused to learn specific dates. It was my theory that the stories were interesting, but I had no interest what date someone settled in Australia, or who the queen or king of England was on a given day in the year.

* * * *

The weekend before we returned to school, we'd spent a day at St Leonards. A large wooden frame had been erected on our block and Papa proudly showed us around, explaining where each room would be located. It was so exciting, I could hardly contain myself.

That week I had also received a letter from Fietje as well as one from my cousin, Hettie, who used to live next door to us in Amsterdam. The thin blue paper airmail letters arrived on the same day. "Marijke," Mama said, handing me the letters, with a broad smile. "It looks like you haven't been forgotten yet in Amsterdam."

I'd been thinking about my friends and family in Holland quite a lot during the school holidays. I wished they were here with me, enjoying the long warm summer days. Many nights I dreamt of an emotional return to Amsterdam. All my friends and family were on the wharf waving like mad and yelling my name as I stood near the railing on a large ship. Long coloured streamers were thrown in my direction, and I'd catch them and hold this tangible line to my past. Then I'd see my late Mama's smiling face in the crowd, but when I looked again, she'd be gone.

This dream became a regular occurrence. It made me feel more and more homesick. Yet, I loved the Australian way of life, which was so relaxed. My Australian friends had so much freedom. It was confusing; I wanted to be here but I wanted to be there too.

"Young people get too much freedom here," Papa said, time and time again.

I argued that we were in Australia, and we should do what they did. "Girls my age are allowed out to the pictures with their friends at night, and even supervised parties. You're stuck in Holland in your mind, Papa. This is a different country." I shouted at him when he once again refused to let me go to a party I'd been invited to. The invitation had come from a girl I met at the Gorge. I didn't know her well, but it seemed to me that Papa only trusted friends I made at school.

"No, Marijke, teenagers here seem to get into much more trouble than in Holland. Unless I know the people and their parents, you're not going out. You're only fourteen, much too young to be out and about. Look at all the drunks and loud people in the streets on Saturday nights."

As we lived on the main street, we often heard rowdy groups of teenagers heading home after a night out. Some had cars and raced up and down the road, yelling and yahooing, and doing wheelies.

"See? Is that what you want us to allow you to do?" Papa asked one night, after another rowdy car raced past our house.

"No, I don't want to drive a car or get drunk. But my friends are allowed to go to dances and parties. I'm responsible and old enough. I won't do anything I shouldn't." I argued, "I'm fourteen now. You should trust me."

"No, you're much too young. Unless a party is supervised and we know the families, you can't go until you're eighteen. By then you'll hopefully have matured enough to know how to behave."

"Eighteen? But, Papa, that is four more years!!!!"

"Yes, it is. You can go to the Dutch Australian Association's teenage dances with your sisters. And of course, you can attend school socials. They're supervised by the nuns. But it'll be a long time before you go to any of those Australian parties, where people get drunk."

"But, Papa!" I turned to Mama for support. "Tell Papa that's unreasonable. I bet my friends in Amsterdam are allowed out."

"I think Papa's right, Marijke. You're far too young. Your older sisters never asked to go out when they were your age. You want to grow up too quickly. You spend so much time doing your hair and preening and priming. You're still a child, you have to learn to accept our rules, they're in your best interest."

"You always take Papa's side," I mumbled under my breath. *Why can't you stand up for me? Every time some friends ask me to go out I have to say no. I wish I was older... We're in Australia now. You decided to come here, but you won't adapt to the Australian way of life! You're both unreasonable.*

"I said no more arguments, Marijke. You're only fourteen, and still at school. Concentrate on your studies so you can get a job when you leave school."

I knew by Papa's tone of voice it was no use. *It's just not fair.*

Chapter 37

"Guess what?" Willie asked me one night when I was getting ready for bed.

"What?" The excitement in her voice told me she had something important to tell me. Willie didn't show her emotions much. As the oldest girl she'd taken on a lot of responsibility when Mama was sick and after she died. She always seemed very much in control, except when she was around her boyfriend, Bill. She was quiet and obedient around him; their relationship was confusing to me.

"Bill asked me to marry him. We're getting engaged on my nineteenth birthday in April, and we'll get married in December." She looked genuinely happy.

"Do Papa and Mama know?" I asked her. It didn't occur to me to congratulate her; getting married was a fact of life. As girls from a working class family, we were groomed to find a husband and have a family.

"Yes, Bill asked Papa earlier today, and he agreed."

I wasn't too sure how to take this news. I was happy for Willie, and I told her so. I was thrilled she had confided in me. But I was worried that Bill bossed her around too much. Papa had always been the head of our house, but he had never spoken to our Mama or this Mama in the tone of voice that Bill used when he spoke to Willie.

"We'll have our engagement dinner at the new house. Bill's going to help get it finished. He gets really annoyed because the builders said the house would be finished before Easter, and now they say it may not be. My birthday is the week after Easter, and Bill wants us to be in the house by then."

Sure enough, thanks to Bill's help, we moved into our brand new house Easter week. This was a very exciting time for me, as it seemed to have taken forever before the house was finally completed.

No matter what Mama and Papa asked me to do, I obliged. I liked things to look nice, and I was happy to put in some extra elbow grease to expedite things.

The house was red brick with a red tile roof. It looked really modern, with painted panels beneath the large windows. From the steps which led to the front door, and from all the windows on the southern side of the house, we could see for miles.

The front door led to a hallway, with the lounge-room on the right-hand side and the toilet on the left. The next door led to the dining-room and kitchen.

The dining-room was separated from the kitchen by a bench and overhead cupboards and was painted in soft apricot with white ceiling. The cupboard doors were a soft orange. Warm autumn colours were fashionable at the time.

Papa and Mama had purchased a dining setting, which consisted of a grey octagonal laminate table and eight orange vinyl chairs. Our old table stood against the wall between the door and the window. Both tables were needed to seat twelve.

The girls' bedroom was at the far side of the house and was about eight meters long and three and a half meters wide. At the end was an alcove with a small window; just big enough to house Willie's single bed as well as Tiny's cot. Partitions divided the long room into three sections. I loved the partitions. They had large cubed shelves painted in bright red, yellow and blue. Each of the three sections held a double bed and a chair. We were allocated two cubes each to put our personal knick-knacks in.

I shared with Ann the far section, adjacent to Willie's single bed. *Only two per double bed, yes!* Once Willie married, Ann would move into the single bed, and then I'd share with Trudy. By then Tiny would be too big for a cot, and she would then share with Ineke. *It's like playing musical beds!*

On Easter Sunday we attended Mass in a little weatherboard church in St. Leonards. Painted white outside, it had a tiny altar and vestibule. A sign next to the altar said, 'There are no strangers in this church. Only friends we have not yet met.' I loved that sign. The church was so little; it only had enough seating for about forty people. Thus the arrival of twelve new friends was a surprise and made things uncomfortable. We received warm smiles and nods, and some men stood and gave us their seats. Others squeezed together, and managed to fit six where only four were meant to sit.

After Mass the Parish priest, Father Reed, introduced himself and we shook hands with other parishioners. Although the weather had cooled down, the sun was out and it was a beautiful autumn day.

At home we had our traditional Easter egg scramble, followed by Easter breakfast and prayers.

We had roast chicken that evening and Papa said a special prayer thanking God for giving us this wonderful opportunity. While we had dinner, brilliant orange and pink hues lit the sky. I felt it was a sign that our life in this house was going to be wonderful. After the sun set Mama pulled the new autumn coloured curtains she had sewn, across the window.

* * * *

To get to school from St Leonards meant catching the eight o'clock bus each morning, which left from the main road at the bottom of our hill. The bus ride took between fifteen and twenty minutes to get into Launceston; then it was a fifteen minute walk to school. Tempers often frayed of a morning as we lined up to use the toilet and the bathroom. If we missed the bus, there wasn't another one until eight-thirty, and that made us late for school. We also had to make sure our beds were made and the dishes were done before we left.

Always first out of bed, I made sure I'd used both the toilet and bathroom before the rush. However, as used to happen before, as I was out of bed early anyway, Papa and Mama asked me to cut lunches for everybody. A big undertaking as this included not only for the school-age kids, but Papa took lunch to work, as did Willie. John had obtained an apprenticeship at a bakery, where he could eat to his heart's content. Ann had left her previous job and soon after we moved to St Leonards, got a job at the hotel at the bottom of the hill, as housemaid and kitchen hand. She was provided with meals as part of her employment.

It didn't take me long to get to know other kids on the bus and around the small township. I met some girls my age who lived in close proximity, and I was invited to their homes on various occasions. I also befriended some boys who used to tease me and flirt with me, and I enjoyed the attention. It felt rather naughty to flirt with them as we had been told at school that we really should be careful and not mix with non Catholic boys.

Willie and Bill's engagement party consisted of a family dinner at home. Over dinner Willie announced, "Bill and I have decided we'll get married in the chapel at Nazareth House. We've talked to Father Reed and the nuns. They are quite excited to have a wedding in the chapel. I believe we will be the first to be married in that chapel."

Nazareth House was a Catholic Home for the Aged in St Leonards. It had been officially opened the previous year by the Archbishop of Tasmania. It included an octagonal chapel. The home was run by 'The Poor Nuns of Nazareth.' The chapel was modern and bright and had a good feel about it. Father Reed said Mass in the chapel at seven-fifteen each Sunday morning. If I awoke early enough I often attended Mass there instead of waiting for the rest of the family, who attended Mass in the little church. In those days we were not allowed to have anything to drink or eat before going to Mass, if we were to receive Holy Communion.

By going to Mass so early, I didn't have to wait until ten o'clock to eat. I was always hungry and found it unreasonable to have to wait so long. We all had to attend church and receive Communion. I never questioned this until I was much older; it was what it was.

Chapter 38

I enjoyed living at St Leonards. In spite of the three year age gap, and our different personalities, Ann and I grew closer. I enjoyed modern things and the latest fashion although I couldn't afford to indulge, while Ann was more homely and was happy with the way she looked naturally. I was skinny and tall, with mousy brown straight hair; Ann was shorter, with pretty dark eyes and dark curly hair.

Like all my sisters, Ann had a heart of gold, but she was also very stubborn. If she was right, she was right; nothing would budge her point of view. I too, could be stubborn and self-righteous! If we had an argument, it could become quite heated, even physical. Since we now shared a double bed, our relationship fluctuated from friendly to volatile. Willie and Ann had consistently clashed for as long as I could remember. Now that Willie had a fiancé, she wasn't home much and the arguments diminished.

After school I'd sometimes pop into the hotel and wait for Ann to finish work. Some Saturdays she invited me to go to the movies in Launceston. She paid for my bus fare and tickets. I knew this was an extremely generous gesture on her part, as Papa insisted all money earned by family members had to go into the family money-pool for living expense. Papa gave Ann an allowance, which wasn't overly generous. When she paid the movies, her allowance for the week had been spent.

I was madly in love with Elvis Presley at that time, and when a new Elvis movie hit town, Ann made a point of inviting me. I was never sure if she liked Elvis, but she seemed to enjoy the movies.

Partway through the year, Ann dated a guy who belonged to a Jazz band. We used to laugh when he picked her up in his little mini-minor car. His trombone took up the front passenger seat and half the back seat. We'd peer out the window to see Ann clamber into the small area left in the back seat behind the driver. Needless to say, this relationship didn't last too long.

After that relationship ended, Ann met a boy from St Leonards. She didn't want Papa to question her about him, so she'd meet him at the bottom of the hill, or walk to where he lived.

One Saturday she told Mama and Papa she was going for a walk, and asked if I could join her. They agreed and we promised we'd be home for dinner. Once outside, Ann told me she was meeting her boyfriend, Graeme. "He's got a car and we'll meet him at his place. You'll like him, he's cute," she giggled. "He's got some friends, and I thought you may like to meet them."

Ann wasn't usually the giggly type. I guessed she was really taken with Graeme. I was surprised but pleased that she trusted me enough to meet him.

We walked past our little church and down a short laneway. "This is where Graeme lives."

A red-headed boy walked around a car parked in a driveway and Ann introduced us. He was cute, in a freckled and red hair sort of way. I liked his smile and I could see Ann was smitten. On the way down the hill she'd told me he wasn't Catholic, and Papa wouldn't approve of him, that's why she hadn't told anyone else about him. Ann was very religious, so I was surprised she would go out with a non-Catholic boy.

Graeme's car was parked in front of his house. Ann got into the front passenger seat and I climbed in behind her. *This is fun. I don't think Papa and Mama would approve, but I'm with Ann and she'll make sure I'm safe. Ann is super conservative; she won't allow anyone to harm me. Besides, Papa always insists Willie has a chaperone, this way I'm Ann's chaperone.*

I couldn't hear what Graeme and Ann talked about during the drive into Launceston. The car radio played the latest hits, and I sang along to amuse myself. We were nearly into town, when Graeme pulled into the driveway of an old house and blew the car horn. Immediately, two boys emerged from the around the back of the house. Although one was thin and the other plump, I could tell they were brothers. The thin one looked about eighteen and the other boy about sixteen. I was introduced and they settled into the back seat on either side of me. I'd never sat so close between two boys before; not even my brothers.

"How do you say your name?" Roger, the older boy asked as Graeme backed his car from the driveway.

"Ma/ray/ke," I said slowly. I had become proficient in pronouncing my name whenever I met someone new. *If I got a penny for every time I had to spell or pronounce my name, I'll be a millionaire by the time I'm twenty-one!*

He repeated it several times. "Marijke, that's a pretty name for a pretty girl," he said.

His younger brother, Robert, also repeated my name until he got it right. "We saw your photo in the newspaper when you came to Tasmania," Roger said. "Do you like it here?" *If I got a penny every time I was asked that question, I would become a millionaire all over again!*

I nodded shyly. My discomfort level was almost off the scale with these two boys in such close proximity. Graeme parked his car near City Park, and we all piled out. It was a pleasant and sunny autumn day; not cold enough to wear a coat but cool enough to wear a light-weight jumper. We walked through the park and watched some kangaroos in an enclosure.

We found a bench in the sun. I can't remember what was said. I felt awkward and shy and only answered questions when they were aimed at me. Graeme and Ann talked between themselves, as the two brothers discussed an old car Roger had bought.

"How old are you?" Roger asked.

"Fourteen-and-a-half."

"Wow! You look older than that," he said with genuine surprise.

"Hello, Marijke." A girl's voice sang out.

I looked up to see three girls from school walk past. I smiled at them and blushed. *Oh, no! Now all the girls in class will hear that I was in the park with these boys. I hope they don't get the wrong idea!*

After a while we went back to the car. Graeme dropped Roger and Robert off in front of their house, and we returned to St Leonards. Ann kissed Graeme goodbye in the front seat. I looked away, feeling uncomfortable. I remembered what we'd been told at schools by the nuns. *"You shouldn't kiss boys. It can lead to other things and that's a mortal sin. Treat your bodies like God's temples."*

I also thought of Mama's comments about kissing boys. She'd shake her head, and say, "Yuk, those slobbering kisses. I don't know why anybody would enjoy them. All that spit and germs and things... yuk!"

"Do you think Papa and Mama will be mad if they knew I'd gone with you and the boys?" I asked her.

"I don't know. You didn't go out with the boys. I went out with Graeme and you and Roger and Robert came for a drive and a walk in the park. I wouldn't think that would be a problem. But I guess we won't tell them, just in case," Ann said. I nodded, although somehow I knew that Papa would be angry.

Over the next few weeks we met the boys several times. Sometimes Roger, who was seventeen and had his licence, picked us up in his car, which had bench-seats. When we went in his car I would sit in the front seat between the two brothers and Ann and Graeme sat in the back . These afternoon trips were innocent, yet I felt guilty.

One Saturday afternoon, Roger asked us inside to meet his mother. She'd baked fresh scones for afternoon tea. When Roger introduced me, she said, "Ah, yes. I wondered when I'd meet this lovely Dutch girl Roger keeps talking about."

I blushed at the thought he'd told his mother about me. Ann was really friendly towards Roger's mother and it was obvious they'd met before. We had a lovely time and the scones, topped with homemade jam and whipped cream, were delicious. By now I felt more comfortable around Roger.

On one outing, Roger and I found ourselves in his car on our own. Robert had declined the invitation to join us for the afternoon, and Ann and Graeme had gone for a walk. I can't recall what we talked about as Roger's arm had unobtrusively draped itself around my shoulders. After a while he gently massaged my arm. I felt uncomfortable. I looked at him, and he bent down to kiss me. As he did, I heard Sister Majella's voice warning us of the temptation of kissing and Mama's warning of germs and spit. I turned my head away from him before his lips touched mine.

"What's wrong?" he asked.

"Nothing," I said. "I don't want you to kiss me."

"Don't you like me?" He looked like a wounded puppy.

"Yes, but I don't want you to kiss me."

As if on cue, Ann and Graeme returned to the car. *Whew! That was close. I don't want to explain to him why I wouldn't let him kiss me.*

That night I tossed and turned. *He shouldn't have tried to kiss me. I don't want to tempt a boy into doing the wrong thing...*

The next day was Sunday. As was my habit, I awoke early. But instead of going to Mass at Nazareth House Chapel, I wrote a letter to Roger. I explained to him that I liked him but that I didn't want that kind of relationship, and that it was against my religion to kiss. I put the letter in an envelope and sealed it. On the back I drew a pair of red lips. When Ann got out of bed I gave it to her. "Next time you see Roger, will you please give this to him?" I asked her.

"Yes, sure. What's the matter?" She looked concerned.

"Nothing, I just don't want to see him again," I said.

I asked her a few of days later if she'd given the letter to Roger yet. "Yes. He was a little upset. He said to tell you he'd put it under his pillow so he can dream of you."

I never saw Roger again. Although I liked the idea of having a boyfriend, I knew I wasn't ready for one. Ann broke up with Graeme after some time, and we went back to going for long walks or to the movies.

During the year I spent most of my lunch breaks with the three van Galen girls. All three planned to enter the convent and become nuns when they completed high school. Because I spent so much time with these girls, Sister Lucy seemed to think that I may also become a nun. One day she asked me straight out if I planned to enter the convent.

"No!" I said, shocked she would think I might.

Me? A nun? In those awful black gowns and veils? Never! Besides, nuns are holy. I could never be holy, no matter how hard I tried! If she only knew how often I still got into trouble at home for telling lies and for stealing things, she wouldn't ask me to be a nun. And if she found out about Roger almost kissing me...

Chapter 39

"Girls, over the next two terms, you'll be making a dress. You will select your own pattern, purchase your materials and accessories, such as zippers, buttons, cotton reels, etcetera, etcetera. You'll draft your patterns to suit you. I know it's a big job, but I'm sure you can do it." Our Home Arts and Crafts teacher looked around the class of thirteen and fourteen year-olds with a big smile on her face.

"Yes! Oh, how exciting!" I exclaimed. Usually I got into trouble for my spontaneous outbursts, but this time, she smiled at me. "I'm thrilled you're so keen, Marijke. Let's see what you can produce."

I couldn't wait to tell Mama and Papa. We'd made aprons the previous term, and Mama told me that I'd done quite a good job with it. She'd even complimented me on the neatness of my stitches. My teacher had been surprised at my sewing skills. *I guess Mama and Papa's constant fussiness paid off!*

"Mama, where are you?" I called as soon as I arrived home.

"In the lounge-room. What's the matter?" She came running out.

"I'm going to make a dress. I have to pick the pattern, and the material. I need them by next week's class. Will you help me pick them out?" I blurted.

"Slow down, Marijke. You're going to make a dress at school? That'll be nice. Maybe you can choose something really nice so you can wear it to Willie's wedding in December."

"Can I pick my own material, please? I want-"

"Yes, but we have to be reasonable. First we'll choose the pattern. I have some lovely pattern books. You may want to browse through them and see if there's anything there you like. You know Papa and I can both draft patterns. That way we can make sure we do the right sizing for you. You're so thin, yet your chest is quite big. It wouldn't be any good if we just cut a pattern one size. I'll measure you and-"

"Can I have a look through your books now? I've always wanted to make a dress."

Mama pulled out her box of dress making books. It didn't take me long to find a pattern I liked. It was simple but fashionable; a sleeveless fitted bodice with a round boat-neck. It had a gathered full skirt and a wide belt with a large buckle provided the finishing touch.

"Are you sure? I like it, but it's quite plain," Mama said when I showed her.

"Not if we choose the right material, Mama, and I will need one of those new full petticoats that makes the skirt stand out."

"Okay, we'll worry about a petticoat later. Papa and I are going to town on Saturday morning. We can look at materials then. Okay?"

I couldn't wait for Saturday to come around. Not only was this the first time in my life I'd make my own dress, it was the first time I'd been given an option of choosing the style and material for the dress.

I arose early on Saturday morning and ensured I'd finished all my chores by the time Mama and Papa were ready to go to town. Papa decided he had some other things to do and left us to it. Mama knew which shop to go to. I looked around in amazement at the rolls and rolls of various materials. *Where do we start? There are hundreds and hundreds to choose from...*

"We'll look over here first," Mama said, and directed me to the far corner of the shop. "These are off-cuts, and they're usually reduced in price. We need to look at cotton, as your dress will be for summer. One of the things I always do, is scrunch the material in my hand to see how easy it is to crush. If it doesn't crush too much it'll be much easier to iron."

I followed her to the corner. There were dozens of rolls to look at, as well as a throw-out table. I found a piece of pale blue material on the table, but we needed five yards and this piece was only three-and-a-half yards. Mama pointed at a couple of other rolls, but I didn't like them; I thought they were too old for me. I expected her to say I should have one of them, but she didn't.

Then I spotted a roll with a royal blue and white chequered pattern. The squares weren't really squares, they sort of blended together, and were half blue and half white.

"That's the one, Mama. I love it. I think that will suit the pattern of my dress." I looked at her expectantly. I hadn't looked at the amount of material on the roll, nor the price. *I really, really want this one. Please, please, please, let me have it...*

Mama pulled the roll from the wall and looked at the dangling label. "That's lucky, it's nearly seven yards. Now, let's look at the price. Mmm, a bit more expensive than the others I looked at... but not too expensive. If you promise to do your very best with this, you can have it."

"Thank you, thank you." I hugged her.

She smiled sweetly. "Now, we need to buy all the other bits. The back zipper needs to be fourteen inches. We'll have to decide whether we get a blue or a white one. Of course, if it's fitted correctly, you shouldn't be able to see the zip once it's closed. You'll also need good quality cotton, to make sure the seams don't come undone. And of course, the belt on that dress is quite wide. We need a special stiffening material to put in it, so it doesn't roll."

Thank God, she knows what she's talking about. I bet mine will be the prettiest dress in the class.

The sales lady helped us find all the extra bits and pieces. "I'm sure you'll look beautiful in that dress, dear," she said to me after I showed her the pattern we'd brought into the shop with us. I felt myself blush.

She turned to Mama. "I bet you wish your daughter wasn't growing up so fast, don't you?" she smiled knowingly.

"Yes, they all grow up too quick," Mama responded.

I floated from the shop, the precious parcel in my hand.

At home I unpacked the material and held it up in front of me. We didn't have any mirrors in our bedroom, but the feint reflection in the window smiled back at me.

Yes, this will be the prettiest dress....

* * * *

"Marijke, how are things going at school?" Papa asked me one evening after dinner.

I was surprised by his question. He usually checked our school reports and extolled the virtue of hard work and good results, but never questioned us on a day to day basis.

"Good, Papa. Why?"

"Well, you're going to be fifteen in a couple of months. That's the age your older sisters and brother went to work to help out with the family finances. When Willie gets married we'll lose one income. With the cost of living and the cost of the mortgage on the house, it'll help for you to leave school and help with the income."

I hadn't considered leaving school up till then. All my class mates planned to finish Fourth Year (Year 10). I was one of the oldest in our class because I'd had to stay back the first year due to my lack of English. That meant I wouldn't complete Year 10 until I was seventeen.

"By law you need to stay at school until you're sixteen, but they make dispensations for special circumstances. We can't afford for you to remain at school until you're seventeen. And if you're going to leave at sixteen, you'll still only be in Third Year , so that won't be of any benefit. I'll get the forms from the school and sign them. Then you can finish on your birthday and look for a job."

The following week I was asked to remain after class by Sister Lucy. She hadn't given me quite as much of her time since she found out I didn't plan to become a nun. I wondered what she wanted. I'd always had a lot of time for Sister Lucy. Why, if it wasn't for her, my name would have been changed to Maria. I was eternally grateful to her for that.

"Marijke, I heard from Mother Superior you plan to leave school on your fifteenth birthday. Is that correct?"

I nodded.

"I'm sorry to hear that, dear. You're much too smart not to continue on with your studies. Why, your grades are good enough to go to university, if you want. Or perhaps you could go to a business college. It would be such a pity to waste your intelligence ..." Her kind face held concern.

"But, Sister, I'll be able to earn money sooner and help Papa and Mama pay the bills. Only really smart and rich people go to university. I don't know anyone who's ever gone to university."

"You're smart enough to go if you work hard, I'm sure of it. Wouldn't you like to have a really good job instead of a menial one?"

"What is a menial job, Sister?" I asked, confused. *If I finish school and then have to go to university, then I wouldn't earn any money for years and years. Besides, once I get married and have children, I'll have to stay home anyway.*

"Well, menial means one which is hard work and doesn't pay too much money. If you study hard you should be able to get a job in an office as a secretary or something like that, instead of working in a shop or a factory. And if you go to university, why, you can be whatever you choose! A teacher, or a doctor or a business owner..."

"Sister, that's for other people. We don't have people like that in our family."

"I'm sorry that's what you think, Marijke. I'm worried that you'll waste your excellent brain on being no more than a chief cook and bottle washer." Her intense eyes held mine.

"Sorry, Sister." I didn't know what else to say.

You don't understand. We're ordinary people and we do ordinary jobs. There's nothing wrong with that. And if I become a "chief cook" somewhere, that would be good, wouldn't it?

I didn't tell Papa or Mama about Sister Lucy's concerns. After Papa's chat, I'd been looking forward to leaving the strict convent school and getting a job. No more uniform, no more wearing hats and gloves in the middle of summer. *When I'm working, I should be treated like an adult. Maybe*

I'll be allowed out more ... I'll miss my friends, but I've already made a lot of friends at St Leonards.

I went to school on my birthday as I did any other day. The school year only had four weeks to go, and exams were in full swing. When the bell rang, some girls said goodbye and wished me luck. Sister Lucy met me at the door and said, "Good bye, Marijke." She had a tear in her eye. "Come and see us sometime, let me know what you're doing?" I nodded.

"Good bye, Sister. Thank you." I shook her hand and ran after my friends. They walked with me to the Home Arts and Crafts class, where I collected my completed dress. I hung it over my arm and left the school grounds for the last time as a student.

Mama admired my dress and said I'd done a good job with it. She didn't pick any faults with my handy-work. "You'll need a new pair of shoes for the wedding, and you can wear stockings. You're too old to wear socks now."

I took the dress into the bedroom and laid it out on my bed. I sat down next to it and stroked the pretty material. *This dress represents me growing up. No more school, no more socks; a whole new beginning...*

Chapter 40

It was Friday 16 November nineteen-sixty-two; the day after my fifteenth birthday. It felt strange not getting dressed for school.

"Marijke, you can help Mama around the house today. I'm sure she'll appreciate a hand," Papa said before he left for work.

I was surprised how much Mama had to do. I thought we did all the work on Saturdays. It hadn't occurred to me that the house looked spotless every day. With so many in the family, washing had to be done almost daily, and then there was the ironing. It had to be so perfect; no false or double pleats or creased sleeves.

I helped Mama with various chores. It was a sunny day and we had our morning coffee outside. Tiny played on the lawn and chased a butterfly. She would be two years old the next day and Mama said I could bake her birthday cake.

"Tomorrow you can start looking for a job," she said. "There are always lots of jobs advertised in the Examiner newspaper on Saturdays. You can circle the ones that suit you and start applying."

I circled about eight jobs. I didn't want to work in a factory and I didn't want to do housework for other people; I did enough at home!

"It's good that you finished school now, so you can get a job before the others leave school in a few weeks," Mama said, looking over my shoulder at the jobs I'd circled.

"Look, there's one that may suit you. It's for a shop assistant in a milk bar and fruit shop. It says to be present at the shop on Monday for an interview between nine o'clock and eleven o'clock or after one o'clock and before five o'clock."

I noticed the address was in the centre of the city. *That's what I'd like, to work in town. That way I can look around the shops in my lunchbreak, and it'll be easy to catch the bus.*

I decided to catch the early bus with my sisters and be one of the first at the milk bar. It was only a five minute walk from the bus. "Dandy Cafe" a large sign over the door stated. The shop front window displayed rows of boxes of colourful fruit and vegetables. I watched a short and rotund elderly man with short-cropped grey hair polish some apples until a middle-aged lady walked in. I followed her and patiently waited behind her.

She purchased some apples and a large cauliflower. The man was friendly and looked like he belonged behind the small counter. He had rosy cheeks and a warm voice. He was in no hurry to get rid of his customer and it was obvious she was a regular. While they chatted amicably he acknowledged my presence and put a finger up as if to say he'd only be a minute.

I looked around and noted the lay-out of the long, narrow shop. Next to the fruit and vegetable bar was a milk-bar counter. A dark-haired girl not much older than me was wiping all the shelves behind the bar which held metal milk-shake tumblers and glasses of various sizes. Next to those were rows of chocolate and candy bars, as well as packets of chips. There were also rows of cigarettes.

Eight tall stools stood in front of the long counter, and against the opposite wall were some small tables and chairs. Where the counter finished a wide area housed tables of various sizes. A door led to the kitchen, where an older lady bustled about. Several tables were taken up with customers.

"Yes, what can I do for you?" the man behind the counter asked me when his customer finally left.

"I-I'm here for an interview," I said, shyly.

"Well, you've come to the right place. My wife over there's doing the interviews. Don't worry, she doesn't bite. What's your name?"

"Marijke Wegman, sir."

"I'm Mr Woods, dear. Mrs Woods is interviewing someone at the moment. We're very popular this morning. Another girl's still in front of you, so it could be a little while. Would you like a milk shake while you're waiting?"

"I'm sorry, Mr Woods, I can't afford a milk shake."

"Oh, no, you don't have to pay! Mah... sorry, how do you say your name again?"

"Ma/ray/ke," I said slowly.

"Right, Ma/ray/ke, what flavour would you like?"

"Uuhm... what flavours do you have?"

"Vanilla, chocolate, strawberry, banana, caramel, lime and pineapple. If you get the job you'll need to know them off by heart, dear," he laughed.

"I'll have banana, please."

He called out to the girl behind the counter, "Hey, Roslyn, give Ma/ray/ke here a banana flavoured milk shake. I've got it sorted, so don't charge her." He winked at me.

Oh, I would love to work here. Mr Woods is such a nice man. I've never had a milk shake before, but I love milk. I'm sure it'll be nice.

"Would you like a scoop of ice-cream or any malt in that?" Roslyn asked as I sat on one of the stools.

"Is the malt nice?" I asked.

She nodded, pulled a jar from the shelf and placed a large scoop of a brown coloured powder into the milk shake container. Next she placed a scoop of vanilla ice cream into the mix, added a scoop of milk and a generous serve of banana flavouring. When whipped, she added a straw and, placed it in front of me. "Are you here for the job?" she asked quietly.

I nodded.

"I think Mr Woods likes you. He didn't offer a drink to the other girls. Mrs Woods can be a bit cantankerous sometimes, but she's usually nice. She makes the decisions, but I'm sure Mr Woods will have a say. I hope you get it, I think we could be friends."

Another customer came in. I sipped the thick creamy drink slowly, as I observed Roslyn making various drinks and sundaes behind the bar. The older woman from the kitchen collected some drinks to serve on the tables.

Mama

"That's Mrs Woods' sister. She's a real sweety," Roslyn whispered.

Mrs Woods tapped me on the shoulder. "Mahreekie, come sit down, dear." She pointed to the small table in the far corner.

The interview didn't last too long. She seemed more interested in my family history, and told me she too came from a large family. She asked me if I'd worked in a milk bar before, and I was pleased I could honestly say that I had helped my cousin in her parent's shop a few times. Their shop was a combined bakery and milk bar. I hadn't done much, as I'd been there to keep my cousin company when she was on her own.

"Do you have a phone number where I can reach you?" Mrs Woods asked at the completion of the interview. "I'll let you know one way or the other."

"We don't have a telephone, but our neighbour will take a message." I wrote down the neighbour's number.

I walked around the city for a while, window shopping. Next door to the Dandy Cafe was a shoe shop. I admired a pair of high heels in the window. *Maybe if I get the job, I'll be able to afford to buy them.* On impulse I walked into the store and asked to try them on. They had a pair my size and I pranced around in front of the mirror.

"Can I wrap them up for you?" asked the girl after she put them back in the box.

"No, thank you. If I get the job next door I'll come back and buy them. I can't afford them now."

"We take lay-by," she said.

"What is lay-by?"

She laughed at my obvious ignorance. "You can pay a deposit of ten percent, and then pay some off each week until they're paid for in full. That way you won't miss out on getting the shoes you want."

I said I'd think about it and left the shop. But I didn't feel like going home yet. This was such a unique experience; in town in the middle of the day. I strolled around some more, and then went to City Park and watched families and couples enjoy the summer sunshine.

Mmmm, I could get used to this. No school, no homework... I hope I get the job...

I decided to save the bus money and walk home. I didn't rush and it took about two hours. The walk was exhilarating as I thought of the other kids in the classroom, swotting for their exams.

As soon as I walked in the door Mama shook my hand. "Congratulations, you've got the job. And only your first interview, you must have impressed them, they want you to start tomorrow."

"Oh, wow! I really want that job. Tomorrow – that soon?" Mama smiled and nodded.

When Papa came home he congratulated me too. "Do you know how much they'll pay you?" he asked.

"Mrs Woods said the job is Monday from nine to five-thirty, with a one hour lunch break, and Saturday mornings to twelve o'clock. They'll pay me three pounds for the first three months, and if they're happy with me I'll get a pay rise of ten shillings."

"Oh, that's quite generous. Okay, while you're on three pounds, your board will be two pounds and ten shillings. That will leave you ten shillings for yourself. When you get your pay rise, your board will go up to two pounds and eighteen shillings. That will give you pocket money of twelve shillings."

I didn't think that was quite an equitable split, but I knew better than to argue with Papa. The amount of 'board' Papa charged was a bone of contention with my older sisters and brother, John.

"We had to give all our money to our parents when we lived at home," Papa argued if anyone dared to question him. "We've provided for you all your life, now it is your turn to help provide for the rest of the family. That's the way it's done in Holland, and that's what we do now."

"Do I have to pay my own bus fares?"I asked.

"Yes, of course. You need to learn to budget and to manage money. Nothing in life comes easy."

The bus fares are six pence each way. That will leave me four shillings and six pence, unless I walk to or from work and save money that way.

"But I'll save you money because I'm allowed to have my lunch for free when I'm working," I said. "You won't have to provide me with sandwiches or drinks."

"Well, that's lucky for me then, isn't it?" He walked away.

Those shoes I want to buy are two pounds and ten shillings. I won't even have the ten percent deposit, and it'll take me ages to pay then off. I shouldn't have told Papa I would get a pay rise in three months! Then I could have kept that money for myself.

I awoke early the next morning and put on my second best dress. "Why are you wearing that good dress, Marijke?" Mama asked. "It's not for working in."

"But I want to look nice for work. My other clothes are hand-me-downs."

"There's nothing wrong with your other clothes, they're neat and tidy."

Begrudgingly I changed into another dress. I teased my hair to give it some volume and then put some pale lipstick on my thin lips. Ann had given me the lipstick for a birthday present.

"You look fine," Mama said as I said good bye to her. "Don't forget, you're going to work, you need to be comfortable, not fashionable."

I like to look nice. Why can't I be both? I'll save my money and then I can have nice clothes!

The first day in the workforce went well. I spent the first few hours with Mr Woods learning about the various fruits and vegetables. He showed me how to weigh them and pack them. He also told me some funny stories about other girls who had worked there. I had another milk shake for morning tea, but this time Roslyn got me to make my own. "You've got to learn how to make them anyway," she said, and handed me the milk shake container.

"You're allowed morning and afternoon tea as well as lunch. But Mrs Woods does complain if you have too much. You're not allowed to take chocolate bars or chips or any of those things. You can have a pie or sandwiches and drinks. Not the bottled drinks, though, they cost too much." Roslyn chatted away like we'd known each other for years.

I liked her straight away. She had black hair and fiery black eyes and was eighteen years old.

Lunch was busy, as there were only a couple of other cafes in Launceston at that time. I soon found out that the Dandy had a regular clientele. We had to have our lunchbreaks either before or after the main rush, and of course, we had to stagger our breaks. Roslyn said she preferred to have an early break, which suited me. When the rush was finished, I had a pie and sauce and another milkshake and finished with an apple. This was a decadent lunch for me, and so very Australian.

I strolled around the city until I had to return to work. Mrs Woods showed me around the kitchen, and said we all had to prepare our own orders, unless we were serving behind the bar. There were two old hot plates under which sandwiches were toasted. The kitchen was small and basic and I soon found out when busy, we'd all get in each other's way.

"We do any washing up as we go, whenever we can. No-one stands around unless there are no customers in the shop and the sinks are clean. Then, of course, you will look if the floor needs a quick clean over, and you wipe tables and fill up salt and pepper shakers and sugar bowls. No rest for the wicked, my dear," Mrs Woods smiled.

"Now, seeing it is quiet, why don't you get your hands in the sink and do some washing up. I'm going to have my break and Roslyn can look after the bar and the cafe. It she gets busy she'll ask you for help."

I filled the sink with suds and as I grabbed the dishcloth, Sister Lucy's words ran around in my head: *"You'll be nothing but a chief cook and bottle washer if you leave school."*

How did she know I'd be doing this kind of work? She must be psychic. But I don't care; I think I'm going to enjoy it here.

Chapter 41

I soon found working gave me less freedom than being at school did. Long hours on my feet five-and-a-half days each week was tiring. Yet I enjoyed the challenge and the interaction with my co-workers and the clients. I was quick and had a good memory, so was able to take orders without writing them down.

"My goodness, girl," one of the regulars said, "You spark on all fours, don't you?" I didn't understand what that meant, but knew by the big smile on her face that it was a compliment. I went into the kitchen and told Mrs Hargreaves (Mrs Woods' sister) what had been said and by whom.

"Well, you must really have impressed Mrs James. She is a valued regular, but she can be difficult if things aren't up to her liking. She doesn't give compliments easily. To spark on all fours means you are quick and efficient; like the spark plugs of a car." She rubbed my back while she talked to me.

Mrs Hargreaves was in her mid-sixties and had worked at the Dandy Cafe since her sister and her husband purchased it years earlier. She'd taken me under her wing since I commenced work. She was sweet and generous with her time and had a disposition like my Oma in Holland. She was short with a trim little figure and tiny waist. Her curly grey hair was always beautifully groomed, and her thick glasses accentuated her gentle eyes.

Wednesday was pay day. Even though Mrs Woods was the boss in the shop, Mr Woods had a tight rein on the finances, and looked after the banking and the payroll. After giving me my first pay, he said, "Oh, here is another three shillings, your share of the tips received. Whatever tips are left on the tables by our customers are put into a jar and shared by all staff each week. We're very pleased with your progress and we've had some wonderful comments about your service. Well done."

I wasn't sure how to deal with this high praise, but before I had time to respond, Mr Woods' face turned mischievous. "By the way, I've noticed an increase in the number of young men lining up for milk shakes and spiders. Why do you think that would be?" He winked at me and walked off, which was just as well, as I felt the colour rise in my cheeks.

Inside the envelope with my pay was a neatly hand written payslip, which clearly identified the gross pay and the tax which had been deducted. It didn't show the share of the tips I'd been given. I decided I wouldn't tell Papa about the tips. I was sure he would want his share. "Share and share alike," I could already hear him say.

After I'd finished my lunch of toasted sandwiches I sprinted next door to the shoe shop and was thrilled that my shoes were still available. "I'll pay a deposit of six shillings," I said proudly, handing the money over to the same girl who'd let me try them on a couple of weeks earlier.

"I just knew you'd be back for these," she said. "I've seen you working next door. By the way, my name's Pat. Come in any time you want to try some shoes on. We're often quiet; it'll give me something to do. I don't expect you to buy, but I can see you like nice shoes." When we finalised the paperwork I promised I'd pop in from time to time.

I put the paperwork in my purse, but then decided that mightn't be a good idea. *If Papa or Mama see this, they'll know I got extra money.* I took it out and asked Mrs Hargreaves if she could look after it for me. "That way I won't forget to bring it to work to make my payments." I felt this little white lie was reasonable, as I didn't want to tell anyone that most of my money had to be paid to Papa.

"Of course, dear. Look, I keep some of my bits and pieces here in a small box on the shelf. I'll put it there, and you just get it whenever you make a payment." I felt a little guilty, but only for a short period of time. *Those tips are mine. People pay them because they think I did a good job. I won't lie about it to Papa. I just won't tell him... that's not lying.*

* * * *

The weather warmed and things got more hectic around the house. Willie was busy making her wedding dress. Like the rest of us, she didn't have a lot of money, as most of her wages had to be given to Papa.

Willie was also planning the reception menu, which would consist of finger food. A small hall down the road and not far from the chapel had been hired for the occasion. Most of the people invited were Dutch. Bill had come to Australia with one of his Dutch mates some years earlier. Bill also boarded with a Dutch family.

The date had been set for the twenty-sixth of December, or Boxing Day, as this day is known in Australia. This was the main holiday period, with many businesses closing over the Christmas and New Year period, and some for a whole month.

Mama was busy making an outfit for herself as well as a cute little dress for Tiny. I was looking forward to wearing my new dress. I'd paid off nearly half the balance still owing on my shoes and I hoped I'd receive enough tips to pay them off. They were a silver-white colour and I knew they would look really nice with my new dress. Mama had bought me some stockings when I started work, and I was careful not to ladder them before the wedding, as I needed all my money to pay off my shoes.

I found it difficult juggling finances, as I wanted to buy Christmas presents for Mama and Papa and all my siblings. And I wanted to buy a wedding present for Willie too.

Papa checked my payslip when I gave him my board money each week. *You don't trust me!* I thought, annoyed. I'd walked to work several times to save bus fares, but found that by the end of each working day, my feet didn't feel like walking another two hours home again.

I was angry with Papa for taking so much of my money. I'd heard him argue with my sisters and brother about this issue and knew I could never win that argument.

One evening I heard Bill shouting at Papa about how much of Willie's earnings he took. "That's none of your business," Papa shouted back at him. "When she's your wife, then she can bring her money home to you." I didn't listen to any more, but I knew Papa stood his ground.

How am I going to buy presents and pay for my shoes and still have enough for bus-fares?

The tips hadn't been as generous as the first week. "People are spending their money on Christmas now," Mr Woods said. "They can't afford to give generous tips at this time of the year. But usually, the week before Christmas is a good week."

If only you knew how much I need those tips!

True to Mr Woods' word, the tips for Christmas week were about double that of the previous weeks. But my share wasn't enough to pay off my shoes. The previous week I'd bought all the Christmas presents as well as a nice set of embroidered face washers for Willie.

The day before Christmas one lady placed a one shilling coin in my hand. "That's yours, dear. Happy Christmas," she said.

I was in a dilemma. *What should I do? We're supposed to share our tips. But she said this one was mine, for Christmas.* I slipped it into the pocket of my apron.

After the lunch rush Mr Woods called us into the kitchen. "Just in case we don't have time later,

Mrs Woods and I wish you all a very happy Christmas." He handed each of us an envelope.

Mrs Hargreaves and Roslyn put their envelopes in their pockets and went back to work. I was far too inquisitive to do so. I walked through the back door of the kitchen into the small back alley which led to the outside toilet. I locked the toilet door and undid the envelope. Inside was a lovely Christmas card. When I opened it a one pound note fluttered to the floor. I stared at it with disbelief, and then tears filled my eyes. *This was more than enough to pay off my shoes!* As I put the card and the money back in my pocket, I felt the shilling the customer had given me.

I quickly went back inside and put the shilling in the jar. *I'm NOT telling Papa about my bonus!*

"Mr Woods, can I go next door, please? I need to pick up a pair of shoes I put on lay-by for my sister's wedding," I asked when the opportunity arose.

"Yes, but don't take too long. We'll have the afternoon tea crowd in soon." From the broad smile on his face I think he knew his pound had helped me out of my predicament.

After I collected my shoes I still had eight shillings left. *I'm rich!* I remembered to thank Mr Woods for the bonus. "Don't forget to thank Mrs Woods. It was from the both of us. We enjoy having you as an employee." He gave me a quick hug.

Mrs Woods beamed when I thanked her for the bonus. "You deserve it, Marijke. You're an excellent and quick worker and our customers think you're wonderful." Those words, coming from her, were high praise indeed.

As soon as I got home that night, I pulled the shoes from the box and put them on. Trudy came into the bedroom. "Oh, they're beautiful!" she gushed. "Did you buy them yourself?"

As I nodded I noticed the price of the shoes on the side of the box. *If Papa sees that he'll know I'm getting more money from somewhere.* As soon as Trudy left the bedroom I fetched a pen and criss-crossed across the price until it was no longer legible.

I slowly walked around the bedroom until I got used to the high heels. I went to the dining room where Mama was dishing up dinner. "Mama, do you like my new shoes?" I asked.

"Oh, yes, they're lovely, Marijke. They're a bit high, though. Are you comfortable on them?"

I walked to the kitchen and back to show her I was capable of wearing them without tripping over. "I put them on lay-by when I started work. I finished paying for them today. I wanted them for Willie's wedding."

"You've done really well, Marijke. You should be really proud of yourself. They're perfect for your dress."

Wow, so many compliments in one day. This is going to be a wonderful Christmas and I'm looking forward to looking like a grown up at Willie's wedding...

Chapter 42

December 24 1962

"Marijke, quickly, Papa's going to put the star on the Christmas tree." Ineke's excitement was contagious. Now seven-years-old, her pretty face framed by her soft blond hair reminded me of a small Christmas angel.

I followed her into the lounge-room where the family had gathered around the newly decorated Christmas tree.

"Where were you?" Papa asked. "We've been waiting for you."

I didn't answer him; I didn't want to share that I'd been thinking about Mama. This would be our third Christmas in Australia. When Papa had stretched the fine fibre-glass angel hair over the pine branches half an hour earlier, it had reminded me of Mama and our Christmases in Amsterdam. I'd quietly left the room and taken my memories with me into the bedroom. I sat on the bed and thought about Mama and our family and friends in Holland.

For the first time in four years these memories didn't bring tears to my eyes; they made me smile with their warmth. I was pleased the rest of the family were busy preparing for Christmas and didn't miss me for a while as I let the memories wash over me. Yet, I felt guilty. *I haven't missed you as much as I used to, Mama. Some days I haven't thought about you at all, and at other times I have trouble remembering your face. I still miss you, and I know you're here with us. I'm sorry I'm still struggling with my dishonesty; I promise I'll try to do better. One day I'll go back and visit Holland and your grave. I still miss my friends. I got a letter from Fietje this week, and she told me she misses me too ... and one from Hettie. But I've made some good friends here. Roslyn at work is really nice and her family have invited me to spend a weekend at their house. I also stay in touch with a couple of school friends, and I have my friends here in the village. I'm happy, Mama.*

Papa waited for me to join the family around the tree. Mama lifted Tiny up and together they slipped the fine glass ornament on the highest branch. Papa had already clipped candles on the tree and around the room. The Nativity set was placed on a small table covered with a white sheet, in the far corner. The grotto was sprinkled with baby powder to represent snow. In the grotto the statues of Mary and Joseph and the three kings had been carefully placed around the crib. Shepherds and various animals stood in dried grass around the grotto, which also had a light dusting of talcum powder. The baby Jesus was not yet in His crib. Papa would place Him in the grotto after Midnight Mass and light the special candle in front of the crib before Christmas breakfast.

"This will be a very special Christmas for us all," Papa said when he had everyone's attention. "The first Christmas in our new home, and of course, Willie will be married on Boxing Day."

We followed him to the dining room where we said Grace and Papa asked God for His special blessings for Christmas and for Willie's wedding.

After dinner we dressed into our second best clothes. We'd wear our new clothes to Willie's wedding. It was a mild evening and the walk to the little church for midnight Mass was pleasant. The clear night exposed the beauty of the Milky Way above us, which mesmerised me. I could never get enough of the beautiful surrounding in which we lived; so different to the narrow streets of Amsterdam.

"Look," I shouted, as a star skimmed across the sky. "What's that?" I asked no-one in particular.

By the time everybody else looked up it had disappeared. "Next you'll be seeing ghosts," John teased me, "or UFO's." I ignored him; I knew what I'd seen.

We were warmly greeted at the little church by Father Reed and the rest of the congregation, most of whom we now knew. We were no longer strangers they hadn't met; we were now an integral part of this small community.

After Mass we wished everyone a Merry Christmas, as they did us. On our walk home it dawned on me that this felt like Christmas. It was different from our Dutch Christmases; but it was Christmas none-the-less. It didn't matter that it was summer. *I bet our family and friends in Holland are envious of our warm weather.*

Christmas day was a mix of traditional Christmas celebrations and preparations for Willie's big day. Her beautiful wedding dress hung proudly above her bed. I felt her excitement build during the day. It was good that Mama and Papa remained true to Christmas, as this alleviated some of the stresses of the wedding preparations. After dinner that night, Papa lit the candles and we sang several carols in full voice. The younger children blew out the candles before we prepared them for bed.

This was the best Christmas since Mama died.

The house was a hubbub of excitement the next morning, especially in the girls' bedroom. Seven girls aged from seven to nineteen, all getting dressed at once, was fun. We helped each other with zippers and buttons, and oohed and aahed when Willie put her dress and veil on. It was the first time since Papa married this Mama that we'd all had new dresses and shoes at the same time.

I felt so grown up in my high heels and stockings, although I still struggled to feel comfortable with the suspenders I needed to keep the stockings up. But I was willing to put up with the discomfort for the sake of feeling pretty. I'd bought some hairspray to keep my fine hair in place. It was getting quite long and I loved trying different styles. I'd worn curlers to bed and now flicked my hair out, just like some of the latest pop stars. When I started spraying the cheap hairspray, Ann objected.

"You can't spray that stuff in here," she said as she coughed and spluttered. "It stinks."

I had to admit she was right, so I took it outside to finish the job. I looked through the window and liked my reflection. *I think I look about eighteen, I actually feel pretty.*

Along with the other guests we congregated outside the chapel, as the nuns brought in some of the old-age residents in wheelchairs and on walking frames. The sky was clear and the sun was bright. As tradition required, Willie arrived five minutes late.

Soft organ music welcomed us as we settled into our seats. I decided to sit in a pew at the side of the altar, to get a better view of Willie and Bill. Mama settled in the front row directly behind the altar, leaving a space for Papa. Arnold and John were altar boys and preceded Father Reed into the chapel.

When the bridal waltz started, Ineke, being flower girl, entered first; her pretty face serious as she concentrated on the instructions she'd been given. Papa looked proud as punch as he escorted Willie down the short aisle. She looked beautiful in her white wedding dress. Her sheer veil draped her face but couldn't hide her smile.

I was in a good position to observe others around the chapel and as the ceremony progressed I was easily distracted. I studied the nuns as they sat, stood and knelt as required; their faces serene, their voices strong as they joined in the prayers. I swallowed a giggle or two when the congregation joined in the hymns Willie and Bill had selected for their service. A couple of nuns sang off-key, and the elderly patients' voices were all over the place. *Just as well our family can hold a tune!*

The service was long. I tried to keep my mind on what was happening, but time and again I found my attention drawn to other things. One of the guests wore a black fluffy hat, even though it was summer. It clashed with her thin floral dress. Bill's best man, Peter, was as tall as Bill was short. They'd been best mates in Holland and Bill had been Peter's best man when he married.

Father Reed's sermon was long and while he spoke about faithfulness and the future pitter patter of little feet, I thought about the kind of man I'd like to marry. *I'd like him to be taller than me, and he'll have to dress nicely. Black hair, like Elvis, and it would be really good if he could sing; I'd like to be serenaded. He'll have to be fun to be around and have a good sense of humour.*

I looked up at Mama and Papa across from me and tried to remember their wedding, but that memory was still locked away. I thought this wedding may have brought those memories back, but it didn't. I closed my eyes, but still nothing. *I don't know why I can't remember their wedding, or Mama's funeral. I was there and it was only a few years ago. Why can't I remember?*

After Communion, Willie and Bill lit a candle in honour of the Virgin Mary. Our Mama had been a great believer in the Virgin Mary and all nine of her children had Maria (the Dutch version of Mary) in their names, even the boys.

Miep Coenen, a Dutch lady who had a beautiful soprano voice, began singing Ave Maria, as Willie and Bill knelt in front of the statue of Mary. Miep's powerful voice filled the chapel.

This used to be Mama's favourite song. I felt tears well up. I closed my eyes and Mama's face appeared before me; not faded, but clearly. The voice surrounding me was her voice; the Latin words were embedded forever in my soul. The hairs on my neck stood on end and I felt as if I was elevated off the floor; lifted higher and higher. I kept my eyes closed, not wanting to break this overwhelming feeling of connection to Mama. I lost all track of time and surroundings.

I don't know how long I remained in this state; I'd lost touch with reality. The music had stopped and the song was finished when I finally opened my eyes and was drawn back to the present. My eyes were damp and my mouth dry. I looked up to see Mama across from me, this Mama, not my late Mama. Yet, suddenly, they became one. Her face became a blend of two; but they were one and the same.

She looked across at me and gave me her sweet smile; a smile filled with love. For a split second I felt lost, confused. I looked down at my shoes and when I looked up again Mama was whispering something in Papa's ear. I saw the closeness they shared, the love she had for Papa.

I closed my eyes again, and felt completely calm.

Oh, Mama, thank you for guiding me through these difficult years. I still miss you; I'll always miss you. But I know this Mama is now truly my Mama. She won't ever take your place, but she loves me and all of us. She is an amazing woman, and I hope one day I can be half the person you were and half the person she is. I am so lucky to have two Mamas. Today I've finally stopped grieving for you. From today I'll always appreciate what this Mama has done for us as a family. I'm sure we'll still have some problems, but I guess all mothers and daughters do. I have finally released the anger and pain of losing you. Rest in peace, Mama, you deserve it.

The End